INTERNATIONAL POLITICAL ECONOMY SERIES

General Editor: Timothy M. Shaw, Professor of Political Science and International Development Studies, and Director of the Centre for Foreign Policy Studies, Dalhousie University, Nova Scotia, Canada

Recent titles include:

David Kowalewski
GLOBAL ESTABLISHMENT: The Political Economy of North/Asian Networks

Richard G. Lipsey and Patricio Meller (*editors*)
WESTERN HEMISPHERE TRADE INTEGRATION: A Canadian–Latin American Dialogue

Laura Macdonald
SUPPORTING CIVIL SOCIETY: The Political Role of Non-Governmental Organizations in Central America.

Stephen D. McDowell
GLOBALIZATION, LIBERALIZATION AND POLICY CHANGE: A Political Economy of India's Communications Sector

James H. Mittelman and Mustapha Kamal Pasha
OUT FROM UNDERDEVELOPMENT REVISITED: Changing Global Structures and the Remaking of the Third World

Juan Antonio Morales and Gary McMahon (*editors*)
ECONOMIC POLICY AND THE TRANSITION TO DEMOCRACY: The Latin American Experience

Paul J. Nelson
THE WORLD BANK AND NON-GOVERNMENTAL ORGANIZATIONS: The Limits of Apolitical Development

Howard Stein (*editor*)
ASIAN INDUSTRIALIZATION AND AFRICA: Studies in Policy Alternatives to Structural Adjustment

Kenneth P. Thomas
CAPITAL BEYOND BORDERS: How Capital Mobility Strengthens Firms in their Bargaining with States

Geoffrey R. D. Underhill (*editor*)
THE NEW WORLD ORDER IN INTERNATIONAL FINANCE

Henry Veltmeyer, James Petras and Steve Vieux
NEOLIBERALISM AND CLASS CONFLICT IN LATIN AMERICA: A Comparative Perspective on the Political Economy of Structural Adjustment

Sandra Whitworth
FEMINISM AND INTERNATIONAL RELATIONS

David Wurfel and Bruce Burton (*editors*)
SOUTHEAST ASIA IN THE NEW WORLD ORDER: The Political Economy of a Dynamic Region

Social Movements in Development

The Challenge of Globalization and Democratization

Edited by

Staffan Lindberg
Associate Professor of Sociology
University of Lund, Sweden

and

Árni Sverrisson
Assistant Professor of Sociology
University of Lund, Sweden

First published in Great Britain 1997 by
MACMILLAN PRESS LTD
Houndmills, Basingstoke, Hampshire RG21 6XS and London
Companies and representatives throughout the world

A catalogue record for this book is available from the British Library.

ISBN 0–333–67089–2

First published in the United States of America 1997 by
ST. MARTIN'S PRESS, INC.,
Scholarly and Reference Division,
175 Fifth Avenue, New York, N.Y. 10010

ISBN 0–312–16472–6

Library of Congress Cataloging-in-Publication Data
Social movements in development : the challenge of globalization and
democratization / edited by Staffan Lindberg and Árni Sverrisson.
p. cm. — (International political economy series)
Papers presented at a conference held Aug. 18–21, 1993 at the
Dept. of Sociology, University of Lund.
Includes bibliographical references and index.
ISBN 0–312–16472–6
1. Social movements—Developing countries—Congresses.
2. Developing countries—Economic conditions—Congresses.
3. Developing countries—Politics and government—Congresses.
I. Lindberg, Staffan, 1943–   II. Sverrisson, Árni.   III. Series.
HN980.S585   1996
303.48'091724—dc20   96–9721
                                                                CIP

This book is printed on paper suitable for recycling and made from fully managed and
sustained forest sources.

10   9   8   7   6   5   4   3   2   1
06   05   04   03   02   01   00   99   98   97

Printed in Great Britain by
The Ipswich Book Company Ltd
Ipswich, Suffolk

Contents

v

List of Figures and Tables

Figures

Table

Preface

This book includes a selection of papers and discussions from a conference on 'Social Movements in the Third World – Economy, Politics and Culture' held at the Department of Sociology, University of Lund, 18–21 August 1993. In all, 92 researchers participated in the conference and 57 papers were presented in three plenary sessions and two working groups. This volume includes contributions from two plenary sessions and two working groups. Another book about cultural movements and gender is in preparation.

The conference was financed by SAREC (Swedish Agency for Research Cooperation with Developing Countries), SIDA (Swedish International Development Authority), NorFA (Nordic Academy for Advanced Study), HSFR (Swedish Council for Research in the Humanities and Social Sciences), FRN (Swedish Council for Planning and Coordination of Research) and the Department of Sociology in Lund. This generous support is warmly acknowledged.

In addition to the editors, the following helped in various capacities in organizing the conference and the preparation of this volume: Göran Djurfeldt, Bertil Egerö, Ron Eyerman, Kajsa Ekholm Friedman, Jonathan Friedman, Christer Gunnarsson, Andrew Jamison, Preben Kaarsholm, Alhadi Khalaf, Christopher Kindblad, Svante Lundberg, Stig Toft Madsen, Chris Mathieu, Julio Numhauser, Sari Pekkola, Nelson Silva, Arne Tostensen, Marja Liisa Swantz, Timothy Shaw and Mariken Vaa. Warm thanks are due to them as well as the participants in the conference who all contributed in one way or another to making it an educative and stimulating experience.

Lund   STAFFAN LINDBERG
                                                         ÁRNI SVERRISSON

Notes on the Contributors

Caixia Dong, MA, is a sociologist and a PhD candidate at the University of Copenhagen. She is currently finalizing her PhD project on the 1989 student movement in China, with a particular emphasis on in-depth studies of student organizations, and the structural constraints which influence collective action.

Manuel Antonio Garretón is Chair, Department of Sociology, University of Chile in Santiago. He has worked for many years on political systems and social movements in Latin America, particularly various aspects of the democratization process. His most important work so far is *The Chilean Political Process*, (1989).

Dharam Ghai, an economist, is Director of United Nations Research Institute on Social Development (UNRISD), Geneva. He has written on a wide range of development issues. His most recent major publications are *Monitoring Social Progress in the 1990s: Data Constraints, Concerns and Priorities* (1993) and *Development and Environment: Sustaining People and Nature* (1994).

Peter Gibbon is Senior Researcher at the Centre for Development Research in Copenhagen. His current research is focused on private trade in East Africa. Earlier he coordinated a research programme on structural adjustment at the Scandinavian Institute for Development Studies, which published three volumes edited by Dr Gibbon with results from the programme in 1995: *Liberalized Development in Tanzania, Structural Adjustment and the Working Poor in Zimbabwe* and *Market, State and Civil Society in Kenya*.

Pernille Gooch is a PhD candidate in social anthropology at the Department of Sociology, University of Lund, Sweden, and is currently completing her doctoral dissertation on the pastoral Gujjars of northern India with special emphasis on ecological and environmental issues. She has published articles based on her research in international journals.

Eva-Lotta E. Hedman is a political scientist and has been conducting research in the Philippines since 1990 on elections, participatory crises and reformist mobilizations. She has published 'Beyond Boycott: The Philippine Left and Electoral Politics after 1986', in P. N. Abinales (ed.), *The Revolution Falters: The Left in Philippine Politics after 1986* (1996).

Staffan Lindberg is Associate Professor at the Department of Sociology, University of Lund. He has done extensive research on agricultural development, health and development, and social movements in India. Among his major publications are *Behind Poverty* and *Pills against Poverty*, both with G. Djurfeldt (1975), and *Barriers Broken*, with V. Athreya and G. Djurfeldt (1990).

Stig Toft Madsen is a researcher at the Department of Sociology, University of Lund, Sweden. He has worked extensively within the field of human rights and social movements in South Asia. His most important publication is *State, Society and Human Rights in South Asia* (1996).

T. K. Oommen is former President of the International Sociological Association and Professor of Sociology, School of Social Sciences, Jawaharlal Nehru University, New Delhi, India. He has written extensively on agrarian classes, social structure and social movements in South Asia in a comparative perspective. He is author of *Protest and Change: Studies in Social Movements* (1990), *State and Society: Studies in Nation-Building* (1990) and *Alien Concepts and South Asian Reality* (1995).

Lloyd M. Sachikonye is a political scientist and works at the Institute of Development Studies, University of Zimbabwe in Harare, where he heads the Department for Agrarian and Labour Studies. He edited *Democracy, Civil Society and the State: Social Movements in South Africa* (1995). He has published a number of articles, including 'Industrial Restructuring and Labour Relations under ESAP in Zimbabwe' in P. Gibbon (ed.), *Structural Adjustment and the Working Poor in Zimbabwe* (1995).

Alexander Schejtman is an agricultural economist and specializes in peasant economics and food security. He is Senior Policy Officer at the Food and Agriculture Organization's (FAO) Regional Office for Latin America and the Caribbean. He has published, among others, *Economia Campesina y Agricultura Empresarial* (1982) and

Economia Politica de los Sistemas Alimentarios en America Latina (1994).

Tor Skålnes, a political scientist, works at the Christian Michelsen Institute in Bergen, Norway. His main research interests are development theory, democratization and the politics of economic reform. He is author of *The Politics of Economic Reform in Zimbabwe: Continuity and Change in Development* (1995). He is currently working on a book on corporatism and economic policy-making in South Africa.

Árni Sverrisson teaches at the Department of Sociology and the Research Policy Institute, University of Lund. He has worked on technology studies in Africa, and published *Evolutionary Technical Change and Flexible Mechanization* (1993). He edited *Flexible Specialization: The Dynamics of Small Scale Industries in the South* (1994), and is currently working on environmental movements and environmental politics in Europe.

List of Abbreviations

AKF   Aga Khan Foundation
AKRSP   Aga Khan Rural Support Programme
ANAPA   National Association of Small Plot Owners, Peru
ANC   African National Congress, South Africa
ARnI   Association of Rhodesian Industries (later known
           as CZI)
BKU   Bharatya Kisan Union, (Farmers' Union) India
CEB   Communidades Eclesiales de Base
CEDLA   Center for Latin American Research and
           Documentation, Amsterdam
CEPAL   Comision Económica para América Latina y Caribe
           (ECLAC)
CESOC   Center for Social Studies, Santiago
CIA   Central Intelligence Agency, USA
CNC   National Peasant's Confederation
CNEA   Citizen National Electoral Assembly, Philippines
CNPA   Coordinadora Nacional Plan de Ayala, Mexico
COSATU   Congress of South African Trade Unions
CPP   Communist Party of the Philippines (see also PKP)
CSE   Centre for Science and Environment, India
CUC   Committee of Peasant Unity, Guatemala
CZI   Confederation of Zimbabwe Industries
ECLAC   Economic Commission for Latin America and the
           Caribbean (CEPAL)
ESAP   Economic Structural Adjustment Policy (Zimbabwe)
FAO   Food and Agriculture Organisation (United Nations)
GATT   General Agreement on Tariffs and Trade
IAMC   Indigenous Authorities Movement, Colombia
IBRD   International Bank for Reconstruction and
           Development
ILO   International Labour Office
INCORA   Colombian Institute for Land Reform
ISI   Import Substitution Industrialization
ISP   Industrial Strategy Project (COSATU), South Africa
JFM   Joint Forest Management, India
JUSMAG   Joint US Military Assistance Group, Philippines

MERG	Macro-Economic Research Group (ANC), South Africa
NAM	Non-Aligned Movement
NAMFREL	National Movement for Free Elections, Philippines
NEDLAC	National Development and Labour Council, South Africa
NEF	National Economic Forum, South Africa
NGOs	Non-Governmental Organizations
NPA	New Peoples Army, Philippines
NUMSA	National Union of Metalworkers of South Africa
OGIL	Open General Import Licence
OQC	Operation Quick Count
PIL	Public Interest Litigation
PKP	Partido Komunista ng Pilipinas (see CPP)
PRA	Participatory Rural Appraisal
PREALC	Regional Employments Programme for Latin America and the Carribean
RDP	Reconstruction and Development Programme (ANC), South Africa
RLEK	Rural Litigation and Entitlement Kendra, India
RRA	Rapid Rural Appraisal
SACP	South African Communist Party
SACTWU	South Africa Clothing and Textiles Workers' Union
SAPs	Structural Adjustment Policies
SIAS	Scandinavian Institute of African Studies
SAREC	Swedish Agency for Research Cooperation with Developing Countries
SIDA	Swedish International Development Authority
UNDP	United Nations Development Programme (PNUD in Ch. 7)
UNRISD	United Nations Research Institute on Social Development
ZANU	Zimbabwe African National Union
ZANU-PF	Zimbabwe African National Union-Patriotic Front
ZCTU	Zimbabwe Congress of Trade Unions

1 Introduction

Staffan Lindberg and Árni Sverrisson

> In the Third World, region, locality, residence, occupation, strati-
> fication, race, colour, ethnicity, religion, etc. are elements and
> instruments of domination and liberation. Social movements and
> the class struggle they express must inevitably also reflect this
> complex economic, political, social and cultural structure and
> process. (Frank and Fuentes 1987: 1506)

During the last two decades popular movements and political
activism seem to have taken decisively new forms all over the world.
In the industrialized countries the so-called new social movements
– that is, environmentalist, women's and peace movements – appear
to have largely replaced those of workers and farmers as the
dominant forms of activism. In the Third World a similar trend can
be observed, as national liberation and anti-imperialist movements
have been superseded by a plethora of separate movements. It is,
therefore, important to again ask the old questions: how do people
organize and mobilize in the Third World today? Which people and
for what purpose? Is there one pattern or several?

This book, then, as its title indicates, is an attempt to see how
contemporary social movements change and develop, and what role
they play in economic and political development. However, its aim
is not primarily the development of new theory, but rather to
describe and analyse concrete manifestations of changes in social
movements and their context. Moreover, its range is limited. Ethnic
and cultural movements largely fall outside the scope of this book,
and so do women's movements. The focus of this book is on social
movements among underprivileged and middle class groups which
aspire to sustainable and democratic political development.

GLOBALIZATION: A NEW CONTEXT FOR SOCIAL MOVEMENTS

'A social movement is a collective actor constituted by individuals who understand themselves to have common interests and, for at least some significant part of their social existence, a common identity' (Scott 1990: 6). Irrespective of whether their goal is to change or defend society or a particular social order, social movements are usually seen as autonomous of the state and established political parties. Another characteristic is that social movements rely on mass mobilization and participation to pursue their goals.

Over the years the social sciences have developed several sophisticated frameworks for understanding social movements. The multitude of approaches matches the variety among social movements and their changing historical contexts.[1] In spite of these theoretical developments, increasing criticism has been levelled at the inability of social movement theory to conceptualize the global context in which contemporary movements act. According to this view the study of social movements has so far been framed within the fixed orbits of nation-states and their respective civil societies, but this framework is now increasingly eroded by processes of globalization, in which the nation-state has lost much of its former pre-eminence as the arena of political activism (Horsman and Marshall 1994). Instead state systems and an emerging global civil society have become the context for collective action (cf. Shaw 1994a and 1994b). This suggests that new concepts and analytical frameworks are needed which are appropriate to this level of analysis. The way social movements today link local struggles with international networks – for example, in the environmental movements – seems to imply a completely new agenda for research on social movements (Jamison 1995).

There are different ways to conceive of this new context. Warren Magnusson (1994), for example, imagines the extension of urbanism and the capitalist economy into the 'global city' as the realm of contemporary movements, an arena or 'hyperspace' largely beyond the control of states and state regulations.

More often, however, and especially from the point of view of the poor and exploited populations of the Third World, the new context is understood as a global development crisis affecting the common security of the Third World as well as of the so-called developed countries. 'This crisis is simultaneously economical, financial, ecological, social, cultural, ideological, and political,' according to Marc Nerfin (1986: 4), a prominent writer within what has come to be called 'third system theory' (Finger 1994: 56).

According to this perspective there is a growing movement of 'all people who suffer, in one way or another, from the current development crisis, whether economically, socially, culturally, or ecologically' (Finger 1994: 56). Beyond states, governments and powerful economic actors, there is:

> an immediate and autonomous power, sometimes obvious, always present: the power of the people. Some, among the people, become aware of it, get together, act and become citizens. The citizens and their associations, or movements, when they neither search nor exercise governmental and economic power, constitute the third system. By contributing to make visible what is hidden, the third system is an expression of the people's autonomous power. (Nerfin 1986: 5)

This way of linking the local with the global, extrapolating, as it were, 'national social movement theory to the phenomena they see globally' (Finger 1994: 56), leads to a perspective that sees diverse movements of the 'powerless, the poor, the unemployed, the disenfranchised and the marginalized' fighting for a people-centred development across the globe (Korten 1990: 218–19).

What is the relevance of these perspectives for a deeper understanding of social movements in the contemporary Third World? More generally, how do contemporary processes of globalization – economical, political and cultural – influence the structure and meaning of collective actions among the peoples inhabiting the post-colonial world of the 1990s?

On the one hand, strong and clear global trends can be identified. Among these trends are deregulation of economic life, including international trade, growing emphasis on private entrepreneurship in development and reduction of state intervention. Simultaneously, international pressures on totalitarian governments have increased, as have demands for democracy and basic human rights (Slater, Schutz and Dorr 1993; Archibugi and Held 1995).

On the other hand, both the promotion of and the resistance to these global trends are manifested in radically different ways in various parts of the Third World. A plethora of seemingly diverse political actors and social movements have both perceived the opportunities posed by these global trends and mobilized resistance against their consequences at the local level, demanding, for instance, local control over the exploitation of natural resources and the reassertion of traditional rights to autonomy at the community level.

This diversity is created by the separate histories of different regions and societies of the Third World. They have led to distinct social and cultural structures in each country and resulted in differentiated positions in the global world order. Global change processes are mediated by the internal social and cultural structure and history of each region (Friedman 1994).

Hence, although the Third World shared a common fate in the past – colonization, economic imperialism, neo-colonialism and the continued dominance of capitalist industrialized states – it does not possess a *common history*, and today some countries have been successful in initiating a modernization process (with considerable social and cultural variations) while others have remained at extremely low levels of development.

The type of relation established between global and local processes is part of this problem. Deregulation of trade and investments, as well as the introduction of parliamentarism, multi-party systems and voting rights, are inspired by values held to be universal and they are promoted by global agencies and northern governments, ostensibly in the interests of all. However, to make these measures work, for better or worse they must take root in local economic, political and cultural contexts, which vary widely due to specific histories and internal social structures. Concepts such as development and social progress therefore have different social, political and economic implications in each country, and even in each province within a country.

It follows from this that the concept of the 'Third World' appears increasingly as what it has been all along: a label for those outside the circle of industrialized countries, lumped together without consideration of their specific histories, their very different presents and their probably divergent futures. Although such a concept may be useful for certain types of analysis it is certainly inadequate to the task of grasping the motive forces and organizational forms of social movements today. Social movements cannot be studied in isolation from their concrete historical contexts, and these contexts vary despite the strong global trends evident in the contemporary world. The challenge, in other words, is to see what globalization processes mean to different societies and populations, but to resist too easy generalizations. In the words of LaViolette and Whitworth (1994: 587–8):

We would suggest that the greatest contribution that analyses of social movements might make to the study of world politics is precisely to resist homogenization. This is difficult to do, because it is tempting within academic discourse as well as political activism, to stake 'firm' claims around new actors . . . In a system of world politics which regularly demands unity and coherence, social movements are insisting on contingency and flux.

Such a resistance to homogenization is strongly borne out by the contributions which are presented in this volume. They reflect the mosaic of social movements and political processes found in different regions of the world, and some of the different issues which these movements contest.

DEMOCRATIZATION, CLASS AND CIVIL SOCIETY

If economic and cultural globalization is one theme running through this book, the process of democratization is another. This can be a truly stunning event. The fall of the communist regimes in the Soviet Union and Eastern Europe is merely the most dramatic expression of the present trend towards more democratic forms of government all over the world. It is also a phenomenon that has been the object of a great many studies recently (Diamond, Linz and Lipset 1990; Huntington 1991). The aim of this book is not to add another volume describing and analysing political regime changes, but rather to contribute to an understanding of how collective action and social movements relate to processes of democratization in various contexts. We are looking for, as Diamond (1993: 43) has aptly formulated it, 'changes in the development, organization, consciousness, and mobilization of civil society'. It involves, among other things, change in 'norms and values', as well as in the 'alignment of interests' and 'the growth of formal and informal organizations' autonomous of the state (Diamond 1993: 46).

At the conference where this book originated, Mahmood Mamdani provided an analysis pertinent to this problem which it is useful to recapitulate here. According to Mamdani, the democratization process in Africa has only reached the urban population where various professional groups and students have been the driving force. Decolonization and the ensuing redistribution of wealth primarily benefited the growing African middle class. The political parties, most often the ruling party, represent this group or a part of this group. The peasantry remains severely oppressed, and in the local administration, all 'three powers' are fused: that is, the chiefs or local authorities possess the power to judge, enforce and administer. Against the few rural notables and privileged peasants who profit from the system stands the overwhelming majority of ordinary people, who lose. Opposition to this system therefore often includes the entire local population and it is often manifested in explosive, unorganized protests with ethnic overtones.

The urban social movements in Africa, which demand expanded representation, have little in common with the social movements in the countryside. The urban movements are, in the main, middle-class movements: the educated classes and the petit bourgeoisie created by the neo-colonial state have now come of age and turn back on this state on its deathbed, demanding not only a share in the estate, but also a voice in how it is allotted.

Civil society is, of course, a historical construct and it is manifested differently in different societies. In the African case, as Mamdani pointed out, rural society is on the one side dominated by the fusion of powers mentioned above, and on the other by conflicts between different classes and strata which have different interests. The privileged peasants, who produce export crops and surplus food for sale, and who are therefore well integrated in the market, gain from both deregulation and democratization. For the poor peasants, however, who produce small food surpluses and often rely partly on wage labour, the benefits are small; Mamdani suggests that they may be completely offset by increased taxation, less access to education and health services and higher prices for agricultural inputs and basic consumption goods.

In his analysis Mamdani makes a point which must in our view be the point of departure in any analysis of the role of social movements in the construction of civil society. Briefly, it can be stated in this way: class divisions, the controversies and conflicts they create, and their negotiation and settlement are integral elements of 'civil society', although the self-image and demands of the movements and organizations involved are not necessarily cast in interest group or class terms.

This view is not shared by all the contributors to this volume to an equal degree. However, down the different paths which these writers pursue, they all arrive at the same destination, which is cognizance of the role that occupation of similar positions in social structures, (that is, what sociologists usually call class) play in inspiring a sense of unity and of a common destiny among participants in various social movements.

The different authors presented here do, however, recognize the limits of this type of analysis. They all avoid the heedless 'class reductionism' which was all too common in the past. Depending on context, class interests which are abstractly comparable are expressed in widely different ways, to the point that class organizations according to 'classic' models, such as cooperatives and trade unions, may be altogether irrelevant. Moreover, class relations and class issues tend in many cases to be embedded in social and political contexts in which class organizations and class identities are currently ephemeral. In India rich and poor agriculturalists, pastoralists and their intellectual allies unite against what they see as the urban and elitist bias of the state. In Zimbabwe and South Africa racism has created a social void and posed political tasks which have eclipsed class issues and class identities for a long period. In Latin America, large minority groups now claim their rightful place in a society which until now has either ignored them or tried to obliterate their culture, their lifestyle and their identities, and similar movements can be found elsewhere. On every continent demands for democracy and efforts to defend democratic rights unite the most disparate social forces. In such political contexts, class-based identities and class-based ideologies are not always adequate guides to organizational forms and social action, although class positions can be identified analytically among the fundamental driving forces of a movement.

The contributions to this book have been arranged in three parts. The first part includes four chapters, which survey general trends globally and on two continents. The second part includes four studies of the relationship between economic developments and political change. In the third part, four case studies are presented, which each in their own way analyse contemporary social movements in the light of the development of the relationship between civil society and the state.

CHALLENGES AND VISIONS

What is the exact significance of current globalization processes? One the one hand, practically instantaneous communications span the globe. On the other hand, in spite of the globalization rhetoric, poverty as well as restrictions on trade and travel still exclude most from real participation in the 'global village'. These issues are developed by Dharam Ghai in Chapter 2. He maintains that thorough-going social change occurs less between countries and regions than within them, resulting in very uneven – but related – development. Some areas, countries or regions appear to be condemned to virtual stagnation and continued marginal status in global society. Other areas, countries or regions suddenly experience very rapid economic development, followed by the emergence of new social forces which are characteristic of modernity. However, the territories of nation-states are of dwindling importance as an arena for economic decision-making, while the pressure increases to create regional and global forms of cooperation. National standards and national policies can no longer exercise absolute control over the national economy. Neither can they protect people and their environment. The role of the state as an intermediary between the local and the global seems to be diminishing, according to Ghai. Certain, mainly economic, issues tend to be resolved in the global arena. Other, mainly social, issues are increasingly seen as the domain of community-based development, which, in the age of instant communication, should not be equated with parochialism. If indeed there is a global transformation of social relations, it is in terms of global learning processes (Finger 1994).

In Chapter 3 T.K. Oommen gives an overarching account of the growth of social movements and collective action in the Third World today. The new movements represent a 'fifth revolution', according to Oommen. Their inclusiveness and direction separate the new movements from those associated with the previous four revolutions: the aristocratic, the bourgeois, the proletarian and the anti-colonial revolutions. This fifth revolution is the revolution of 'the marginalized – that is, the women, the youth, the unemployed, the Blacks, the foreign migrant workers, the cultural minorities'. The antagonists are 'the establishment constituted by the clergy, intelligentsia, aristocrats, capitalists, bureaucrats, entrepreneurs and technocrats'. A major characteristic of the movements of the fifth revolution, according to Oommen, is that they 'are attempting to evolve a participatory society to improve the quality of life'. The new movements simultaneously combat economic injustice, political oppression and cultural discrimination. They are, in other words, multi-dimensional.

Similar movements have appeared all over the world, and this has led to the creation of various networks connecting movements on the different continents. News coverage of major manifestations has also contributed greatly to the transnationalization of the new movements. Although the concept 'Third World' appears to be dissolving it is clear that economic, social and political cleavages have become particularly severe in these areas and they all provide a fertile soil for new social movements.

The theme of this part is developed further by Manuel Antonio Garretón in Chapter 4. He maintains that a decisive break in political mobilization has occurred in Latin America. The classic mobilizations of the twentieth century aspired to modernization, development and social integration, and everyone saw national autonomy as a prerequisite of the realization of these aims, as well as a goal in itself (for example, import substitution as an economic strategy). The state, the nation and the people were fused in various populist projects, which often had revolutionary overtones, and all social movements, particularly unions and peasant movements, took part in this general national movement.

Military dictatorships and economic crisis have seriously disturbed this classic pattern of political action in Latin America, according to Garretón. Because of military repression, independent social movements were unable to influence directly the form and policies of the state. They therefore resorted to symbolic rather than instrumental struggles. The many human rights movements are typical of this period. Instead of national revolution, the fight for a democratic system of government became central for the first time.

After the disintegration of military oppression an embryonic form of a more democratic political culture has emerged. However, the process of democratization in Latin America implies a paradox: the small but very active groups which pressed for democratization and played a large role immediately after the fall of the dictators generally lost most of their political influence when parliamentary democracy was re-established. Other and more established interest groups have instead revived their interest-based agendas and claimed political and economic power. In Latin America, there are strong trade union and peasant movement traditions. Base-community movements and protest movements against reduction of public services and rising prices, often led by women, played an increasing role during the 1980s.

An all-encompassing social movement, such as the national populist movement in earlier epochs, has not reappeared, however.
Manifest social conflicts today often express the demands and
grievances of 'outsiders', that is persons and groups which are
excluded from mainstream society and whatever modernization and
democratization is taking place there. This conflict divides social
classes and categories as traditionally defined: within the peasantry,
the proletariat, among women, in rural areas as well as urban areas,
there are both insiders and outsiders in this sense. United social
action through the 'old' organizations is therefore exceedingly
difficult. In this segregated situation, collective identities are
ephemeral and ambiguous and the search for a collective subjectiv-
ity, an adequate definition of 'we', takes precedence over instrumental action against concrete and well-defined opponents. The
new movements are therefore less confrontational and more ready
to negotiate for a legitimate position in the national constellation
of interest articulation.

In Africa, both structural adjustment and democratization have
been launched in the context of an unprecedented and escalating
social crisis on the continent, increasing poverty, disintegration of
state apparatuses, almost to the point of total anarchy, and the
deepening marginalization of Africa in the world economy. Because
of the indebtedness of African states, which was created by the
development policies of the 1960s and 1970s, reductions in public
employment are unavoidable. This particularly hits various categories of government employees, which have up to now been the
main carriers of the modernization project in Africa. The working
class, once a privileged group, is also on the retreat. Big industries
are laying off workers, and mines and plantations are being closed
down. New industrialization initiatives are confined to the rehabili-
tation of defunct industries and horizontal growth in the small and
medium enterprise sector, which mainly caters for local demand. At
the same time, the main productive sector, that is the peasantry, has
been exploited heavily, but to no avail. Rather, large segments of
African societies have been further marginalized.

Currently, 'donor' policies are openly and unabashedly forced on
African governments by their creditors. As Mahmood Mamdani
has aptly put it, the introduction of democracy in Africa means that
Africans are allowed the privilege of deciding who is to preside over
the implementation of policies designed elsewhere. Further, development funds increasingly bypass governments and go directly to

charities and other non-governmental organizations which, if anything, have even less leverage *vis-à-vis* their sponsors than national
governments (see Mamdani 1990).

In this context, Peter Gibbon focuses our attention on the crisis
of the developmentalist state in Chapter 5, and on the concomitant
crisis of the civil society which evolved in symbiosis with that state.
This type of state has above all been characterized by the incorporation of existing interest organizations, or alternatively, the establishment of corporatist organizations which ostensibly represent
social interests. However, the disintegration of developmentalism
has led to escalated competition for resources controlled by the
state and foreign 'donors'. This has forced the leaders of corporatist
'estates' to compete actively among themselves for a share. Thus,
although the social basis of the corporatist interest organizations is
withering away, their leaders are as active as ever before.

BETWEEN ECONOMY AND POLITICS

The second theme of this book is social movements in the field of
forces constituted by two interrelated poles, the economy on the
one hand, and politics and the state on the other hand.

In Chapter 6 and Chapter 7, Staffan Lindberg and Alexander
Schejtman develop the point that deregulation of trade creates
significant opportunities for relatively prosperous peasants, who are
able to increase the production of commercial crops. At the same
time poor peasants, who do not benefit from increased commercialization, face increasing hardships.

The consequences, in terms of social movements, have been
different, however. In India the peasantry has united, allied itself
with commercial farmers, and focused demands on the state. In
Latin America, an opposite trend has prevailed. The very legitimacy
of state intervention has been contested as peasants, farmers and
agricultural workers increasingly link their fortunes to commercial
rather than political forces.

In parts of India, the new peasants' and farmers' movements have
in a short period of time become very important, and they have
challenged the political system upheld by the traditional parties.
Earlier, peasant movements demanded land redistribution, improvements in leasing conditions and higher wages; they represented the lower and proletarian strata of the peasantry. The new

movements, in contrast, typically represent the upper and middle strata of the peasantry, who are more commercially oriented. The increased prominence of this group is a result of profound changes in the agrarian structure in India. The new movements emerged as a consequence of the breakthrough of the Green Revolution and they are demanding better terms of production, cheaper inputs and higher output prices. As these prices are largely set by government agencies, these demands are addressed directly to the state, and are leading to calls for changes in agricultural policy.

However, deregulation of international trade will create a new context for Indian agriculture. The pros and cons of this are intensively debated there. Among the participants in this debate are various representatives of the new farmers' movements, including intellectuals drawn to these movements. Perhaps this debate is a test of the extent to which the farmers' movements can play an active role in shaping broad-based development policies for Indian agriculture.

In Chapter 7, Alexander Schejtman discusses basic and enduring patterns of agrarian change in Latin America, in which landlords and peasants contested issues of land ownership and other conditions of production. The result, Schejtman claims, is a bimodal agrarian structure in which capitalist enterprises coexist with a large segment of peasant and family farms. In both these categories there are large variations in terms of resources and logic of production.

Structural adjustment policies have created new conditions for the agricultural producers. The situation has improved for those who produce cash crops for export. The labourers working on such farms have also been able to better their lot because the demand for labour has increased. For the large majority of basic food producers as well as for subsistence peasants and labourers the situation has, however, deteriorated.

Schejtman paints a broad canvas of peasant collective action in a Latin America dominated by structural adjustment policies (SAPs), and emphasizes both strategy and social identity as important elements in the analysis of social movements. His analysis reveals an interesting pattern which persists today. On the one hand, the movements which represent the poorest peasants and agricultural workers, the groups which are hardest hit by economic crisis and structural adjustment, continue their struggle for land and wages. However, these mobilizations now have regional or ethnic connotations more frequently than in the past when socialist overtones were common. The goal today is not total transformation of society, but rather local autonomy.

On the other hand, peasants who produce for the market, who are usually better off, have in many places organized themselves into more or less effective pressure groups. They have attempted to influence prices and other conditions for commercial agriculture. They also organize themselves cooperatively for purchasing, marketing and common productive efforts. These peasant movements are therefore also distinguished by their aspiration to escape state control and create an autonomous role for themselves. In effect, they try to avoid the state rather than fight the state, and the budding civil societies of Latin America are ripening in the process.

In Africa, the gradual transition to a democratic political system means that opposition voices which were formerly repressed with vigour even by the most benevolent dictators can today make themselves heard. Hence, in the wake of economic crisis, deregulation of trade and disintegration of party-states, new forms of resistance and organization appear, which simultaneously try to address both the economic crisis and the inability of the elite to transform the political system into an efficient agent of democracy and development.

In this situation, it would be a catastrophe if each social group pursued its own defensive strategies without regard to the legitimate interests of other groups. However, the legitimacy of national leaders, which earlier was precarious at best, is being eroded to the point of insignificance and it is difficult for discredited governments to assume the role of arbitrator. In Chapter 8 Tor Skålnes addresses this intricate problem. He poses the question whether interest group politics currently facilitate or impede the success of structural adjustment policies in Africa. After a review of past experiences on the continent, he considers two cases in some detail, Zimbabwe and South Africa.

Skålnes concludes that the view that interest groups must be kept at bay in order to ensure successful implementation of structural adjustment is mistaken. Governments must in the long run rather ensure the support of interest groups. Suppression of group interests in the name of the 'national interest' has been and will be self-defeating.

Skålnes also shows that interest group leaders are quite as likely as political leaders to take a long-term view of economic policies. This view is supported by the harmony of general interest which obtains between governing groups in Africa and the leaders of various organizations, and which builds on the twin foundation of common class interests and a long-standing corporatist form of government. This general unity of purpose is difficult to practise in the current situation. Popular forces place increasing demands on the ruling coalitions in most African states. Different factions link up now with this external ally, and now with that internal group, both politically and financially. However, in this process a social space for active opposition, criticism and genuine political innovation has been created.

This theme is pursued further by Lloyd Sachikonye in Chapter 9, where he discusses the implications of structural adjustment in Zimbabwe. They are, in many ways, different from those in the rest of Africa because of powerful settler interests and the recent liberation of the country. After documenting the consequences of structural adjustment for workers within and outside the state, as well as for industrial enterprises, he goes on to discuss the consequences at the political level. He focuses his analysis on the crisis of the hegemonic project which the Zimbabwe African National Union (ZANU) government embarked on at independence.

The 15 years which have passed since the installation of majority rule in Zimbabwe contain the essential elements of the post-colonial experience in Africa. After a brief period of uncontested legitimacy, maintained by expansion of the public sector as well as subsidization of consumption goods, the government of Zimbabwe ran into serious obstacles. It was unable to fulfil the most basic demand of the general population – that is, redistribution of land – except in a symbolic and largely inefficient fashion. High-level corruption came to the light in 1988, and instances of petty corruption multiplied. An attempt in 1990 to formalize the *de facto* one-party state was unsuccessful, and demonstrations by students and leading public figures against heavy handed authoritarianism gained momentum. After 1992 criticism of the effects of structural adjustment have further eroded the legitimacy of the government and jeopardized its hegemonic project.

Sachikonye is more pessimistic than Skålnes as regards the possibility of bringing together different sectoral interests and negotiating viable national development policies. However, each in its own way highlights the importance of effective social mechanisms for interest articulation, in order to transcend parochial interests and construct a workable *modus vivendi* which simultaneously allows economic regeneration and avoids the social and political risks associated with hyperexploitation and marginalization of large social groups. This, in turn, cannot be achieved through dictates from above. Quite the contrary: the historic task in Africa today is rather the creation of a civil society distinct from the state, and a space for independent class and/or interest organizations which can voice the concerns of the people to the rulers of the day.

STATE AND CIVIL SOCIETY

The construction of civil society is addressed by all the case studies collected under this third theme. In Chapter 10 Caixia Dong describes and analyses the events that led up to the violent suppression of the Chinese student movement in 1989, symbolized by the massacre in Tiananmen Square. Dong's study takes up an important problem, the significance of which is not limited to China: namely, the role of the educated and moderately privileged classes who have often been the most articulate spokesmen for political reform. In China, current changes have created deep-seated insecurity among students about their future prospects, but also about the capability of the current leadership to guide the country. Hence the students demanded a dialogue with the government, and recognition of their independent organizations. This the government ignored, and when the students persisted, the government answered with armed violence.

Another problem of general interest to everyone who studies social movements is the question of alliances. The Chinese students, a privileged minority, felt this problem in a particularly acute way. Among them are prospective members of the ruling group, but also putative professionals and intellectuals as well. As a result, the movement was not free from internal contradictions.

Caixia Dong focuses particularly on the relationship between students and intellectuals, which emerges as essential in any democratic movement: these groups are the primary carriers of demands for the right to discuss, meet and organize. The struggle for space for public discourse, free from government control, is largely the work of these groups, who also readily use whatever openings there are to voice their more specific concerns.

These issues reappear in Eva-Lotta Hedman's contribution. In Chapter 11 she discusses election watch movements in the Philippines after the Second World War. The contexts are different: communist China and the capitalist Philippines are as far from each other in social structure and form of government as countries can be. The time scales are also different: the Chinese study derives its focus from a single event, whereas in the Philippine case a broad panorama of post-war developments is painted from the perspective of electoral politics.

However, election watch movements in the Philippines can also be traced to deep suspicions on the part of the relatively privileged about the leadership of the country, and about the authenticity of the democratic intentions professed by a succession of presidents. As in China, such doubts have been well founded. Hence social groups which are basically in accord with the direction that development has taken in the Philippines have nonetheless felt that monitoring of elections and other initiatives to ensure the accountability of governments were called for.

In the Philippines, alliance-building has been problematic too. Eva-Lotta Hedman maintains that the election watch movements she analyses have not only been aimed against anti-democratic presidents and their military cronies, but have also been intended to prevent the spread of demands for radical reforms in Philippine society. They have therefore attracted a range of supporters, businesspeople, clergy and trade union leaders, all of whom have a vested interest in strengthening the workings of democratic institutions without changing the fundamental parameters of social structure. Hedman concludes that civil society mobilization is strongly influenced and meditated by powerful institutions (such as the US government and the Catholic Church) and class interests (the business community/class).

The alliance problem points to the importance of 'civil society', a major manifestation of which is the variety of voluntary organizations or NGOs (non-governmental organizations), their differences, their interaction and sometimes conflicts. It is therefore particularly apt to conclude this volume with two case studies which focus on the relation between popular movements and the influential NGOs which promote their causes.

In Chapter 12, Pernille Gooch describes and analyses the struggle of a semi-nomadic people in Northern India, the Van Gujjars, and their attempts to retain control over their natural environment. In 1983 their winter forest was proclaimed as a National Park with no room provided for the Gujjars, although they had lived in this area for many generations. The policy was sponsored by a powerful conservationist lobby. Right from the beginning, however, the Van Gujjars' struggle against this scheme was supported by a local NGO, and it quickly became a symbol of people's resistance against eviction from an area which they have traditionally inhabited.

Gooch shows how this movement and the activities of the NGO have given rise to an intense political and ideological debate over how to best preserve nature in areas already used by people for their survival. A chain of actors has been drawn into this debate: local intellectuals of the movement, various activists of NGOs, middle-class professionals, government officials and politicians at various levels. The Gujjar case has become something of a national showcase for a people-oriented conservation strategy, in which the local people are seen as guardians and preservers of nature rather than as the ones who destroy it.

The catalytic role of NGOs in the Gujjars' case, as well as in other similar environmental protection cases, is also the subject matter of Chapter 13 by Stig Toft Madsen, which also implies a practical model for constructive movement-NGO-state relations. It is often claimed by NGOs that they mobilize local people for participation in development programmes in societies where the state and other institutions, like political parties or social movements, are weak. Madsen, however, deals with prominent NGOs which in fact play a completely different role. They have become successful brokers between local collective action and movements, on the one hand, and the outside world of state administrations, national governments, the media, commercial interests, and so on, on the other hand. His first example concerns the Rural Litigation and Entitlement Kendra (RLEK) in Dehra Dun. Madsen shows how RLEK successfully intervened to bring to a halt the destructive limestone quarrying in the Doon valley by using scientific facts to elicit the support of a 'critical mass of influential, knowledgeable and respectable persons, officials', and so on, and by taking their case to an increasingly activist Supreme Court. He compares this case with RLEK's intervention in the Van Gujjars' struggle. He finds that there are neither national legislation nor undisputed scientific facts to support of the Van Gujjars' case. Instead of going to court RLEK has resorted to, among other things, international human rights declarations on tribal rights of entitlement to 'survival' and 'culture'.

A second example of successful brokerage presented by Madsen is the case of the Aga Khan Rural Support Programme (AKRSP), a highly professional NGO which has acted as 'troubleshooter and innovator' in cases relating mainly to forests and irrigation. In cooperation with activist academics the NGO has introduced new methods for monitoring projects which effectively tap the knowledge resources of the participants. They have also contributed to the draft of a new legislation for Joint Forest Management (JFM) between Forest Departments and organized villagers.

Together these two case studies illustrate the ways in which local struggles for control over natural resources has been supported, negotiated and theorized by concerned activists and intellectuals in order to reach the national or even the international scene effectively. In this process the local issue is connected with a universal discourse on environmental protection and human rights, which greatly improves the chances of success of the struggle, but also develops the environmental discourse itself.

Madsen's and Gooch's contributions provide a healthy antidote to the long-standing emphasis on national modernization projects. Their analysis shows, however, that locally-based movements need allies who will take the issues into the national whirlpool of political debates and political struggle, and enlist international support through their networks as well. Intellectuals from within the movement or recruited from the outside also interpret the movement for the participants themselves as well as outsiders. This is particularly important because, in order to succeed in the long term, locally-based social movements must contest hegemonic interpretations of the issues at hand as well as the resolution of the issues by bureaucratic dictates. In this way the two chapters provide a deeper understanding of the concrete processes at work 'linking the local and the global' in world environmental politics and the crucial role of NGOs in this process (see Princen and Finger 1994).

The possibilities for this in turn depend on the national political climate. This issue strikes at the core of the civil society problematic. When economic activities as well as intellectual activities are strictly controlled by the state, to the point where state and society are in effect fused, heterogenous activities and unorthodox and oppositional views cannot mature. However, variability is the prerequisite of evolution, and that applies particularly to the process of social innovation referred to by the term 'development'.

Constructing civil society therefore means, fundamentally, the creation of an expanding space of activities not controlled by the state apparatus or by governments. Alongside formal administrative hierarchies and patron-client networks which characterize quasi-feudal states in particular, but which can be found in some form or another in the interstices of all structures of governance, new and different types of social relations take root. The activities of 'developmental' NGOs of all kinds which create new networks of relations between the people and state are a part of this process.

However, the case studies presented in this book also bring out the fact that other actors and other kinds of social network are equally necessary. These include everything from democratic mass media and national interest-based associations to mundane phenomena such as local mutual help associations and savings banks. They also include forms of organizing economic life, the structures of which are independent of the structures of the state. In the end, this involves a transformation in which the tables are turned on the state.

Modernization starts from a situation in which the state is the main locus of power and in which social power emanates from the state. State and society are in this sense united, and economic relationships tend to be simultaneously and primarily relations of power and political domination. However, in the modernization process, the state is increasingly put under the control of the forces of civil society. Eventually, civil society becomes the major source of social as well as political power, and governments (democratic or otherwise) are created or removed at the behest of social forces which are largely beyond their control. This, rather than the formal trappings of democracy, is the hallmark of development.

In this process, social movements are essential. By their very existence, they contest not only the monopoly of power and the legitimacy of abject inequalities, but they also challenge the hegemony of interpretation which deprives the peoples of the Third World of the insights, concepts and visions with which they can interpret their world and understand how to change it.

References

Archibugi, D. and D. Held (1995), *Cosmopolitan Democracy: An Agenda for New World Order* (Cambridge: Polity Press).

Diamond, L. (1993), 'The Globalization of Democracy', in R. O. Slater, B. M. Schutz and S. R. Dorr (eds), *Global Transformation and the Third*

World (Boulder, Col.: Lynne Rienner and London: Adamantine Press), pp. 31–69.

Diamond, L., J. J. Linz and S. M. Lipset (eds) (1990), *Politics in Developing Countries: Comparing Experiences with Democracy* (Boulder, Col.: Lynne Rienner).

Esman, M. J. and N. T. Uphoff (1984), *Local Organizations: Intermediaries in Rural Development* (London: Cornell University Press).

Eyerman, R. and A. Jamison (1991), *Social Movements: A Cognitive Approach* (Cambridge: Polity Press).

Farrington, J. and A. J. Bebbington (1993), *Reluctant Partners? Non-Governmental Organizations, the State and Sustainable Agricultural Development* (London: Routledge).

Farrington, J. and D. J. Lewis (eds) (1993), *Non-Governmental Organizations and the State in Asia: Rethinking Roles in Sustainable Agricultural Development* (London: Routledge).

Finger, M. (1994), 'NGOs and transformation: beyond social movement theory', in T. Princen and M. Finger (eds), *Environmental NGOs in World Politics: Linking the Local and the Global* (London: Routledge), pp. 48–66.

Frank, A. G. and M. Fuentes (1987), 'Nine Theses on Social Movements', *Economic and Political Weekly*, 29 August, pp. 1503–10.

Friedman, J. (1994), *Cultural Identity and Global Process* (London: Sage).

Hirschman, A. O. (1970), *Exit, Voice, and Loyalty: Response to Decline in Firms, Organizations and States* (Cambridge, Mass.: Harvard University Press).

Horsman, M. and A. Marshall (1994), *After the Nation-State: Citizens, Tribalism and New World Disorder* (London: Harper Collins).

Huntington, S. P. (1991), *The Third Wave: Democratization in the Late Twentieth Century* (Norman: University of Oklahoma Press).

Jamison, A. (1995), 'The Shaping of the Global Environmental Agenda: The Role of Non-Governmental Organizations', in S. Lash, B. Szerszynsky and B. Wynne (eds), *Risk, Environment and Modernity* (London: Sage).

Korten, D. (1990), *Getting to the 21st Century: Voluntary Action and the Global Agenda* (West Hartford, Conn.: Kumarian Press).

LaViolette, N. and S. Whitworth (1994), 'No Safe Haven: Sexuality as a Universal Human Right and Gay and Lesbian Activism in International Politics', *Millennium*, Vol. 23, No. 3, pp. 563–88.

Magnusson, W. (1994), 'Social Movements and the Global City', *Millennium*, Vol. 23, No. 3, pp. 621–45.

Mamdani, M. (1990) 'Social Movements, Social Transformation and the Struggle for Democracy in Africa', *CODESRIA Bulletin*, No. 3.

Melucci, A. (1989), *Nomads of the Present: Social Movements and Individual Needs in Contemporary Society* (Philadelphia: Temple University Press).

Nerfin, M. (1986), 'Neither Prince nor Merchant – An Introduction to the Third System', *IFDA Dossier*, No. 56, pp. 3–29.

Olson, M. (1965), *The Logic of Collective Action: Public Goods and the Theory of Groups* (Cambridge, Mass.: Harvard University Press).

Princen, T. and M. Finger (1994), *Environmental NGOs in World Politics: Linking the Local and the Global* (London: Routledge).

Scott, A. (1990), *Ideology and the New Social Movements* (London: Unwin Hyman).

Shaw, M. (1994a), 'Civil Society and Global Politics: Beyond a Social Movement Approach', *Millennium*, Vol. 23, No. 3, pp. 647–67.

Shaw, M. (1994b), *Global Society and International Relations: Sociological Concepts and Political Perspectives* (Cambridge: Polity Press).

Slater, R. O., B. M. Schutz and S. R. Dorr (eds) (1993), *Global Transformation and the Third World* (London: Adamantine Press).

Tarrow, S. (1994), *The Power in Movement: Social Movements, Collective Action and Politics* (Cambridge: Cambridge University Press).

Touraine, A. (1981), *The Voice and the Eye: An Analysis of Social Movements* (Cambridge: Cambridge University Press).

Note

1. Some theories focus on economic transactions and rational choice (see, for example, Olson 1965; Hirschman 1970). Others highlight changes in political systems and opportunity structures, particularly the role of interest groups and political alliances (Tarrow 1994). Still others emphasize community development, local institutions and voluntary organizations (Esman and Uphoff 1984; Farrington and Bebbington, 1993; Farrington and Lewis 1993). Finally, the emergence of new social identities and ideologies in post-industrial or so called post-modern societies have been seen by many as the essence of the political and economic transformation which is taking place both in the centre and in the periphery of global society. This view has led to a whole new approach within social movement research (see Touraine 1981; Melucci 1989; Eyerman and Jamison 1991).

Part I

Challenges and Visions

2 Economic Globalization, Institutional Change and Human Security

Dharam Ghai

There has been a marked acceleration in the tempo of globalization in recent years. Its scope has also widened beyond the realm of economy to embrace the domains of social, cultural and political norms and practices. This powerful thrust has been associated with far-reaching consequences for economic well-being, social structures and political processes in countries around the world. The different parts of the world have become so interdependent in so many ways that it is no longer possible to understand their socio-economic problems, much less to do something about them, without taking into account the play of global forces. The process of globalization has been accompanied by major changes in the role and responsibilities of a wide range of institutions: families, communities, civil society institutions, business corporations, states and supranational organizations. One of the important consequences of the changes associated with globalization has been increased insecurity at the level of the individual and the family. This in turn not only affects individual welfare but has broader economic, social and political impact. This chapter seeks to analyse the sources and consequences of human insecurity and explore policy and institutional alternatives for its mitigation.

This chapter begins with a discussion of the concept and processes of globalization. It then looks briefly at the principal socio-economic, political and institutional consequences of accelerated globalization. These are brought together to assess their impact on human security. Some of the principal effects of increased human insecurity are outlined before considering policy and institutional reforms to ameliorate individual security. In view of the vast scope of the themes covered, it has been possible only to consider the broad picture, omitting important supporting evidence and necessary qualifications.

CONCEPT AND PROCESSES OF GLOBALIZATION

In recent years there has been a good deal of discussion in academic circles, especially among sociologists, on the concept and defining characteristics of globalization.[1] In a fuller treatment of the subject, it would be important to review the variety of concepts and approaches to globalization put forward in the literature. For the purposes of this chapter, it is sufficient to indicate briefly the sense in which this term is used here. In common parlance, globalization is often equated with growing integration of national economies; but, as employed here, the concept also refers to the rapid spread worldwide of some dominant social, cultural and political norms and practices.

In the sphere of economics, globalization is reflected in the increasing acceptance of free markets and private enterprise as the principal mechanisms for promoting economic activities. Its growing importance is captured in such indices as trade in goods and services, private capital flows in different forms, foreign investment, technology transfers, operations of transnational enterprises, business travel and communications, and migration and remittances (Griffin and Khan 1992; Dunning 1993). The social sphere comprises social relations and customs (family relations, social organizations, etiquettes of social behaviour) and consumption patterns and lifestyles (consumer goods and services such as consumer durables, fashion and design articles, food and beverages). The cultural dimension includes the important domain of values, religion and identity. It also embraces leisure activities such as television, videos, popular music, dance, night clubs, sports, foreign travel. At the political level, globalization is reflected in the spread of plural systems, multi-party democracy, free elections, independent judiciaries and human rights.

It would be naive to argue that globalization in any of these spheres has proceeded in a smooth and uniform manner, or that it is anywhere near completion. On the contrary, it has proceeded by fits and starts, generated contradictory effects and can claim only partial achievements. In the economic domain, the financial markets come closest to achieving global integration. Despite impressive progress in removing trade impediments in the post-war period, world commerce continues to be subject to a range of tariff and non-tariff barriers. The biggest contribution to trade liberalization in recent years has come from developing and ex-centrally planned countries. Outside the framework of regional free trade areas, the trend in most industrialized countries over the past decade and a half has been towards imposition of various barriers to free trade, especially in their trade with developing countries. The conclusion of the Uruguay Round may reverse this trend and speed up trade in hitherto highly regulated markets such as textiles, leather products and certain agricultural commodities.

Another major exception to liberalization is provided by the global labour markets (Stalker 1994; Harriss 1995). The growing volume of migration flows is often cited as another aspect of increasing globalization. It is, however, doubtful whether this popular perception is supported by empirical evidence. In the 1950s and 1960s, the booming economies of Western Europe fuelled large-scale immigration from the North African region, the ex-colonial empire and countries such as Turkey and Yugoslavia. In the 1970s and early 1980s, the oil boom provided employment opportunities in the Middle East for millions from North Africa and Asia. Rapid economic growth in South Korea, Japan, Taiwan and Malaysia has in recent years attracted growing number of migrants from poorer Asian countries. The general trend in the past decade in most parts of the world has, however, been towards increasing restrictions on immigration from poorer regions. To the extent that migration of unskilled workers takes place, it is mostly of an illegal and clandestine nature. The few countries which still retain significant quotas for migrants, such as the USA, Canada and Australia, give preference to relatives of nationals or to highly qualified and affluent applicants.

The pattern of global economic integration also displays some sharp inequalities. Whether measured in terms of trade, capital flows, foreign investment, technology transfers or activities of transnational enterprises, most of the transactions take place among developed countries. The linkages with developing countries have expanded significantly in recent years but there is a marked concentration of direction: a handful of countries account for the great bulk of flows. The fact that this group includes some large Asian and Latin American countries means that, in terms of population, the pattern of flows is distinctly less uneven. Nevertheless, most of the poorest and least developed countries are largely bypassed by the intensified circuits of trade, capital and investment.

Globalization in the social and cultural spheres has also been marked by discontinuities and contradictions. The consumption patterns and lifestyles of the middle classes in rich countries have penetrated only a thin layer of the affluent minorities in poor countries (Barnet and Cavanagh 1994). In most manifestations of cultural and social life – dress, food, music and dance, social relations and personal beliefs and values – the vast majority of populations in the non-Western world continue to adhere to inherited traditions. Even where Western forms have taken root, they have often been adapted to the indigenous style. In the domain of politics also, the ideals of liberal democracy have not been uniformly embraced. In some situations where this appears to be the case, the underlying reality may be quite different. Furthermore, the conceptions and content of democracy and human rights show wide variation even among countries generally accepted as falling in the camp of liberal democracy.

The processes of globalization have been driven by a number of forces. World-wide expansion of capitalism and technological progress are at the core of the dynamics of globalization. These forces have been in operation for centuries but have increased in scale and intensity in recent decades. The new spurt in the expansion of capitalism has found expression in the shift towards greater reliance on markets and private enterprise in all parts of the world. Almost everywhere there has been a reduction in the state intervention in the economy, privatization of public enterprises, deregulation of the economy and liberalization of foreign trade and capital flows. The collapse of communism in Europe is only the most dramatic manifestation of this global phenomenon. Economic reform in China and other communist countries in Asia and elsewhere is further striking evidence of the global reach of free markets and private enterprise.

The transnational enterprises have played a central role in this process through internationalization of production, transfer of technology, managerial and technical skills, foreign investment, marketing, international staff recruitment, promotion of trade and advertising (United Nations 1992; Dunning 1993). The rapidity of technological change, especially in transport, communications and information processing, has been a decisive element in the acceleration of globalization. The increasing competitiveness of a growing number of countries through market-friendly policies, infrastructural investment and the development of technical skills and entrepreneurial abilities has further boosted globalization through rapid economic growth and expansion of trade and other economic links with the outside world. Similarly, the rapid expansion of mass media has made a powerful contribution to globalization in the political, social and cultural domains. Enormous growth in communications, travel and tourism has been critical in advancing globalization along all fronts.

ECONOMIC CONSEQUENCES

The process of globalization has been associated with wide-ranging socio-economic consequences. In many cases these have been aggravated by the fact that the current phase of accelerated globalization since the 1970s coincided with a period of low growth in most industrialized countries and of stagnation and decline in many Latin American, African, Middle Eastern and some Asian countries. These years have also witnessed a systemic change in the former centrally planned countries in Europe. At the same time, as mentioned above, globalization has been associated with a number of other changes, such as technological progress, liberalization and deregulation. It is quite impossible to separate out the economic impact of globalization, however defined, from that of the above factors. There is the further difficulty arising from the time period over which the analysis is carried out. The immediate and short-term impact may turn out to be very different from that of the medium and long term. Despite these qualifications, it is important to stress that the process of globalization tends to produce certain socio-economic effects.

Concentrating first on the economic impact, among the key issues are the effects of globalization on efficiency, growth and distribution. It is clear that the process of globalization has promoted efficiency gains in a number of ways. The static gains accrue whenever market distortions are reduced or eliminated. Globalization has been associated with wide-ranging reductions in barriers to movement of goods, services and factors of production. The greater competition brought about by globalization has also produced dynamic efficiency gains through improvements in management and technology. Likewise, the replacement of state enterprises by private corporations has in many cases resulted in efficiency gains. The value of efficiency gains is clearly greater when they occur in periods of full utilization of resources than when they merely add to unemployment and excess capacity. Unfortunately, the coincidence of globalization with economic crisis and stagnation has meant that in most countries the efficiency gains due to improved resource allocation appear to have accentuated the problems of poverty, unemployment and inequalities. It can be argued that these reforms have laid the basis for more rapid and efficient growth in the medium to long term, but this remains to be seen.

With regard to growth, there may again be conflict between short- and medium-term considerations. The short-run impact of globalization has undoubtedly been contractionary. The increased competition nationally and internationally has resulted in relentless pressures to reduce costs and enhance productivity *inter alia* through reductions in employment and wages. Furthermore, this has contributed to increased uncertainty about job prospects. The effect has been to reduce aggregate consumer demand. The governments have also been constrained to restrain or reduce public expenditures to diminish budget deficits and control inflation. The increased integration of factor and product markets has effectively undermined the ability of most countries to pursue expansionist policies to stimulate demand and promote employment. At the same time there is no effective machinery at the international level to coordinate the macro policies of individual countries (Michie and Smith 1995). The markets themselves have had powerful contractionary effects. Any initiative to lower interest rates or increase public expenditure or bank lending leads to market 'over-reaction' in terms of capital flows, exchange and interest rate changes, creditworthiness and so on. In effect, the markets hold a veto on the macro-economic policies of governments. The countries thus have become prisoners of global markets.

The longer-term effects are more uncertain. It can be argued that increased efficiency, greater competition and the creation of a hospitable environment for business activities are likely to spur investment, enterprise and technological progress, thereby contributing to faster growth on a more sustainable basis. There is little doubt that individual countries or groups of countries may be able to forge ahead rapidly, as has been the case with many Asian countries; but whether, in the absence of effective mechanisms for coordinating policy at the world level, the new environment and global market forces can counteract the contractionary influences noted above and provide a stimulus for sustained expansion of the world economy remains to be seen.

The issue of distribution relates to benefits and losses from globalization. More specifically, it concerns the important question of who gains and loses from the changes associated with globalization? The distribution of income is affected, among other things, by changes in the level of economic activity, public taxation and expenditure, trade and resource flows and in factor and product prices. It is therefore extremely difficult to estimate the direction, let alone the extent, of changes in income distribution attributable to globalization. All that can be attempted here is identification of the main tendencies associated with globalization that impact on income distribution.

In the short run, most of the changes associated with globalization are likely to deepen income inequalities (Ghai 1992; Griffin and Khan 1992). The greater role of market forces in the labour and capital markets can be expected in most countries to raise interest rates and to lower wages, especially of unskilled workers. This is so because the government regulations in these markets were designed to control interest rates and ensure minimum wages. The effect is likely to be reinforced by changes in taxes and public expenditure, such as moves towards indirect taxes, lower marginal rates of individual and corporate taxes, reduction of subsidies and social security and welfare expenditure. The deflationary effects on economic activities may put further pressure on employment and wages which may be reinforced by labour-saving technological progress.

The increased competition nationally and internationally is likely to work in the same direction for most countries. The increase in the speed and volume of resource flows, expansion of trade and internationalization of production can be expected to have considerable effects on income distribution. Countries which are successful in attracting foreign funds, investment and technology and in enhancing expansion of output and exports are likely to experience rising employment and wages and possibly reduction in inequality. At the other extreme, less competitive and more unstable countries may suffer from outflows of capital, investment, skills and entrepreneurship. They are likely to get caught in a downward spiral of production, employment and wages, exacerbating both poverty and inequalities (Amin 1993).

The overall impact of these changes is likely to be negative on the working class in most countries. In the industrialized countries, their employment and wages are under pressure from three sources: increased competition (both internally and from abroad), techno-

logical progress and internationalization of production. The fate of
the working class in the industrialized countries would be even
worse if there were no restrictions on labour migration. Likewise,
owners of many small and medium sized enterprises may suffer
from increased national and international competition. The major
beneficiaries from the globalization process are likely to be large
corporations, owners of mobile capital and professional, technical
and managerial personnel (Ghai 1991, 1992).

In the medium to long term so many dynamic factors come into
play that it becomes exceedingly difficult to assess the impact of
globalization on income distribution. A central question is the
effect of globalization on growth rate of the world economy and on
its constituent parts. The pattern of growth also assumes critical
importance in determining the distribution of benefits and costs.
Much will depend on the extent to which various markets – goods,
services, capital and labour – become truly integrated at the global
level. The economic policies pursued at the national level will
obviously be critical in determining the distributional implications
of globalization.

SOCIAL AND CULTURAL IMPACT

The social and cultural impact of globalization has also been
widespread. It is manifested most clearly in the world-wide spread
of certain patterns of consumption and lifestyles. These include
cars, television, videos, fashions and designer clothing, popular
music, films, television and video shows, dances, alcohol, beverages
and fast foods, just to mention a few of the more prominent
symbols of world culture. The social and cultural impact is especially noticeable on two sections of the population, the affluent
minorities and youth. While many of the consumption goods and
services are available only to affluent minorities in developing and
former communist countries, others (such as television and video
programmes and fast foods) reach much larger proportions of the
population in these countries.

Several consequences have flowed from social and cultural globalization (UNRISD 1995). Most obviously, there has been a trend
towards social and cultural homogenization at the expense of
richness and diversity. Even if the global spread of some consumer
goods and services and of leisure activities does not destroy the

local and national equivalents, it greatly weakens them. Related to this is the influence of dominant social and cultural practices on indigenous social relations, behaviour and values. These can affect relations between parents and children, men and women, and among members of the extended families and different social groups. They are also likely to affect the attitude of the population towards authority, whether this be the government, school administrations or religious establishments. It is inevitable that such modification or disruption of traditional relations, values and modes of behaviour should generate tensions in various parts of the society. A much-publicized aspect of this problem concerns the local impact of foreign films, videos and television programmes. The dominance of violence, crime, sex and drugs in many of these programmes is alleged to have generated or intensified these problems worldwide, including the industrialized countries.

Cultural and social globalization has aroused widespread opposition and resistance. This has occurred both in industrialized and developing countries and has taken many forms. The states have tried in various ways to restrict the exposure of the people to imported products and programmes in an attempt both to minimize their alleged negative effects as well as to preserve and promote national culture and social practices and values. Their actions have been promoted or supported by other important bodies such as political parties, cultural associations and religious organizations. The implacable opposition of fundamentalist and xenophobic movements is only an extreme example of widespread concern at foreign influences on local society and culture (Bangura 1994; Haynes 1995).

Another important consequence of globalization is that it creates or strengthens groups which are linked with people in other parts of the world by common interests and lifestyles. The affluent minorities in poor countries can thus relate to the middle classes in the industrialized world. A common culture binds together youth from different parts of the world. These cultural and social links strengthen those already created by the web of international commerce, production, finance and investment. All these provide points of common interest going beyond the state borders, thus further loosening national ties.

A fundamental aspect of social and cultural globalization is that vast multitudes of people in poor countries (but increasingly also in the rich countries) are left outside these circuits of consumption and leisure activities. The sense of frustration engendered by deprivation is fuelled by their relentless exposure through the media to the temptations and seductions of good life enjoyed by the fortunate few. It is hardly surprising if this leads them into get-rich-quick activities which are typically associated with illegal acts such as crime and arms trade, prostitution, pornography and production and sale of drugs.

POLITICAL AND INSTITUTIONAL ASPECTS

As noted above, the pace of globalization has been quickened by the shift in policies towards free markets and private enterprise. The spread of globalization in turn has reinforced the trend in favour of market liberalization and privatization. This shift in economic policy and ideology has been accompanied by significant changes in power relations among social groups and in effectiveness of established institutions (UNRISD 1995, Wolfe 1994). Enhanced national and international competition, the greater mobility of capital and the increased reliance of governments on global capital markets have greatly increased the power of business and financial groups, especially those linked to international transactions of one sort or another. The relative power of organized labour has been weakened by economic restructuring, more precarious forms of employment and high levels of unemployment.

These changes are also reflected at the level of institutions. Mass organizations such as trade unions, cooperatives and peasant associations have seen an erosion of their power and effectiveness. Political parties incorporating the interests of organized workers and the working poor have either become marginalized or have adapted their electoral platforms and policies to the dominant neo-liberal ideologies (Guéhemo 1993). At the same time, business and employers' organizations have greatly increased their power and influence, not least through their ownership of mass media. Everywhere the power and reach of the state have been diminished. Especially in the domain of economic policy, the ability of the countries to regulate the economy through monetary, fiscal, trade and exchange rate policy has been restricted in varying degrees. The liberalization of markets and the growing integration of the world economy are mainly responsible for this situation. Additional contributory factors are regional economic and political groupings and international commercial and financial agreements. The degree of freedom enjoyed by a country to pursue an independent policy is evidently related to its economic size and integration in the world economy. But other factors, such as its reliance on foreign governments, commercial banks and international financial agencies for servicing its debts or covering its budgetary and foreign payment deficits, often impinge severely on its economic sovereignty. This has especially been the case with many developing and transition economies.

The net result of these changes in power relations, ideological discourse and institutional effectiveness has been to greatly tilt the balance against public expenditure on social programmes. The touchstone of public policy has become its impact on efficiency and competitiveness. Any redistributive policies and programmes for social expenditure are routinely denounced for their adverse effects on incentives and for undermining individual initiative and responsibility. The reduced effectiveness of 'popular' institutions and progressive parties has further weakened the countervailing power against neo-liberal policies. The state, with its reduced autonomy, mounting debts and growing reliance on capital markets, has often little choice but to follow the dictates of the dominant domestic and foreign interests.

ACCELERATED GLOBALIZATION AND HUMAN INSECURITY

One of the main consequences of accelerated globalization and associated changes has been to intensify human insecurity (Dahrendorf 1996). This appears to have occurred across a wide spectrum of countries varying in socio-economic systems and levels of development. The sources of this insecurity can be traced to changes in the domains of economy, society, politics and culture (Buzan 1991; United Nations Development Programme (UNDP) 1994). Any dynamic system generates human insecurity but, when changes occur with startling rapidity, the cumulative impact can be quite frightening; and when the institutions and mechanisms in place to cushion insecurity begin to crumble under the impact of the same forces, the effect is intensified.

Increased economic insecurity is at the centre of the rising spiral of human insecurity. The key contributory factors are intensified competition, internationalization of production, changes in methods of production, surges of financial speculation and rapidity of technological innovations. These dynamic forces have generated unprecedented pressures on livelihood security that are expressed in different ways for different groups in different countries. In most countries, a central element in economic insecurity is intensification of the unemployment problem. This characteristic is common to many OECD countries, the ex-centrally planned countries in Europe and most countries in Africa, Middle East and Latin America (Khan 1994; International Labour Office (ILO) 1995; World Bank 1995). Even those with jobs have experienced a deterioration in conditions of employment reflected in a decline in employment security, an increase in casual and part-time work, greater work pressure from employers and the need for constant adjustments to rapidly changing circumstances. Increasingly these pressures are felt not just by unskilled workers but also by personnel in higher grades such as technical, professional and managerial cadres. Neither are owners of enterprises spared the anxiety and uncertainty generated by intensified competition and innovation. These forces have also contributed to pressure on wages in low skilled jobs. In many countries, such wages have declined, stayed constant or risen more slowly than the earnings of persons with higher skills, thereby widening income inequalities.

These sources of economic insecurity have been reinforced by changes in state policies in the field of income redistribution and social security. Influenced by new ideologies and buffeted by the factors noted above, the states in most countries have been cutting down on subsidies on items of mass consumption, increasing charges for social services and reducing the level and range of benefits under social security and welfare programmes. Thus unemployment benefits, health coverage and old age pensions are being adversely affected for most citizens (Vivian 1995; Esping-Andersen 1996). The family and community structures are also undergoing important changes under the influence of globalization and associated changes. They are thus less effective in cushioning the impact of adverse economic changes. Some existing and new institutions, such as religious bodies and citizens' organizations, are trying to fill in the void but their efforts at best have had limited impact.

The sources of insecurity are located also in other domains of human activity. In the sphere of politics, the close bonds between political parties and their supporters have become loosened in recent years. The workers, the unemployed and other categories of low-income groups lack confidence in the traditional parties to defend their interests. It is not surprising that there is a growing disenchantment and lack of interest in the political process. In the social domain, it is the weakening of community and family structures that exacerbates a sense of personal insecurity. Changes in the established patterns of relations between generations, sexes and peer groups add a potent new source of anxiety for many (Giddens 1996). In the sphere of culture, it is the clash between traditional values and those propagated by the media and the consumer society that contribute to conflicts and uncertainty.

The intensified individual and social insecurity resulting from these multiple sources has been associated with a range of adverse effects. Its immediate effect at the individual and the family level is an increase in mental stress and strain. This is manifested in different forms of psychological and physical ailments including depression, alienation, suicide, high blood pressure, strokes and heart attacks (Galtung 1996). The human, social and economic costs of such consequences of insecurity are staggering but are almost never taken into account by decision-makers.

When confronted with the malaise induced by insecurity, people tend to turn for support to institutions such as the state, work organizations, communities and families. However, as argued above, the ability of such institutions to offer material and psychological support is much reduced. The void so created is filled increasingly by ethnic and religious bodies. At moments of deep anxiety for their people, such organizations supply material needs, cultural identity and secure values. Unfortunately in many circumstances, these organizations espouse extremist visions characterized by intolerance, exclusion, hatred and violence. Material deprivation and cultural crisis provide a fertile ground for the operation of ethnic and religious entrepreneurs with their own power and ideological agenda. All too often these initiatives end up in religious and ethnic violence and wars of secession with their inevitable accompaniment of mass killings, physical destruction and forced displacement of people as external and internal refugees.

People turn in many directions in their search for security of livelihood. The processes of globalization create new and enlarged opportunities. Not all of them are legal and benign, and neither are all the beneficiaries indigent and helpless. Growing numbers of people turn to illegal and clandestine ways to earn vast fortunes or to augment their meagre means. This expanding complex of activities ranges in space from the transnational to the village level and in number from teams of thousands to operations of individuals. Trade in armaments and illegal drugs runs into scores of billions of dollars and involves a complicated chain of industrialists, growers, merchants, banks, retailers and consumers (Tullis 1995). Robberies and thefts also come in many shapes and sizes. Commerce in sex and pornography has taken new and perverse forms. Entrepreneurs have even found ways of profiteering from moving people around illegally and dealing in human parts!

ENHANCING ECONOMIC SECURITY

Human insecurity is the product of diverse and complex factors. In one form or another, it has always formed part of human condition. It can never be eliminated altogether, but neither is it clear that total security would be a desirable state of living. Nevertheless, human beings have sought through the ages to reduce insecurity to tolerable levels. Although insecurities in different domains are interrelated and feed on each other, the primary focus here is on economic insecurity. It is undeniable that economic insecurity has worsened in most parts of the world in recent years compared with the preceding decades in the post-war period. As argued above, this insecurity derives from high levels of unemployment, precarious job conditions, deepening poverty and diminishing state support.

Economic security cannot be enhanced by reverting simply to the conditions and policies of earlier years. The forces of globalization cannot be rolled back. Technology alone has forever changed the world we live in, and it does not make sense to reverse the reliance on free markets and private enterprise as the primary mechanisms for promoting economic progress. The great challenge for analysts, reformers and leaders alike is to devise policies and institutions to ensure greater security in the new situation created by accelerated globalization and technological advance. It must be admitted that this is a daunting task and little progress has been made so far in this respect either at the level of thought or action. This section can do no more than sketch the broad directions for policy and institutional reform for enhanced human security. Even so, more questions are raised than answers provided.

The problems of human security differ in industrialized, transition and developing countries and so must the policies to deal with them. A case in point concerns the prescription of higher growth rates to combat unemployment and poverty. Most developed countries were able to achieve near full employment in the first three decades of the post-war period in large part due to historically unprecedented rates of economic growth. It is unrealistic to assume that this experience can be repeated in the future. It is more probable that the growth rates of the past two decades, more in line with the historical experience, are likely to prevail in the future. In any case both environmental considerations and the nature of technological progress raise serious doubts as to whether higher growth is the best route to handling unemployment problems in rich countries. Reforms in labour market and in educational and training systems can help in enhancing employment possibilities. But significant progress towards full employment would call for more imaginative policy and institutional reforms in such areas as technological progress, new combinations of work, learning and leisure, work sharing and novel arrangements for financing of socially and economically useful work.

For most developing and transition countries, rapid economic growth is indispensable for employment generation and poverty reduction. In the past the growth rate in poor countries was largely tied to economic conditions in the industrialized countries. Increased integration of the world economy might be expected to intensify this dependent relationship. But for many countries this link appears to have been attenuated, if not severed. They have succeeded in attaining high growth rates even in years of stagnation or low growth in the rich countries. This is especially true of the Asian region. If similar trends appear in other developing regions, this could create the possibility of poor countries being able to attain high growth rates independent of economic performance in the rich countries. Ironically the world may be moving in the direction where growth in the industrialized countries comes to depend increasingly on expansion in the erstwhile developing countries!

What is the explanation of this apparent paradox? The increasing integration and competitiveness of some developing countries means that they are able to achieve high growth rates by increasing their share of the markets in the rich countries even in periods of stagnation or low growth. For this to be possible, it is clearly important that developing countries be in a position to supply competitively a range of consumer or capital goods with substantial markets in the industrialized countries. It is also crucial that the movement towards trade liberalization signalled by the Uruguay Round be sustained and strengthened. Other developing countries can profit from the new centres of dynamism by forging closer economic and political links with them. Thus globalization may contribute to the long cherished ideal of increased trade and economic cooperation among developing countries.

Rapid growth alone cannot suffice to make a significant dent in unemployment and poverty. To ensure broad diffusion of the benefits of economic expansion, the pattern of growth must be labour intensive. This in turn calls for appropriate macroeconomic, trade, technology, asset distribution and human investment policies. Several countries in South-East Asia and elsewhere have succeeded in combining high rates of economic growth with rapid labour absorption. There are also many instances of countries where rapid growth made only a limited contribution to relief of unemployment and destitution. This was due primarily to highly unequal pattern of asset distribution, especially land, and emphasis on capital-intensive technology.

The first line of defence is thus pursuit of economic policies that are successful in generating a rate and pattern of growth which reduce poverty and unemployment to manageable proportions. To the extent that this is achieved, there will be correspondingly less need for programmes of social support. In recent years, a number of countries came close to meeting these objectives. Among the industrialized countries, these include Japan, Switzerland and Austria, and among the developing countries, Hong Kong, Taiwan Province of China, Singapore and South Korea. They have been joined recently by other countries such as Chile, Malaysia and Mauritius. If, however, economic policies continue to generate substantial unemployment and poverty, it will become necessary to put in place programmes of social support to prevent or mitigate secondary social problems which can be extremely expensive in terms of human suffering and financial outlays. In recent years, Scandinavian countries, the Netherlands, Germany and France have pursued comprehensive policies of social support for the poor, the unemployed and other vulnerable groups. In the developing countries, examples of social support programmes with wide coverage are provided by a diverse range of countries including the

Middle East oil producers, Cost Rica, Chile, Cuba, Sri Lanka and China (Ahmad *et al.* 1991).

As indicated above, social security and welfare programmes are under strain almost everywhere. In the poor countries, stabilization and structural adjustment policies seek to cut social spending. In the former centrally planned economies, the previous systems of comprehensive social security have been scrapped and replaced by selective programmes of varying degrees of effectiveness. In the industrialized countries the range and level of benefits are being trimmed. Many factors have contributed to this outcome. These include high levels of debt, balance of payments difficulties, budget deficits, resistance to tax increases and demographic changes. The problems of the welfare state are also in no small measure due to increased international competition, reduced state autonomy to pursue independent fiscal and monetary policies, and the discipline of the market, all associated with accelerated globalization.

Provision of social support for the poor, the unemployed and other vulnerable groups raises important issues of public policy in the era of market liberalization. One of the issues relates to identification of core needs for which public authorities need to assume responsibility. How do these vary with social and economic structures and the level of economic development? There is also the important question of the relationship between the methods of financing social support programmes and their effects on incentives to save, invest and work. It would seem desirable that, wherever possible, the social support programmes should encourage socially and economically productive work and facilitate the acquisition of skills and capabilities which enhance the recipients' potential contribution to the economy and the society.

A major question concerns the institutional and agency responsibility in the domain of social and economic policies. It is clear that, in the light of the market liberalization and globalization of the past two decades, there is need to rethink the roles and responsibilities of institutions at all levels. There are two aspects to this issue. The first relates to the division between public, private and voluntary agencies and the second refers to the level at which they operate: local, national, regional and international. It can be argued that in the post-war years, there was a tendency for the state to assume too many powers and responsibilities. This has often resulted in inefficient performance and stifling of initiatives by other agencies, both public and private. It is thus likely that an optimal solution would call for a better balance in the division of responsibility among different agencies. Some of the functions and tasks performed by the state may advantageously be taken over by NGOs and lower tier public authorities. This would be a movement in the direction of decentralization and participation. The other trend is likely to favour the assumption of responsibility by institutions at regional and global levels. This is inherent in the logic of globalization. With the steadily increasing interdependence in many social, economic and political activities, the effective level for their regulation has expanded beyond the national borders.

The issue of accountability applies to institutions of all forms and at all levels. Thus as responsibility for different functions is re-divided among institutions, the issue of their public accountability becomes critical. The concept of accountability is closely linked with that of democracy and participation. An important aspect of the issue therefore concerns the mechanisms and procedures for ensuring public accountability of both private and public institutions at different levels.

In any global social policy, priority needs to be accorded to meeting the basic human needs of the world's population. This includes food, shelter, clothing, literacy, primary education and health care. In the allocation of global and national resources, priority should be given to meeting these needs. What are the appropriate institutional arrangements for bringing this about? There is clearly a need to strengthen local government and community institutions. These should be first lines of defence. They have the additional advantage of possessing detailed knowledge of local social and economic conditions, and of offering the benefits to the population of participation and institutional accountability. There is also the need to reform and strengthen central governments. For the foreseeable future, the primary responsibility for meeting the essential needs of the people will continue to devolve on the states. In countries which have reached a certain stage of development or which have the necessary resources, appropriate policies and institutional reforms can adequately meet most of the basic needs. But the problem arises in situations where governments are weak or incompetent and where the resources are scarce and the level of development low. In such situations, international agencies and NGOs have a critical role to play in meeting the essential needs of the people.

CONCLUSION

This chapter has been concerned with the economic, social and institutional consequences of accelerated globalization over the past two decades. It has focused particularly on heightened human insecurity resulting from the processes of globalization. Apart from being a source of much human suffering and hardship, intensification of economic insecurity is associated with social problems, ethnic conflicts and political instability. The systems of social support for disadvantaged groups built up in the post-war period are under severe strain and increasingly ineffective in coping with these problems. Policy and institutional reforms to provide a modicum of social and economic security must reflect the reality of open markets, fierce competition and rapid technological change. In the long run, the globalization of the economy must be matched by a globalization of social policy.

References

Ahmad, E., J. Dreze, J. Hills and A. Sen (eds) (1991), *Social Security in Developing Countries*, (Oxford: Clarendon Press).

Amin, S. (ed.) (1993), *Mondialisation et Accumulation* (Paris: L'Harmattan).

Bangura, Y. (1994), *The Search for Identity: Ethnicity, Religion and Political Violence* (Geneva: UNRISD).

Barnet, R. J. and J. Cavanagh (1994), *Global Dreams: Imperial Corporations and the New World Order* (New York: Simon & Schuster).

Beyer, P. (1994), *Religion and Globalisation* (London: Sage).

Buzan, B. (1991), *People, States and Fear* (Hemel Hempstead: Harvester Wheatsheaf).

Dahrendorf, R. (1996), 'Economic Opportunity, Civil Society and Political Liberty', in Cynthia Hewitt de Alcántara (ed.), *Social Futures, Global Visions* (Oxford: Basil Blackwell).

Dunning, J. H. (1993), *The Globalisation of Business* (London: Routledge).

Esping-Andersen, G. (1996), *Welfare States in Transition* (London: Sage).

Featherstone, M. (ed.), (1990), *Global Culture: Nationalism, Globalisation and Modernity* (London: Sage).

Galtung, J. (1996), 'On the Social Costs of Modernisation: Social Disintegration, Atomie/Anomie and Social Development', in Cynthia Hewitt de Alcántara (ed.), *Social Futures, Global Visions* (Oxford: Basil Blackwell).

Ghai, D. (ed.) (1991), *The IMF and the South* (London: Zed Books).

Ghai, D. (1992), *Structural Adjustment, Global Integration and Social Democracy* (Geneva: UNRISD).

Giddens, A. (1996), 'Affluence, Poverty and the Idea of a Post-Scarcity Society', in Cynthia Hewitt de Alcántara (ed.), *Social Futures, Global Visions* (Oxford: Basil Blackwell).

Griffin, K. and A. R. Khan (1992), *Globalisation and the Developing World: An Essay on the International Dimensions of Development in the Post-Cold War Era* (Geneva: UNRISD).

Guéhemo, J.-M. (1993), *La Fin de la Démocratie* (Paris: Flammarion).

Harris, N. (1995), *The New Untouchables: Immigration and the New World Worker* (London: I. B. Tauris).

Haynes, J. (1995), *Religion, Fundamentalism and Ethnicity: A Global Perspective* (Geneva: UNRISD).

ILO (1995), *World Employment 1995* (Geneva: ILO).

Khan, A.R. (1994), *Overcoming Unemployment* (Geneva: ILO).

McGrew, A. G. and P. G. Lewis (1992), *Global Politics: Globalisation and the Nation-State* (Cambridge: Polity Press).

Michie, J. and J. G. Smith (eds) (1995), *Managing the Global Economy* (Oxford: Oxford University Press).

Robertson, R. (1992), *Social Theory and Global Culture* (London: Sage).

Stalker, P. (1994), *The World of Strangers: A Survey of International Migration* (Geneva: ILO).

Tullis, L. (1995), *Unintended Consequences: Illegal Drugs and Drug Policies in Nine Countries* (Boulder, Col.: Lynne Rienner).

UNDP (1994), *Human Development Report 1994* (New York: UNDP).

United Nations (1992), *World Investment Report 1992: Transnational Corporations and Engines of Growth* (New York: United Nations).

UNRISD (1995), *States of Disarray: The Social Effects of Globalisation* (Geneva: UNRISD).

Vivian J. (ed.) (1995), *Adjustment and Social Sector Restructuring* (London: Frank Cass).

Waters, M. (1995), *Globalisation* (London: Routledge).

Wolfe, M. (1994), *Social Integration: Institutions and Actors* (Geneva: UNRISD).

World Bank (1995), *Workers in an Integrating World* (New York: Oxford University Press).

Note

1. See Featherstone 1990; Mcgrew and Lewis 1992; Robertson 1992; Beyer 1994; Waters 1995.

3 Social Movements in the Third World

T. K. Oommen

As a preamble to the analysis in this chapter, a conceptual clarification regarding the relationship between social movements and development is necessary, for several reasons.

First, in conventional social science, social movements[1] used to be viewed as mechanisms of coping with stress and strain and they were rarely seen as sources of change and development (see, for example, Smelser 1962; Eisenstadt 1965). Most studies of change concentrated on factors such as technology, migration, urbanization, industrialization and communication as sources of change. Even when the role of ideology was recognized, social movements were not perceived as vehicles of creative ideas.

Second, when movement studies surfaced, the initial tendency was to look upon movements as indicative of social pathology. Movement participants were defined and described as 'deviants' who are creating instability in the system. Third, the dominant tendency, particularly in sociology and until recently, was to emphasize social equilibrium and stability, often ignoring that most of the time it is coercive equilibrium which prevails.[2]

As against the above trends, there is accumulating evidence to suggest that movements are increasingly perceived as vehicles of innovative and creative ideas. Today movement participants are described as martyrs to their faith rather than deviants indulging in anti-establishment activities. Consequently, the nature of societal equilibrium must be viewed as consensual, which is qualitatively different from coercive equilibrium. In addition movements are also increasingly viewed as creative confrontations propelled by collectivities in search of a society based on a qualitatively different collective consciousness. That is, movements are perceived to be playing a positive, indeed creative, role.

In order to understand the role of social movements in development it is necessary to discuss the notion of social development and distinguish it from the concept of social change. This latter idea,

46

whether it refers to change within the structure or change of the structure, implies a point of departure, a point of destination and a process of replacement occurring between these points. The directionality of change could be from system state A to, say, system states B, C or N. Hypothetically, the process can even be in the reverse: that is, the point of departure may perhaps be B, C or N and the point of destination A. Viewed thus, the notion of social change is neutral to the point of destination; it is a value-free concept. In contrast, social development occurs when the process of replacement is taking place in a specific direction, when the point of destination is a desired and a desirable one; it is desired by the vast majority of the system participants, and it is desirable from the perspective of their welfare. Then social development is that type of social change taking place through the active participation and conscious volition of the people, geared mainly to the welfare of the disadvantaged, dispossessed and disinherited. Social change can take place without social development. However, while social change is a prerequisite for social development, it is not sufficient, because social development also prescribes the destination of change. It is a value-loaded concept.

Mobilization for social development entails involving groups in collective action. Group formation is based on a variety of factors. However, for the present purpose I propose to categorize them into biological collectivities (such as gender, racial or age group), civil collectivities (such as workers, peasants, students, professionals) and primordial collectivities (such as regional, linguistic, religious, caste groups). The rationale of this three-fold categorization of collectivities – biological, civil and primordial – is that they can be placed on a fixity-flexibility continuum. While the attributes of the biological collectivities are largely given, although necessarily buttressed by socio-cultural stereotypes, the attributes of civil collectivities are invariably acquired, a product almost entirely of the socialization process. In the case of primordial collectivities it is partly given and partly acquired. Given the relative fixity or flexibility of attributes, the possibility of crystallization of a collective conscience varies among these entities. In the case of biological collectivities it is relatively easy; in the case of civil collectivities it is very difficult. The case of primordial collectivities comes in between. The intermediate status of primordial collectivities on the fixity-flexibility continuum is significant when viewed in the context of social development. As indicated earlier, my notion of social development implies conscious volition and active involvement of the system participants in the developmental process. That is to say, social mobilization of collectivities is a prerequisite for their social development. In turn, the crystallization of collective consciousness is not only a precondition for their mobilization but takes place as the very process of mobilization proceeds. The understanding of this dialectical intertwining between the attributes of a collectivity, the prospects of their mobilization and the shaping of their consciousness is of utmost importance in analysing the ongoing process of social development.

All the three types of collectivity listed above are found everywhere. However, the importance of primordial collectivities (based on religious, linguistic, regional and caste attributes) is often exaggerated, because the goals of these collectivities are often manifestly in conflict with 'national' interests. In the Third World, such conflicts acquire salience easily.

There are two reasons for this. First, the emergence of the nation-state as a territorially defined socio-political entity is relatively recent in the long span of human history and, in the case of the new states of the Third World, the notion of the nation-state is not yet deeply rooted. Formed through the consolidation of a large number of pre-modern political entities, such as princely states and tribal kingdoms, they are nations-in-the-making, to recall a cliché. Hence, all threats to the unity of the state are viewed very seriously by their rulers, and particularly the threat of alternative allegiances typically generated by the mobilization of primordial collectivities.

Second, in Western Europe where modern nation-states first emerged and solidified, the polity-society gap was minimal in several cases. In those cases where it was substantial, the gap was narrowed through a rapacious process of homogenization, as in France (Weber 1976; Berger 1977; Reece 1979). In other cases, diversity was conceded and tolerated, as in the UK. However, for several countries in the Third World, which are deeply embedded in regional historicity, linguistic and cultural diversity, religious multiplicity and social pluralism, the West European model of the nation-state is largely irrelevant. Fuel for ideologies promoting autonomous primordial collectivities is plentiful, however, and the possibility of their development towards outright secessionism is always present.

THE END OF THE THIRD WORLD?

The notion of the Third World was much in currency and perhaps seductive in the 1960s, so much so that Peter Worsley published a book in 1964 with the title, without even defining the term. The unstated assumption was that the Third World was constituted by ex-colonial, newly independent and non-aligned countries. On the other hand, Wallerstein (1974) argued that there is only one single world system, which in the final analysis was a capitalist one. According to Wallerstein, the communist state is merely a 'collective capitalist firm as long as it remains a participant in the capitalist market' (1979: 68). The building blocks of the world system are put into a continuum: core countries, semi-peripheral countries and peripheral countries. Wallerstein's model is essentially economic and it abstracts from the cultural dimension.

Having realized the ambiguity of the term Third World, Worsley attempts a conceptual clarification and an elaborate analysis of the three world model in his later work (1984: 298–344), in which he squarely recognizes the role of culture in development. However, the paradox – that the Third World is constituted of countries and regions extremely varied in cultural heritages – is not adequately dealt with. Given the theme of this chapter, it is necessary to take cognizance of this variation and its implications for the analysis.

In popular parlance, three broad geographical regions (whose total population makes for the majority of humanity) together make up the artificial entity called the Third World; but they are racially and culturally different.

First, Latin America is racially and culturally close to the First World. Predominantly Christian and Catholic, most Latin American states have a European language – Spanish or Portuguese – as their official language. At its core Latin America is an extension and a cultural reproduction of the European periphery (Spain and Portugal). Most Latin American countries today are settler-majority countries and their native populations are either completely annihilated and/or marginalized.

Second, Africa is racially distinct or mixed (for example, South Africa) and culturally an amalgam of the native and the alien-colonial West. Of the 50 African states, 80 per cent have one of the European languages as their official language, and the dominant religions – Islam and Christianity – have been transplanted through conquest and colonialism. There is no settler-majority country on the African continent.

Third, Asia contains two major civilizations: the Chinese and the Indian. Of the 40 states in Asia, only one is predominantly Christian (the Philippines) and, except for Singapore, the small port-state, none has a European language as its official language. There is no country in Asia with a substantial presence of an 'alien' race. So the three regions put together and labelled as the Third World have hardly anything in common in their socio-cultural milieu except Western influence.

The common source of Western influence admittedly is colonialism. However, all Third World countries did not experience colonialism (Thailand) and all ex-colonial countries have not remained in the Third World. Some colonies were not only incorporated into the First World (such as the USA, Canada, Australia, New Zealand) but they even surpassed and assumed leadership over their erstwhile masters. Therefore, a distinction between *transplantive or replicative* colonialism (which reproduced the culture, society, polity and economy of the imperial power in the colony) and *intrusive and oppressive* colonialism (which dominates the colony even after the withdrawal of the imperial power) ought to be made. While the countries which experienced oppressive and intrusive colonialism shared a common economic deprivation, their cultural milieus vary vastly, as I have noted elsewhere (Oommen 1991: 67–84).

Further, some of the ex-colonial countries located in the regions traditionally identified with the Third World are very affluent today. Japan heads the list of developed countries, and the development ratings of Singapore, Korea, Taiwan and so on are quite high (UNDP 1991). The point I want to make at this juncture is that the nature and types of social movements and collective action which emerge and crystallize in 'Third World' countries may have precious little in common.

THE FIFTH REVOLUTION

Therefore it is necessary and useful to situate collective action and social movements historically. Broadly speaking, so far humanity has experienced five social revolutions, each of which may be viewed as a series of social movements and collective action.[3] First, there was the revolt of the aristocracy (those who claimed nobility based on birth) against the clergy (God's representatives on earth) which secularized the social order, separating the state and the Church. The focus of this revolution was to arrive at a consensus regarding a *division of labour* resulting in the allocation of the secular realm exclusively to the state and confining the activity of the church to the spiritual realm.

Second came the revolt by the economic categories (the merchants, the capitalists, the entrepreneurs, the bourgeoisie) against the clergy and the aristocracy, thereby questioning the *bases of status* in society. Next there was the proletarian revolution against the bourgeoisie for an appropriate share in the social product, produced by them, so as to bring about *distributive justice* in the economic realm. Fourth, there was a revolt by the colonized peoples of Asia, Africa and the Americas, challenging the political dominance and economic exploitation of their colonial masters in order to establish political *equality* between peoples, irrespective of their race, creed or geographical origin. The fifth revolution is that of the marginalized – that is, the women, the youth, the unemployed, the Blacks, the foreign migrant workers, the cultural minorities – questioning those in the establishment constituted by the clergy, intelligentsia, aristocrats, capitalists, bureaucrats, entrepreneurs and technocrats, attempting to evolve a *participatory society* to improve the *quality of life*.

A few general points may be noted about these revolutions as a prelude to my discussion. The first three revolutions occurred in particular state-societies, or blocks of them, mainly in Europe. The fourth revolution was necessarily confined to the ex-colonial countries but there came about a substantial differentiation amongst these new state-societies after this revolution. While one set of ex-colonial countries got incorporated into the affluent First World, the state-societies of Asia, Africa and Latin America came to constitute the underprivileged and poverty-stricken 'Third World' in the wake of their political liberation from colonialism.

The fifth revolution is truly transnational in its scale and scope, in that although particular events may occur only in specific state-societies their reverberations are felt globally because of increased interdependence between societies and thanks to the impact of the mass media. It may also be noted that while the first four revolutions were contentions about single dimensions, be it status, power or wealth, the fifth revolution is multi-dimensional in its thrust, because the marginalized are the victims of cumulative dominance and inequality. Finally, while the first four revolutions have already terminated, the fifth is still ongoing. It is the womb out of which new mobilizations and actors are continually emerging.

To answer the question why collective actors who experience cumulative deprivation have emerged at the present juncture in history, we must understand the *changing cognitions* about the nature of deprivation and the societal mechanisms invoked to cope with the deprived. Broadly speaking, the mechanisms passed through three phases (Titmuss 1958). In the beginning, only material deprivation, and that too of an abject kind, was recognized. The poor and destitute were merely the recipients of benefits; they were objects of relief and charity. They were believed to be responsible for their predicament and yet the ameliorative acts of different institutions (family and kin, village and neighbourhood, religious charity and so on) sought to mitigate their material deprivation. The needs of the poor were met through the charity extended by the relatively well-off members of society. However, the motivation behind charity was not so much the physical survival of the recipient in this world but the moral survival of the donor in the other world. That is, the material deprivation of the poor was a necessary prerequisite for meeting the moral ends of the rich. Admittedly, such a societal ethos could not provide for the emergence of a self-conscious collective actor.

With the emergence of the socialist states and the welfare states, development and welfare replaced charity as the mechanism of meeting the demands of the poor. Strategies were initiated both by the state and by voluntary associations, popularly referred to as NGOs, to bring about the 'self-sustaining development' of the poor. In concrete terms this meant introducing a set of income-generating measures for the poor which would lead them eventually to the portal of economic self-sufficiency and autonomy. The leadership was provided either by the developmental bureaucracy of the state and/or by 'altruistic' professionals. But both groups were drawn from the middle class, and they viewed development essentially as a non-political, techno-managerial activity. In this model of development people's participation had no space, and the beneficiaries of development were defined as clients and targets. In fact, development itself was defined as a function of capital and technology; development goals were conceptualized in terms of urban middle-class aspirations. If the people did not show the expected level of enthusiasm about this strategy and goal of development, they were instantly labelled conservative and change-resisting. Understandably, this paradigm of development deprived the people of their participatory potential. However, gradually a new understanding about development crystallized; it dawned on a few of the experts and bureaucrats as well as the people at large that, to be authentic, development ought to be participatory.

The above realization ushered in the current phase of collective action. Accordingly, for this paradigm of development, the critical inputs are not capital and technology but mobilization and protest. The middle-class experts of the NGOs and the developmental bureaucracy of the state are replaced by a set of militant, ideologically-oriented, social activists. The focus is on conscientizing the deprived of their legal and political rights as equal citizens. Development is defined as a human right of the poor and not as charity or as a benefit bestowed on them. It is viewed as political activity (see Kothari 1988).

This understanding of development brought in the much-needed focus on people's participation.[4] But it also suffered from several defects. *First*, it did not clearly articulate a political theory, let alone a political strategy, of capturing state power through the electoral process or through revolutionary means. It operated in the extra-parliamentary space, demanding effective implementation of the existing laws or formulation of new legislation in response to the changing situation.

Second, notwithstanding the above, since law-making and its implementation are a state monopoly, the protagonists of this paradigm invariably took a negative stance towards the state which turned out to be dysfunctional: dysfunctional because not only will the state not wither away, it cannot be wished away either. Further, if and when mobilizations constitute a nuisance or threat, the state will attempt to coopt or coerce them, both of which are detrimental from the perspective of the cause pursued. If cooption leads to ideological erosion, coercion may result in physical annihilation. Success, therefore, would depend on keeping the required amount of pressure on the state by acting as a countervailing power (Oommen 1990: 183–209).

Third, protest and the resultant mobilization are not substitutes for capital and technology, both of which are essential for development. Protest and mobilization are only instruments to moderate the hegemony of capital and to determine the choice of technology. That is, it should be squarely recognized that protest and mobilization are but means for achieving participatory development. What I am suggesting is that to be effective and meaningful, collective actors should give adequate weight not only to democracy but also to development.

In the first two revolutions referred to above, the confronting collectivities constituted proximate layers in the social structure (the clergy, aristocracy and the economic categories), and their deprivation was confined to the non-material domain. The third revolution, the proletarian one, although representing an onslaught on all the upper layers, was also essentially one-dimensional in its thrust. Its assumption, although unstated, was that economic equality will bring about social justice. Even the anti-colonial struggle, the fourth revolution, was one-dimensional in the final analysis, focusing on transfer of power from the imperial agencies to the national elites. Once again the assumption was simplistic: national governments would necessarily and automatically bring about equality and social justice. None of these assumptions proved to be correct. Consequently, collective action and social movements had to be based on a different set of assumptions and strategies and had to pursue a new set of goals.

A democratic polity, by definition, is one in which the hiatus between the government and the people does not exist. It is a system in which the people participate along with their representatives in the government to create a common future; it is a tryst with destiny, to recall the evocative phrase invoked by Jawaharlal Nehru. Political institutions, development plans, technology, information, knowledge and so on are inputs and instruments through which the destiny is to be achieved. But when these institutions, instrumentalities and inputs do not deliver the goods and instead become the tools of oppression, people's action becomes imperative. This is the context of the emerging social movements which is common to *all the Three Worlds*. It is indicative of the failures of the liberal expectancy of the First World, the radical expectancy of the Second World and the nationalist expectancy of the Third World. The elites of all the Three Worlds, the variations in their modes of recruitment and social composition notwithstanding, have failed to incorporate the people – the masses – into the participatory process and to create an open civil society. Instead, the state, the government and even the political parties have become instruments in the hands of the elite to perpetuate their power. The people have become aware of the abysmal gap between what the system had promised and what it delivered, and they are demanding the correction of this aberration. Established institutions have become suspect and even stigmatized. People's actions in contemporary societies are piloted through agencies variously labelled as non-party organizations, voluntary associations, people's committees and so on, and all of them want to avoid the 'iron law of oligarchy' which has sapped the vitality of established institutions.

It follows from the above that the second objective of the emerging social movements is to establish the much-needed balance between the logic of development and the demands of democracy. The situation has been complicated by two contrasting tendencies. Development fostered the cult of affluence and the ethic of consumerism, leading to the concentration of wealth in a limited number of state-societies and in the hands of groups and individuals within them. On the other hand, democracy nurtured the notion of decentralization and the process of participation. The assumption on which the liberal democracies of the First World have been built, namely that political democracy can be sustained without economic democracy, is being seriously questioned. The premise of the Second World, namely, that the ideology of distributive justice in the economy and a concentration of authority in the polity can coexist, was stripped naked, leading to its very collapse. The widespread belief in the Third World that the rising aspirations of the people can be contained and kept at bay indefinitely in the name of the abstract notion of nation-building has come to grief. Contemporary collective actors seek to provide economic content to political democracy; they insist that food without freedom is not worth consuming!

Further, emerging social movements do not endorse either of the prevalent evaluations about technology. These evaluations see technology either as good in itself and as a humanizing agent or as an unmitigated evil, inherently violent and ultimately destructive of humankind. In contrast, the emerging perspective seems to endorse the view that technology is a conditional good and opts for technological pluralism which implies decentralization in its production, distribution and deployment (Oommen 1992: 131–9).

There are, however, two important factors which militate against technological pluralism. One is that the most advanced technology is war technology, which is the monopoly of a handful of state-societies. The other is the fact that the most sophisticated technology is virtually the monopoly of a few multi-national corporations whose aggressive market behaviour cannot be controlled either by particular states or by multi-state organizations. Technological pluralism consciously nurtures harmony between humanity and nature, preventing ecological degradation and fostering sustainable development. Understandably, the emerging social movements are anti-war, anti-centralization and anti-high technology. Conversely, the new collective actors are pro-peace, pro-decentralization and pro-appropriate technology.

Finally, the emerging social movements recognize three basic sources of deprivation: exploitation, discrimination and oppression. Presently, it is imperative to acknowledge the three basic identities of the collective actors: class-occupational, socio-cultural and pol-itical-ideological, as well as their changing saliency. According to the conventional class analysis anchored to homogeneous state-so-cieties, economic exploitation was the major, nay, the only source of deprivation. But gradually it is being conceded that discrimina-tion based on gender and age also exists in those societies. How-ever, in the case of culturally plural and socially heterogeneous societies, discrimination based on race, nationality, religion and so on exists irrespective of class background. Further, exclusion of citizens from the decision-making process, rendering them mar-ginal, powerless and alienated, is not uncommon in many societies even when they are not economically down and out and socially discriminated. That is, political oppression is as much a source of deprivation as economic exploitation or socio-cultural discrimina-tion. This persisting dispersed inequality has given birth to numer-ous mobilizations asserting cultural identity, even when the collectivity is economically well-off but culturally dominated.

As I hinted above, however, to the extent that a collectivity simultaneously experiences all these deprivations it is a victim of cumulative inequality and dominance. Thus, the category 'women' cuts across race, class and cultures and the deprivation common to all of them is gender-specific: that is, powerlessness. Therefore, it is only natural that feminist collective actors pursue empowerment as one of their basic goals. Similarly, the Blacks in the USA and the lower castes in India locate the primary source of their deprivation in racial and social discrimination respectively. And the poor everywhere find their disability is rooted in class exploitation. But the ongoing processes of development and transformation also create new privileged categories: the empowered women, the Black bourgeoisie, the affluent worker. The corollary to this is the creation of deprived categories, such as poor black rural uneducated women, the sources of whose deprivation are multiple and of a cumulative intensity. At the global level this polarization is manifest in the White, affluent, urban man at one end of the continuum and the Black/low caste, poor, rural woman on the other. Thus we get three empirically plausible collective actors: victims of cumulative domination, victims of dispersed domination and the cumulatively dominant. The real content of contemporary collective action and social movements is located in the confrontation between the cumulatively dominated and the cumulatively dominant.

It is far from my intention to suggest that there are no social movements or types of collective action which are specific to Third World countries; indeed there are. But I want to affirm two points. First, women's movements, environmental movements, human rights movements, peace movements and so on are not specific to Third World countries; they are global movements. This, however, is not to deny that these movements assume certain specific features as they appear in the Third World. Nevertheless the specificity acquired by these movements does not stem from their 'Third-World-ness', but from the cultural specificity which varies substantially within the three geographical-civilizational regions – Asia, Africa and Latin America – of the Third World. And this is my second point.

Notwithstanding the above there is a set of movements and a type of collective action which are predominantly found in Third World countries. I shall briefly discuss two examples of these, one of which is trans-state and the other invariably occurs within state-societies: the collective action of non-aligned states and movements for cultural identity, respectively.

THE NON-ALIGNED MOVEMENT

To start with, it may be noted that the Non-Aligned Movement (NAM) was not initiated by people to cope with their deprivations. NAM was initiated by the top leaders of a few states who sought to create an independent path in world politics so that the developing countries would not be reduced to the status of mere client states of superpowers or power-blocs. And yet NAM sought to change global structures and create a more just, equitable and peaceful world order. On the other hand, it is not particular individuals who joined and/or participated in NAM, but representatives of states. Formed in 1961 with 25 states, under the leadership of Nehru (India), Tito (Yugoslavia), Sukarno (Indonesia), Nkrumah (Ghana) and Nasser (Egypt), it grew into a forum of over 100 states (Rajan 1990).

It may be noted here that of the states which initiated the NAM, two (India and Indonesia) are among the largest in the world. (Of the 220 odd states in the world, fewer than a dozen have a population of a hundred million or more each (the biggest size), and 54 per cent have a population of five million or below). Therefore, the general impression that NAM is a coalition of small or middle-sized states is not correct. Similarly, it is not true that all the member-states of NAM are drawn from the Third World or were ex-colonial countries; they are predominantly drawn from the developing countries of all continents.

What distinguishes NAM from other trans-state associations is that it views the world as a single system and tries to create and maintain an independent voice for the less powerful and developed states. To this end it pursued the following goals: (a) reduction of tension between major world powers through disarmament so as to create a peaceful world order; (b) ensuring the right to self-determination to all colonial peoples so that they can achieve political freedom leading to equality between races; (c) reducing the growing economic disparity between the rich and the poor countries of the world so as to evolve a New International Economic Order; (d) doing away with the prevailing Western monopoly in information so as to create a more equitable global information and communication system; and (e) extending strong support to the United Nations, which is also founded on the principles of universalism, multilateralism and non-alignment (see Singham and Hume 1986).

The membership of the NAM is drawn from those countries which have adopted or have an inclination to adopt an independent foreign policy based on non-alignment, which consistently support national liberation movements; and which are not members in the multilateral military alliances. Thus NAM may be viewed as the collective voice of those states which are economically and militarily weak but aspire to maintain their political independence.

Several valid criticisms have been levelled against NAM: the imprecise conceptualization of non-alignment leading to the inclusion of several members who do not have adequate commitment to its principles and practice; the incapability of prescribing a set of norms and disciplining the member-states to ensure adherence to these norms; the inability to process and settle disputes peacefully even among the members; the tendency towards institutionalization giving additional advantage to the bigger/stronger members; the imbalance created by the tendency to be more critical of the capitalist bloc and relatively tolerant of the communist bloc; the incapacity to contain the unhealthy influence the big powers exert on member-states which undermines the basic principles of the movement; the failure to provide security to members against attacks by strong and powerful states; the incapacity to discipline even the members who violate human rights thereby (a) creating a wedge between profession and practice of the NAM and (b) rendering domestic and foreign policies inadequate for economic cooperation among members.

Even if all these criticisms are valid, the fundamental contradiction faced by NAM is to be located in its tendency to uphold the existing sovereign states as inviolable units. Part of the problem arises out of the uncritical acceptance of Western conceptualizations and part of the problem is to be found in refusing to take cognizance of the critical differences involved in the process of emergence of nation-states both in Europe and post-colonial states. Indeed, conceptual inadequacy and empirical insensitivity are two sides of the same coin.

MOVEMENTS FOR CULTURAL IDENTITY

In the West, particularly in Western Europe, the coterminality between state and nation was assumed to be a necessity and hence the effort was to create nation states. Where this coterminality existed, nation-building was smooth; and where it did not exist, smaller and weaker nations, that is cultural entities, were destroyed and/or marginalized to build states (see Connor 1994). This principle was applied more or less mechanically by the Western powers to their colonies. The storm-troopers of anti-colonial movements were the Western-trained elites of the Third World countries, quite a few of these countries being ex-colonial and non-aligned. Thus the mechanical applications of the Western conception of nation to

Africa, Asia and Latin America by the colonial rulers and its uncritical acceptance by the Western-oriented Third World elites provide the context for the emergence of a large number of social movements which are specific to the Third World (see Young 1976), the second type of social movements which I propose to discuss. But it is necessary to allude to the ambivalence in orientation shown by the ruling elite of non-aligned countries to the movements for cultural identity, particularly when they emerge and operate within their own country. As noted above, ensuring the right to self-determination to all colonized peoples is one of the principles upheld by NAM. But this right is invariably denied to peoples who are victims of internal colonialism in non-aligned countries, a phenomenon largely, if not exclusively, a legacy of external (that is, Western) colonialism.

In Western definition and perception, nations are peoples with history and the source of sovereignty is essentially the nation (Mamdani 1992). Notwithstanding the difference in the definitions of nation (as an entity of freely associating individuals as upheld by liberal democrats or as a product of tradition inherited by people, as enunciated by conservatives) they conceded the right to self-determination to nations, which essentially meant the right to establish their own states. But this right, according to Western colonizers, could not be extended to colonies as there were no nations (that is, people with history) among the colonized. Of course, the situation varied between the colonized peoples; Africa and Latin America were lands of tribes who were presumed to have no history, but Asia had some peoples with history!

The patterns of state formation varied drastically between Africa and Latin America. In Africa, political territories (states) were carved out by the colonizers without any respect for cultural territories (nations). This rupture between state and nation is not recognized and/or if recognized, not respected, even by the indigenous political elites. In fact, what passes for nations in Africa are the artificially created state territories which often vivisect and apportion the same tribe to different states and/or put a large number of tribes in the same state. I am not suggesting for a moment that the European solution – namely, for each nation (tribe) there ought to be a state – is viable for Africa. For one thing, it is simply not practical, given the fact that there are some 6000 tribes in Africa. For another, the European solution is pernicious and not practised even in Europe; the number of states in Europe is far lower than the number of nations.[5] However, it is possible and often desirable to avoid the mindless vivisection and apportioning of the same tribe to different states. Similarly, it is necessary to concede a certain level of political autonomy to tribes within a multi-tribal state. Both these measures would contain and terminate a large number of movements for cultural autonomy among the tribes of Africa. Instead, these movements are simply labelled as anti-national and secessionist.

The situation in the settler-majority Latin American states is quite different. Having either completely liquidated and/or substantially marginalized (demographically, politically, economically and culturally) the native peoples, the issue of self-determination had become redundant. From the perspective of the European settler-majority, conceding self-determination as a right to the indigenous peoples would have endangered the very prospect of becoming permanent settlers and establishing their own states. Further, as the populations of the Latin American states are drawn from a variety of sources – European, indigenous, African, and so on – their identification with specific territories is often problematic. The European solution could not be applied to Latin America and hence the shift from the right to self-determination of nations to the right to non-discrimination of individuals (Mamdani 1992). This quantum jump rendered Latin American states aggregates of individual citizens instead of nations, (that is, organic collectivities). Admittedly, this shift from group identity to individual freedom has given birth to the emergence of a large number of social movements with individual human rights as their central focus.

In South Asia, the colonial strategy was somewhat different. Having denied nationhood to linguistic and tribal collectivities, the artificial notion of religion-based nationhood was injected into the body politic resulting in religion acquiring saliency in state formation. Religion is an artificial element in state formation either because no part of the territory could be claimed as the exclusive homeland by one or another religious collectivity or because a religious collectivity is not a linguistic community, or both (Oommen 1994: 455–72). On the other hand, several tribal communities are divided either between two states (thus the Nagas and Mizos are distributed across India and Burma) or between two administrative units within the same state (thus the Santhals and Bhils are divided between several Indian states). Both these factors, according recognition to religion as an element in nation-formation and apportion-

ing tribes across different states and administrative units within
states, have given birth to numerous social movements in South
Asia.

CONCLUSION

It is clear from the above analysis that (a) the NAM, although
predominantly a Third World movement, is not confined to it and
(b) while movements for cultural identity are found in all the
regions of the Third World, their content and context vary across
these regions. Why is it so? The answer to this question should
reinforce my contention that state-societies, or blocks of them, are
not appropriate units for the analysis of social movements.

State societies, invariably wrongly referred to as nation-states,
are artificial entities viewed in terms of their contested boundaries
and shifting loyalties to them. This is so not only because the
socio-cultural compositions of the state-societies vastly vary, but
also because their announced objectives differ. This point may be
explained by briefly reviewing the changing character of the unit of
our analysis – the state-societies – as well as the transformation that
occurred in their goals.

The Western capitalist democratic states of Europe were by and
large culturally homogeneous. And, if they were characterized by
cultural heterogeneity (multi-religious/denominational, multi-lin-
gual), it was either ignored or efforts were made to assimilate the
weak and smaller nations. In the beginning, the state functioned as
a police state, creating conditions for citizens to operate freely in
terms of their chosen goals. But the emergence of welfare states in
Western Europe and socialist states in Eastern Europe brought a
sea change in the functions of the state. Development, distributive
justice and social transformation became the central concerns of the
state. But to the extent that both capitalist democracies and
socialist states were homogenous – one race (white), one religion
(Christian) and consisting of a linguistic community – the vulnerable and deprived groups (the poor, the destitute, the physically
handicapped, the mentally deranged) were drawn from the same
people. Understandably, the background of the deprived determined the nature of social movements: they pursued the interests of
particular classes or special groups.

The scenario changed drastically when multi-national (former

Soviet Union), poly-ethnic (the USA) and multi-national and poly-ethnic states (India) with differing objectives emerged. On the one hand, these states had to be responsive to collective action and contain protests at manageable levels. On the other, the commitment of the state to the welfare of the poor had to be upheld. The nationality policy of Soviet Union, affirmative action in the USA, protective discrimination in India and linguistic re-organization of Indian states are examples of such responses by modern states. Mark that in this context, the deprived categories are not classes but nationalities, minorities, ethnic groups, races, castes and tribes.

What is common to the situations discussed so far is that, be they police states, welfare states, socialist states, multi-national or poly-ethnic states, the unit of operation of movements was particular state-societies. But with the emergence of the world system model as a tool of analysis, groups of state-societies came to be viewed as units of analysis. The emphasis in analysis shifted from modes of production to unequal exchange, particularly between the First and the Third World. This in turn gave birth to trans-state collective mobilizations leading to formation of blocs of states for collective action. The NAM is an example of this. But viewing the world as a system also brought to the fore the relative deprivations specific to certain categories irrespective of their location in the affluent or developing countries. Mobilizations of and by gender and age-groups are examples of such collective action.

Even the world-system model had taken into account only the human world, ignoring the non-human environment. The unintended consequences of the reckless application of technology for developmental purposes was not recognized until recently. When this happened a New Consciousness emerged which came to be articulated in the form of green movements and green parties which take different forms in different parts of the world (see Galtung 1986: 75–90). Further, the background of the deprived also changed: those who came to be displaced because of huge projects (be they dams or steel plants), those who got thrown out of employment (for example, women) or those who were denied entry to the labour market (the youth) became the new vulnerable groups (see Cernea 1985). The fact that there is an intermeshing between these deprived groups and particular primordial collectivities makes the situation all the more explosive.

The point I am making is this. As development and social transformation continues, the structure of deprivation changes and consequently the composition of the deprived undergoes a change too. Naturally, the nature and type of social movements and collective action would also necessarily undergo transformation. We need to take into account this dialectical intertwining between the nature of the system and the process of development in order to appreciate the what and why of social movements.

References

Berger, S. (1977), 'Bretons and Jacobins: Reflections on French Regional Ethnicity', in Milton J. Esman (ed.), *Ethnic Conflicts in the Western World* (Ithaca, NY: Cornell University Press), pp. 158–78.

Cernea, M. M. (1985), *Putting People First: Sociological Variables in Development* (New York: Oxford University Press).

Connor, W. (1994), *Ethnonationalism: The Quest for Understanding* (Princeton, NJ: Princeton University Press).

Eisenstadt, S. N. (1965), *Modernization: Protest and Change* (Englewood Cliffs, NJ: Prentice-Hall).

Galtung, J. (1986), 'The Green Movement: A Socio-Historical Exploration', *International Sociology*, Vol. 1, No. 1, pp. 75–90.

Kothari, R. (1988), *Rethinking Development: In Search of Humane Alternatives* (New Delhi: Ajanta).

Mamdani, M. (1992), 'Africa: Democratic Theory and Democratic Struggles', paper presented to International Workshop on Social Movements, State and Democracy, New Delhi, 4–8 October.

Oommen, T. K. (1990), *Protest and Change: Studies in Social Movements* (New Delhi: Sage).

Oommen, T. K. (1991), 'Internationalization of Sociology: A View from Developing Countries', *Current Sociology*, Vol. 39, No. 1, pp. 67–84.

Oommen, T. K. (1992), 'Restructuring Development through Technological Pluralism', *International Sociology*, Vol. 7, No. 2, pp. 131–9.

Oommen, T. K. (1994), 'Religious Nationalism and Democratic Polity: The Indian Case', *Sociology of Religion*, Vol. 55, No. 4, pp. 455–72.

Rajan, M. S. (1990), *Non-alignment and Non-aligned Movement* (Delhi: Vikas Publishing House).

Reece, J. (1979), 'Internal Colonialism, the Case of Brittany', *Ethnic and Racial Studies*, Vol. 2, No. 3, pp. 275–92.

Singham, A. W. and S. Hume (1986), *Non-Alignment in an Age of Alignments* (London: Zed Books).

Smelser, N.J. (1962), *The Theory of Collective Behaviour* (London: Routledge & Kegan Paul).

Smith, A.D. (1983), *Theories of Nationalism* (London: Duckworth).

Titmuss, R. M. (1958), *Essays on the Welfare State* (London: Allen & Unwin).

UNDP (1991), *Human Development Report 1991* (Oxford: Oxford University Press).

Wallerstein, I. (1974), *The Modern World System: Capitalist Agriculture and the Origins of the World Economy in the Sixteenth Century*, 2 vols (New York: Academic Press).

Wallerstein, I. (1979), *The Capitalist World Economy* (Cambridge: Cambridge University Press).

Weber, E. (1976), *Peasants into Frenchmen: Modernisation of Rural France, 1870–1914* (Stanford, Calif.: Stanford University Press).

Worsley, P. (1964), *The Third World: A Vital New Force in International Affairs* (London: Weidenfeld & Nicolson).

Worsley, P. (1984), *The Three Worlds: Culture and World Development* (Chicago: Chicago University Press).

Young, C. (1976), *The Politics of Cultural Pluralism* (Madison, Wisc.: University of Wisconsin Press).

Notes

1. Some authors consider social movements as a particular type of collective behaviour/action. In this scheme of categorization elementary collective behaviours, such as panic response and crowd behaviour, are instant responses to cope with unanticipated sudden events. In contrast, social movements are collective action informed by an ideology and based on an organizational structure (see particularly Smelser 1962). In this chapter, no sharp distinction is made between social movements and collective action and both refer to collective mobilizations which are intended to bring about social transformation and social development.

2. The structural functional school, particularly of the Parsonian variety, typifies this approach.

3. Galtung (1986: 79–80) listed four of these revolutions and confined his analysis to Europe but Oommen (1992: 131–9) added the revolt of the colonized peoples to the list, thereby including the rest of the world in the analysis.

4. People's participation in development became such a popular idea by the 1980s that it came to be prescribed as a conditionality for extending financial assistance to Third World countries by agencies such as World Bank. Needless to say, the significance of people's participation was discovered through the observation and analysis of state-sponsored development projects which are found to be failures (see Cernea 1985).

5. For example, Smith (1983) notes that in early 1980s there were 73 nations but only 24 states in Europe.

4 Social Movements and Democratization

Manuel Antonio Garretón[1]

Social movements can be defined as collective action with some stability over time and some degree of organization, oriented towards change or conservation of society or some sphere of it. The idea of social movements tends to move between two poles in social theory. One is the vision of social movements as collective action responding to specific tensions or a contradiction in society and oriented towards resolving that specific contradiction. The other is social movement as bearers of the meaning of history and the incarnation and the main agent of global social change.[2]

Both poles can be seen as two dimensions of social movements. On the one hand we can conceive of a *Social Movement* (SM with capitals) which is oriented towards the 'historical problematique' of a given society and defines its central conflict and contradiction.[3] On the other hand, there are *social movements* (sms, plural), that are concrete actors oriented towards specific goals and are parts of the capital *SM*. The relations between both dimensions are historical and their nature specific to each society.

Social movements in general always combine the reference to a certain principle of globality with a reference to a particular identity. The degree of corporatism and political orientation varies for every social movement. This reference to a principle of action must be distinguished from the level of action (that is, personal interaction, organizational framework, institutional setting or rules of the game), as well as the historical problematique of a society (see Touraine 1993).

Finally, it is important to keep in mind that social movements are not the only type of collective action and some periods in some societies are characterized by the absence of social movements. Two other types of collective action especially must be distinguished from social movements. One is *demands*; the other is *mobilizations* (Garretón 1989b).

DEMOCRATIZATION AND POLITICS IN LATIN AMERICA

Political democratization refers to the process of establishing or extending the institutions that define a democratic regime. It can take the form of founding a new regime or resurrecting democratic rule that in some way existed before an authoritarian regime or a dictatorship (Garretón 1991).

During the last decades in Latin America we have seen a few foundings of democracy (Central America), some democratic extensions or deepenings (like Mexico and Colombia) and, especially, some transitions from authoritarian military regimes (Southern Cone). Transitions, in turn, should be distinguished from the consolidation of a new democratic regime (O'Donnell and Schmitter 1986).

What the different experiences of transitions to democracy have shown us in recent decades is that what is usually inaugurated after the transition period is an incomplete democratic regime because of the continued presence of authoritarian enclaves inherited from the authoritarian regime (institutions, human rights, actors).[4] This is because contemporary military regimes have been extremely repressive and reactive against society. However, they have also attempted to establish a particular social order. Thus, even if they failed, they have disarticulated previously existing relations between the economy, state and society (Collier 1979, Garretón 1989c).

This means that the first democratic governments after a transition have two main tasks. One is to complete the transition and overcome the authoritarian enclaves. The other is to initiate the process of consolidation of the new democratic regime. In order to achieve this second task, it is necessary to avoid authoritarian regression, but also to initiate a process of social democratization and integration. These last two processes have been part of the democratic ethos and of the idea of democracy in Latin America.

The question therefore is whether we are in a new cycle of authoritarianism-democracy, as earlier in Latin America, or whether we are inaugurating a new epoch in our societies and in our politics (that is, something that goes beyond the change of a regime, but includes it).

This potential transformation can be characterized as the disarticulation and possible recomposition or refoundation of the Latin American socio-political matrix.[5] This concept refers broadly to the way in which social actors are constituted as such in a given society and to the relations between state and society. More specifically, a socio-political matrix defines the relations between the state in its different dimensions, the system of representation (institutions, party system) and the socio-economic and cultural base of social actors (economy and civil society). The institutional meditations between these three components constitute the political regime.

In general terms, we can say that the Latin American socio-political matrix, which we will define as the 'classic' one and which prevailed from the 1930s until the 1970s, was formed by the fusion of different processes: development, modernization, social integration, and national autonomy (Touraine 1989). Every social action was conditioned by these four dimensions, and all the different conflicts reflected their fusion. The economic base of this matrix was the inward model of development characterized by the import substitution industrialization (ISI) strategy, with a strong role for the state (Hirschman 1969). The political model was the 'state of compromise' and different types of populism independent of political regimes (Graciarena and Franco 1981). The cultural reference was at the same time the state, the nation and the people, and a vision of radical global social change that gives political action revolutionary connotations (Touraine 1989).

The main characteristic of the classic socio-political matrix, in ideal type terms, was the fusion of its components: that is, state, political parties and social actors. That means weak autonomy of each of these components and a mixture of two or three of them, with the subordination or suppression of the others. The particular combination depends on historical factors and varies from country to country. In any case, the privileged form of collective action was politics and the weakest part of the matrix was the institutional linkage between components of the political regime regardless of that regime's nature (democratic or authoritarian).

The military regimes of the 1960's and later, and the process of globalization with its economic consequences, brought about the crisis of this matrix and its decomposition or disarticulation. This does not mean that we are now facing a new matrix, but that we have several different processes including decomposition, persistence of old elements, attempts to recreate the same matrix and also the construction of new ones. These complex processes create three different scenarios. The first is decomposition without a new pattern of social action. The second is regression to the classical matrix. The third is the building of a new matrix characterized by the autonomy and mutual complementarity of each component. The results are different for each country and it is too early to predict the outcome. What seems relatively clear is that the institutional framework will be democratic, but it is unclear how relevant this democracy will be (Garretón 1994b, 1992; O'Donnell 1994).

FROM NATIONAL POPULAR MOVEMENT TO DEMOCRATIC SOCIAL MOVEMENT

The main hypothesis of this chapter is that the transformation of the socio-political matrix has brought about a significant change in the nature of social movements in Latin America. In ideal type terms, it is possible to affirm that along with the classic socio-political matrix there existed a central Social Movement, which can be defined as the National Popular Movement (Germani 1965), and which embraced the different social movements, despite their particularities. That means that every *sm* was at the same time developmentalist, modernist, nationalist, oriented towards global change and identifying itself as part of the *pueblo* (Touraine 1989). This last category was considered the only subject of history. Usually the workers' movement was the emblematic concrete *sm* of the National Popular Movement, due more to its symbolic significance than to its structural strength. But in different periods this leadership was challenged by the idea that urban workers were forced to compromise and had lost their revolutionary momentum, and then other movements, like peasants' or students' vanguards, were called on to take over revolutionary leadership.

Thus the principal characteristics of this *SM*, shared in different ways by *sms* (and I am referring mainly to urban movements) were, first, the combination of a very strong symbolic dimension, calling for global social change, and a dimension of very concrete demands. This means the implicit or explicit assumption of the revolutionary orientation even if the concrete movements were very 'reformist'. Second, the state was conceived as the interlocutor for demands as a well as the locus for taking power over society. From this follows a complex relation with politics, varying from a complete subordination of organizations to the political, to a more independent style of action. The weakness of the class structure as the base for social movements was compensated for by political and ideological appeals (Touraine 1989).

The attempt to dismantle the classic socio-political matrix by the military regimes of the 1960s and 1970s, and the structural or institutional transformations that also occurred in other countries without this kind of authoritarianism, implied important consequences for social movements.

First, there were at least two meanings interwoven in the action of any *sms*. One is the reconstruction of the social fabric destroyed by authoritarianism and economic reforms.[6] The other is the orientation of every action towards the ending of the authoritarian regimes, which politicized all demands.

Second, because of the repressive nature of the regime, the reference to the state and the links with politics changed dramatically, and *sms* became more autonomous, more symbolic and more identity-oriented rather than instrumentally or demand-oriented.[7] During the most intensive repressive moment at the beginning of the military regime, the main orientation of any collective action was self-defence and survival: that is, the central theme was life and human rights. When the regimes had established themselves, the movements were diversified, acting within different spheres of society and culturally and socially oriented rather than economically or politically oriented. Finally, when the regime started to decompose and its ending was a real possibility, social movements turned to politics and to an institutional formula of transition that tended to involve all the previous expressions of collective action.

Third, at the level of *sms*, authoritarianism attempted to change the role of the state and its relation to economy and society. This transformed the spaces in which *sms* were constituted. Their structural and institutional positions were weakened through repression, marginalization and the informalization of the economy. Rather than organized movements, the main form of collective action during the military regime was *social mobilizations*. They tended to stress the symbolic dimension instead of instrumental or demanding orientations. It is significant that the leading role in this was attained by the human rights movements. The more instrumental orientation appeared only when the movements began to address the end of the regime and its replacement by a democratic one.

Fourth, at the level of the central *SM*, there is a shift from the National Popular Movement towards the Democratic Movement: that is to say, towards a central *SM* that for the first time is not oriented to global and radical social change but to change of political regime. Authoritarian rulers were seen as the main advers-

aries, and the ending of the regime and the installation of democracy became the main aim of collective action. With this change the
SM gains in instrumental terms, but this is counterbalanced by the
fact that particular demands tend to be subordinated to political
goals. This in turn gives a leading role to political actors. Negotiations and agreements at the top and the elite level tend to replace
social mobilizations during the democratic transition and consolidation processes. In this sense, the political democratization process
tends to split every collective action into two different types of logic
that penetrate all *sms*: one is the political logic oriented towards the
establishment of a consolidated democracy as a condition for all
other types of demands; the other is the particular logic of each *sms*
oriented towards concrete gains in social democratization as the
condition of active support to the new democratic regime.

SOCIAL MOVEMENTS IN THE WAKE OF DEMOCRATIZATION

The human rights movements remained important after the inaug-
uration of the new democracies both because of the continued
existence of authoritarian enclaves, and because of the risk of
authoritarian regression. This situation gives political actors, in
government and in opposition, the key roles in social action, and
they in turn subordinate other actors to their own logic. At the
beginning of the consolidation process, in particular, the requirements of economic adjustment and stability had high priority, and
collective action which could jeopardize these aims was discouraged. The result is a decrease in the activity of social movements.

More important, however, is that the establishment of a democratic regime, even if there are some pending tasks, leaves the social
movements without a central principle for the future. So the
question is what type of *SM* will replace the National Popular
Movement and the Democratic Movement? Will there be a new
central *SM* in Latin America?

There are at least three problems that make the emergence of a
new *SM* very difficult and complex. First, the consolidation of
democracy is linked, as we have said, to the overcoming of the
exclusion of between one-third and two-thirds of the population
from mainstream society. The central contradiction in these countries is between people who are 'inside' the socio-economic and

political system, no matter what their relative position, and the people who are 'outside' this system. This segmentation penetrates, in different proportions, every social category or actor or group, making collective organized action very difficult. However, the model of modernity is not only challenged by the 'outsiders', whose interests, beyond inclusion, are very contradictory. It is also challenged by people who are 'inside' the system, and who question their subordinate position in it. The peasants and the urban poor are examples of people who are 'outside', even if it is not entirely true in cultural terms because of their integration through the mass media. Women, youth, and (especially) workers are examples of categories which are divided by the 'in-out' contradiction. There is no real conflict in sociological terms between insiders and outsiders, but there are conflicts among insiders over the model of development. Outsiders tend to be people who are not needed, and today there is not – as there was in the 1960s – any revolutionary model that takes them into account, except perhaps some appeals to desperate fundamentalism. But fundamentalism is very weak in Latin America today.

Second, democratic consolidation is also linked in our terms to the construction of a new socio-political matrix, after the disarticulation of the 'classical' one, and that creates a new difficulty for a central *SM*. In fact the old matrix had the advantage of focusing the different problems and dimensions of society. The new emergent matrix, if it is to succeed, will be made of differentiated components, with more autonomy, tension and complementarity among them. This means that the role of politics will be different and that it is not clear what will replace the state or the party system or the populist movement, in organizing social movements. What seems most probable is that the differentiation of each sphere of society with its own specific contradictions will give place to very heterogeneous collective action with perhaps a few principles in common. This will create enriched and diverse social identities, but weaken the symbolic and organic links that could unify this diversity in a new *SM*.

Third, beyond transition and consolidation, there are some cultural changes in collective behaviour that will profoundly affect the type of *SM* and *sm* (Slater 1985; Jelin 1993; Schuurman 1993). During the prevalence of the classic socio-political matrix, struggles and conflicts were mainly oriented, as we pointed out, to egalitarian, libertarian and nationalist principles and goals, and they were well captured by anti-capitalist, anti-oligarchic, democratic and anti-imperialist and nationalist movements. These principles and struggles still remain to be attained and stimulate many of the collective actions in Latin America.

There are two new elements that must be taken into account, however (Garretón 1994a). On the one hand, each of these principles has become more technical, autonomous and complex. The old forms of organization, like unions or parties or corporatism, have become inadequate and there is no single formula for all these dimensions to be found in the vocabulary of classical politics. Moreover, sometimes the achievement of some gains in one of these dimensions was accompanied by severe regressions in the others.

On the other hand, changes in civil society have brought about new kinds of demands and principles of action that cannot be captured by the old struggles for equality, freedom and national independence. New themes referring to daily life, interpersonal relations, individual and group achievement, aspirations to dignity and social recognition, sense of belonging and social identities, belong rather to the dimension of happiness or subjective experience, and cannot be sustained by the old principles. These themes no longer belong exclusively to the private realm. They are increasingly brought up in the public sphere. Of course this new dimension in turn does not replace the old ones, but adds more diversity and complexity to social action. The main change that this dimension introduces to the action of *sms*, beside the fact that the old form of organizations appears to be insufficient for these particular purposes (unions, parties), is that it defines a very diffuse principle of opposition and it is based not only on confrontation but also on cooperation. Consequently, it does not address a clear opponent or antagonist, as was the case in the classical social struggles.

If in the past we witnessed a central *SM* in search of *sms* and social actors, the scene today seems closer to that of *sms* in search of a central *SM*. But even more, it is perhaps better to say that collective behaviour and social mobilizations are in search of any kind of social movement: *sms* and *SM*. In fact what seems predictable for the near future is a variety of forms of struggle and mobilization. They will be relatively autonomous, of shorter duration, less politically oriented, more concerned with institutions rather than protests, and oriented towards sectoral inclusion, partial modernization, gradual social democratization and integration, rather than towards radical global changes. In the absence of satisfaction of their demands, abrupt and punctual explosions will probably occur, or withdrawal through apathy will develop, rather than the creation of revolutionary movements.

What we have said so far has crucial consequences, from my point of view, for the way that social scientists study social movements. We must resist two temptations. One is the temptation to become prophets of 'the' *SM*, inventing concrete *sms* and ignoring the real meaning of their actions. The other temptation, in the absence of an *SM*, is to become prophets of one particular identity, ignoring its meaning for global society. These opposite kinds of certainty about social movements should give way to a more modest attempt to cope with the ambiguity of social life. This means elaborating new theoretical visions of social change. It means also an effort of solidarity and commitment, and simultaneously, it means maintaining the distance necessary for understanding and criticism.

References

Cavarozzi, M. (1992), 'Beyond transitions to democracy in Latin America', *Journal of Latin American Studies*, No. 24, pp. 665–87

Collier, D. (ed.) (1979), *The New Authoritarianism in Latin America* (Princeton, NJ: Princeton University Press).

Corradi, S., P. Weiss and M.A. Garretón (eds) (1992), *Fear at the Edge: State Terror and Resistance in Latin America* (London: University of California Press).

Eckstein, S. (ed.) (1989), *Power and Popular Protest: Latin American Protest* (London: University of California Press).

Garretón, M.A. (1984), *Dictaduras y democratización* (Santiago: FLACSO).

Garretón, M.A. (1989a), *La posibilidad democrática en Chile* (Santiago: FLACSO).

Garretón, M.A. (1989b), 'Popular mobilization and the military regime in Chile: The complexities of the invisible transition', in S. Eckstein (ed.), *Power and Popular Protest: Latin American Protest* (London: University of California Press).

Garretón, M.A. (1989c), *The Chilean Political Process* (London: Unwin Hyman).

Garretón, M.A. (1994a), *La faz sunmergida del iceberg: Ensayos sobre la transformación cultural* (Santiago: CESOC).

76   *Social Movements and Democratization*

Garretón, M.A. (1991), 'Political democratisation in Latin America and the crisis of paradigms', in J. Manor (ed.), *Rethinking Third World Politics* (London: Longman).

Garretón, M.A. (1994b), 'Transformaciones socio-políticas en América Latina', in M.A. Garretón (ed.), *Los partidos y la transformación política de América Latina* (Santiago: FLACSO).

Germani, G. (1965), *Política y Sociedad en una época de transición* (Buenos Aires: Paidós).

Graciarena, J. and R. Franco (1981), *Formaciones Sociales y Estructuras de Poder en América Latina* (Madrid: Edit. Centro de Investigaciones Sociológicas).

Guido, R. and O. Fernández (1989), 'El Juicio al Sujeto: un análisis de los Movimientos Sociales en América Latina', *Revista Mexicana de Sociología*, No. 4, pp. 45–76.

Hirschman, A. (1969), 'The political economy of import-substituting industrialization in Latin America', *Quarterly Journal of Economics*, February.

Jelin, E. (1993), '¿Qué hay de nuevo en los nuevos movimientos sociales? Una actualización para los años noventa', paper presented to the seminar 'La democratización chilena en perspectiva comparada', FLACSO, Chile, 19–21 July 1993.

McAdam, D., J. D. McCarthy and M. N. Zald (1988), 'Social Movements', in N. Smelser (ed.), *Handbook of Sociology* (London: Sage), pp. 695–739.

Nun, J. (1989), *La Rebelión del Coro* (Buenos Aires: Ediciones Nueva Visión).

O'Donnell, G. (1992), *Delegative Democracy?*, Working paper No. 172 (New York: Kellogg Institute).

O'Donnell, G. (1994), 'The state, democratization and some conceptual problems', in W. Smith, C. Acuña and E. Gamarra (eds), *Latin American Political Economy in the Age of Neo-liberal Reform* (New Brunswick: Transaction).

O'Donnell, G. and P. Schmitter (1986), 'Tentative conclusions about uncertain democracies', in G.O'Donnell, P. Schmitter and L. Whitehead (eds), *Transitions from Authoritarian Rule* (Baltimore, Md: Johns Hopkins University Press).

Schmitter, P. and T. Karl (1991), *What Kind of Democracies are Emerging in South America, Central America, Southern Europe and Eastern Europe?* (Stanford University, Calif.: Center for Latin American Studies).

Schuurman, F. J. (1993), 'Modernity, postmodernity and the new social movements', in F. J. Schuurman (ed), *Beyond the Impasse: New Directions in Development Theory* (London: Zed Books).

Slater, D. (ed.) (1985), *New Social Movements and the State in Latin America* (Amsterdam: CEDLA).

Smelser, N. (1963), *Theory of Collective Behavior* (New York: Free Press).

Touraine, A. (1978), *La voix et le regard: Sociologie des mouvements sociaux* (Paris: Seuil).

Touraine, A. (1984), *Le retour de l'acteur* (Paris: Fayard).

Touraine, A. (1989), *América Latina: Política y Sociedad* (Madrid: Espasa).

Touraine, A. (1993), *Production de la société* (Paris: Seuil).

Notes

1. This chapter is part of a project carried out by the author and Malva Espinosa: Tendencias de cambio en la matriz socio-política chilena Una aproximación empírica, with the support of FONDECYT-Chile.

2. The first perspective is the classic one developed by Smelser (1963). The second is the Marxist and post-Marxist approach. An original position more linked to this second vision can be found in Touraine (1978 and 1984). An interpretation of social movement theory can be found in McAdam, McCarthy and Zald (1988: 695–739). An important revision of popular movement concepts, applied to Latin America, is Eckstein (1989).

3. This concept is related to the concept of 'historicité' developed by A. Touraine (1993).

4. On authoritarian enclaves, see Garretón (1989a). On different outcomes of political democratizations of recent years, see Schmitter and Karl (1991).

5. This concept has been developed in, among other texts, Garretón (1984 and 1994b). A somewhat different meaning is found in Cavarozzi (1992).

6. On the resurgence of civil society under authoritarianism, see Nun (1989). A critical analysis of the perspective developed here is provided in Guido and Fernández (1989: 45–76).

7. On the meaning and evolution of social movements under military regimes, see Garretón (1989b). See also the other contributions in the same volume edited by S. Eckstein, especially the ones by María Helena Moreira Alves, Marysa Navarro, and Levine and Mainwaring. For human rights movements and other types of resistance to authoritarianism, see part three of Corradi, Weiss and Garretón (1992).

5 Civil Society, Politics and Democracy in Developmentalist States

Peter Gibbon

The question of why political liberalization is currently on the agenda in many less developed countries has generated considerable discussion recently (for example, O'Donnell and Schmitter 1986 on Latin America and the contributors to Gibbon, Bangura and Ofstad 1992 on Africa). In this, much attention has been focused on the changing conjuncture of international relations and on structural adjustment and economic crisis. These are important aspects of the situation, but only a few works (notably Stepan 1985) have sought explicitly to address structural features of state-civil society relations in these processes, which can be considered equally important. This chapter tries to redress this balance with regard to 'developmentalist' states in Africa, without in any way denigrating the significance of other factors.

'Developmentalist' states will be discussed here as a species of a broader category of 'authoritarian' states. The central features of state/civil society relations in the latter can be highlighted via a comparison with the liberal democratic state form. Under bourgeois liberal democracy, politics in the sense of organized practices and discourses concerning the general interest tends to be confined to the state and to political parties, which are themselves effectively part of the state. The overwhelming bulk of their practical activity is within state institutions, both national and local, and only exceptionally takes the form of organizing mass activity. On the other hand, civil society tends to take the form of sectional 'special interest' groups, both economic and cultural. A form of popular politics also exists, mainly based on articulating general claims based on the status of citizenship and hence threatening to go beyond civil society, but this is episodic and in general contained by the operations of the political parties. Consistent with Marx's prognosis, a tendency exists in such states for politics to become steadily more concentrated in the state and for civil society organizations to play a modified and less expansive role. While political parties classically tended to articulate or aggregate a combination of civil society group interests, they now increasingly appeal simply to individuals as 'customers', both subjects and consumers of state policies and state services.

In contrast to this, the authoritarian statist state is one in which the state/civil society distinction is eliminated. This occurs not, as under radical or popular democracy, through the mutual dissolution of state and civil society. Rather, it occurs through the dissolution of civil society into the state. In the name of the general interest and on the basis of a claim for the identity of the state and the general interest, political parties are declared redundant and civil society is directly reorganized from above to eliminate all 'special' interests. In practice this means that civil society is dissolved, for the only organizations which continue to occupy the former civil society terrain are state organizations. Of course, this does not imply the elimination of political conflict and contradictions: these tend to become concentrated in the state itself instead.

'Developmentalist' states are distinguished from the category of 'socialist' authoritarian statist states (since 1945 probably the most significant group) by their maintenance of strong links with international finance capital (at least partly on the basis of 'overseas development assistance') and by a corresponding absence of centralized economic planning mechanisms and abrogations of private property rights. However, as in the state socialist countries, there were severe restrictions on civic and political freedoms and the compulsory organization of the bulk of the population (workers, peasants, women, youths, students, businessmen, artists, parents, and so on) into monopolistic agencies of social integration whose leaders were appointed and whose agendas were set by the state and which the state used as instruments of social control. In developmentalist states the role played by these organizations was less one of social orchestration within an administered economy than of economic mobilization, linked to monopolistic forms of surplus-value extraction within a general framework in which small-scale private property was physically predominant. These states have tended to be located on the continents where capitalism has been less developed. They have sought to establish internal political legitimacy primarily on the basis of claims to overcome the gross inequalities between nations inherent in the international division of labour.

I do not want to present these states as a homogeneous category or as deviations from early Western capitalist or state socialist 'norms' regarding state-civil society relations. However, light can be thrown on processes of political liberalization in these states by sketching certain specifics of the context and content of the state-civil society separation currently under way in them, as compared with earlier historical forms of the same process (including earlier colonial forms in these same countries).

In early capitalist Western Europe the ruling-class (landed property), together with embryonic elements of a number of other classes, was incorporated directly into the state in the form of 'estates'. The process of capitalist development saw these different forces become increasingly differentiated from each other, as their collective reproduction was detached from the state. As Marx (1843a, 1843b, 1844) showed, this process corresponded to the emergence of an internally divided but largely apolitical civil society on the one hand and a bureaucratic state on the other. This whole change was simultaneously accompanied by another, in which a large working class was formed from elements expelled or differentiated from the estates, or which had from the outset been excluded from them. (Nevertheless the estates themselves had generally been tightly organized.) Marx, Engels and Gramsci saw this formation of a class opposed both to state and civil society as exercising an initially restraining influence on democratization, for it encouraged the capitalist middle class to form an alliance with landed property on the basis of a retention of some aspects of state-civil society integration (such as fusion of economic and political power in rural areas). But in the long run – that is, in most countries, over the following century – civil society became gradually but decisively separated from the state and in part less privatized, as the working class developed a relative political-ideological autonomy from other social forces and through this exercised a systematic democratic influence. From the late nineteenth century the politicization of civil society was also accompanied by a gradual opening of the state. This process was limited by judicial assertions of the 'rule of law' (see Thompson 1984) and was extremely drawn out, but probably reached a high point in most of Western Europe between 1945 and 1970. It has been – and still is – subject to reversals of varying magnitudes. The worst of these (for instance, Germany,

Italy, Spain under fascism) were associated with a drawing of the working class and (the rest of) civil society directly back into the state, in the form of new artificial estates.

The principal context of this general pattern of political development in Western Europe was the succession of a dynamic period of competitive industrial capitalism by a still relatively dynamic phase of monopoly industrial capitalism. That is, not only did the classical capitalist division of labour become reflected in the pattern of state-civil society relations but so too did the later evolution of the international division of labour. Amongst the latter's consequences were that a working class whose political and ideological formation continued to bear the marks of competitive capitalism still occupied a central role under conditions where state intervention in class formation intensified markedly.

FROM COLONIALISM TO DEVELOPMENTALISM

Developmentalist states were the successors of colonial ones, themselves either constituted or fundamentally transformed by monopoly capitalism: *inter alia* this was reflected in the nature of their state forms, civil societies and state-civil society relations. The colonial state was essentially a mechanism for producing capitalist social classes – particularly a working class and a peasantry – from generally (but not entirely) pre-capitalist social relations. More precisely, it was a mechanism to produce these classes in a manner consistent with the generalization of monopoly relations and an international division of labour corresponding to them. Monopoly relations encompassed a tendency for commodities (including labour power) to be exchanged at prices systematically diverging from their prices of production, while the monopoly capitalist international division of labour encompassed a tendency for this to apply specifically to the production of primary commodities in tropical regions.

In the colonial state and certain of its variants (such as the apartheid states of southern Africa), a state-produced capitalist division of labour emerged where certain classes (peasants, but more especially worker-peasants, or migrant labour) were constituted to a greater or lesser degree (usually a greater one) on the basis of ethnicity/'tribal community'. These ethnicities, which were certainly no less (and probably significantly more) 'real' in their effects than class identities, were of course not simply or only *ex nihilo* state creations. Neither was their consequence unambiguously inhibitive of the formation of class identities. The point rather is that they were (and to some extent still are) inextricable from class identities. That is, there are not and virtually cannot be 'national' peasant or worker-peasant movements.

Though not themselves produced by the state, the other major class of the colonial and early developmentalist period – the informal sector of the working class and worker-peasantry – was also largely synonymous with ethnic/tribal community divisions. The only partially 'national-territorial' groups were the (usually tiny) proletariat and the slightly larger indigenous petty bourgeoisie. These groups were 'national-territorial' mainly and precisely in so far as they were linked to the state and its administrative and commercial functions. Even then they tended to reflect the custom of the colonial state to recruit its local personnel from particular regions/groups/clans. Further, their constitution through the state's own internal division of labour as bearers of subaltern 'native' roles meant that their occupational identity was fraught with racial implications. It was sometimes also overdetermined by age, particularly in Africa where the urban population and especially the urban petty bourgeoisie professed its 'youth' in contrast to the state support lent to the authority of elders in rural areas.

Following the observations of Mamdani (1990), the colonial period can thus be characterized as corresponding to the formation of a dualistic civil society (rural/semi-rural and ethnic-oriented on the one hand and urban/state employment and class and territorial-national oriented on the other). As well as being dualistic it was also relatively politicized, in so far as identities and counteridentities were produced mainly in and through the state or in relation to state-created political actors (such as chiefs) and in so far as access to economic resources (such as land) was explicitly politically mediated (that is, it occurred only through the chiefs).

Broadly generalizing once more, this created conditions for a somewhat complex pattern of state/civil society relations. To the extent that it spontaneously reproduced 'approved' divisions of labour identities, rural and semi-rural/worker-peasant civil society was mostly subject to relatively low-level political intervention. On the other hand, active efforts were made by the state to 'educate' and mould urban 'national' civil society entities into responsible and respectable forms. The most intensive and repressive intervention tended to be reserved for movements which gave explicitly social dimensions to ethnic identities, and which in the process might have disrupted not only rural civil society but also the approved pattern of rural-urban relations.

Unlike the colonial state, the developmentalist state constituted itself as an intervening factor in the international division of labour, corresponding to the assumption of power by 'natives'. The essence of this mediation was a double one: to retain a greater share locally of the surplus value generated through the colonial division of labour, on the basis of taxing existing production forms; and to create new production forms which would be nationally owned. Almost without exception an extension and/or deepening of monopoly relations was the chosen means, entailing a corresponding extension/deepening of class formation and extra-economic coercion.

During developmentalism's first, expansive phase (roughly up to the mid-1970s) the conditions for such intervention were internationally quite favourable. The prices of primary commodities tended to rise towards their prices of production, transnational monopoly capitals undertook considerable direct investment, overseas development assistance (public and private) became available on a large scale, demand for international migrant labour increased, and so on. In this context the developmentalist state intervened to extend the process of peasantization and to deepen that of proletarianization. In the name of development it simultaneously intervened to expand its own economic, social and political functions and thereby to rapidly accelerate the process of territorial petty bourgeoisie formation. Also rapidly expanding, though in the absence of state encouragement, was the urban informal working class, involved in petty production and trade for the working class and petty bourgeois markets.

It was partly as vehicles of state-induced 'extended' class formation (under monopoly conditions) that a distinctive complex of state organizations was set up by developmentalist regimes in the 1960s and 1970s, often supplanting the 'civil society' organizations of the later colonial period and thereby corresponding to a reabsorption of civil society by the state and the reappearance of quasi-'estates' reminiscent of the early capitalist period in Western Europe.

The most obvious example of this trend was the constitution of nation-wide peasant cooperatives organized by the state in a num-

ber of African countries, ostensibly to organize the fragmented
producers of specific crops but actually more commonly to create,
control and exploit them, particularly in the context of the donor-
driven regional/rural integrated development programmes of the
1970s. As has been pointed out by various commentators (for
example, Bernstein 1990; Raikes 1992), the rapidity and extent of
commodification implied by these programmes necessitated levels
of regulation and post-investment extraction which voluntary
organizations could not have managed by consensus.

This was not the only basis on which state or semi-state bodies
were created and civil society organizations of the colonial period
disbanded by those inheriting post-colonial state power. In urban
Africa the extended constitution of territorial working classes and
petty bourgeoisies through the state coincided with the opening-up
of new forms of political differentiation and struggle. These tended
to be mainly associated with the issue of 'Africanization' in general
and Africanization of the public sector in particular. Their content
was a polarization of nationalism around the elite promotion of a
legalistic definition of citizenship, which left the inherited racist
division of labour largely intact. Counterposed to this was a
popular 'Africanism', whose programme was to turn this racist
division of labour on its head. This was simultaneously a political
differentiation between 'state nationalism' and 'civil society nationalism'. For reasons which cannot be explored here, the result almost
everywhere was a victory for state nationalism and the banning,
absorption or state-organized substitution of the civil society organizations in question. Certain substitute organizations (such as state
trade unions) subsequently took on broad functions of guiding the
class formation of the formal sector urban social classes

In a number of African countries a sequel to the elimination of
'Africanism' in civil society was its reappearance in a party political
guise, thus presenting a serious challenge to generally already
near-dormant ruling parties. A common state reaction was the
banning of opposition parties, a 'state socialist'-inspired reconstitution of ruling parties as state parties, the promulgation of doctrines
of single-partyism and a systematic party-led statization of public
activity, in which the various remaining civil society organizations
were dissolved or incorporated in the name of consistency.

Under rising developmentalism can thus be found a reproduction
of capitalist relations and an extension of state intervention in the
division of labour, with the creation of political contradictions in

this process, resulting in a partial severing by the state of the link between the division of labour and the formation of civil society. Developmentalist states, like early capitalist and later fascist ones, thus became characterized by a corporatist system of 'estates': that is, a more or less limited set of compulsory sectional membership organizations incorporated into or created by the state and supported by state resources. Relative to early capitalism and fascism this system was far from inclusive, however, with certain sections of the population simply left outside (see below). Moreover many 'estates', though technically inclusive, soon exercised only a very weak influence with regard to organization/domination. Consider in this connection peasant cooperatives and state women's organizations (see Hedlund 1988 on cooperatives and Woodford-Berger 1993 on Ghanaian women's organizations).

Just as in early capitalism and fascism, a system of hierarchy was built into that of the 'estates'. This differed from one developmentalist state to another but typically certain well-off rural male and middle-class urban-centred male estates enjoyed disproportionate levels of resources. Corresponding to this hierarchy were important qualitative differences in how interest groups were incorporated (for example, through collectively – versus individually – consumed forms of patronage).

As Poulantzas (1976: 93–4) has noted of corporatist states in southern Europe, within and across 'estates' there tended to develop 'fiefs' or state-based informal networks, often carrying significantly more influence than the formalized 'estates' themselves. These informal 'fiefs', usually arbitrated by a relatively strong executive or personal ruler, constituted the state's own specific 'civil society' (that is, a set of private interests born within the state itself). In cases where elements of national- and local-level political competition were maintained (such as Kenya) these fiefs moreover had ethno-regionally structured links with sections of the masses. Equally importantly they also cross-cut state relations with international capital (private and public).

Besides re-emerging in the form of the constitution of 'private' interests within the public sector, civil society usually persisted in this period in the shape of certain institutions which managed to resist proscription/incorporation or which made sufficient adjustment to the new situation to avoid it. In Africa, common examples of the latter included certain religious organizations (others of which were of course part of the state), certain forms of voluntary development initiative, certain non-monopoly private business operations (monopoly – including private monopoly – ones were invariably indistinguishable from the state), and certain professional associations and trade unions. But such more or less continuously present civil society forms tended to possess at least one of two important characteristics. They were demonstratively private/corporate in their social and ideological content, and/or they were indirectly linked to the state.

A civil society entity sharing both these characteristics was the famous Kenyan phenomenon of *harambee*, or peasant community-based self-help projects, – at least prior to their total subversion by the state in the early 1980s (see Kanyinga 1993). Simplifying greatly, from independence until this time *harambee* was mainly a means whereby the Kenyan peasantry, constituted on a village/community basis, contributed surplus value in money or labour-power forms to the construction of local infrastructure. In the process, peasant communities also collectively extracted resources from the state by extracting contributions also from local state/party politicians. The economic base of this civil society form was the tendency for the dominance of (state) monopoly forms of accumulation within cash-crop agriculture to be mitigated by a tendency for peasant cash crop prices to rise nearer to their prices of production, creating (with other factors) the basis for a limited but definite peasant accumulation from below. At the same time severe differentiation around this accumulation was restricted (*inter alia*) by the absence of complete private property in land. The organizational structure of peasant participation in cash-crop agriculture (via primary community-level cooperatives), as well as prevailing relations of distribution in the sector, became directly reflected in *harambee* alongside the general rise in surpluses. In other words, *harambee*'s horizon remained the exclusive corporate interest of the pre-structured local community of producers. That is not to say that it was apolitical; however, the politics it generated and reproduced was one of corporate intercommunity resource allocation.

Less narrowly corporate forms of public politics – that is, politics articulated around claims about general social interests – were also intermittently part of developmentalist civil society. Or rather, they had a tendency to be asserted in a subordinate and temporary way within (some of) the civil society forms mentioned earlier, and more strikingly in episodic independent organization by students, workers and intellectuals. In certain Francophone African countries they were also sustained much more consistently, albeit in underground forms, by national communist parties, for example. The bases of these organizations were the extended processes of peasantization, proletarianization and formation of a state petty bourgeoisie in developmentalism's early expansive phase. However, the location in the state (in some cases), as well as organization of these processes by the state – along with their limited scale – allowed any consistent expression of these processes in civil society to be contained.

In early capitalist Western Europe economic growth and class formation occurred outside and in tension with the state. This meant not only that a strong civil society was incubated but so too was a force (the working class) excluded from both and with an interest in opening up both. But in the developmentalist state, capitalist development occurred primarily in monopoly forms and was more or less identical with state development. Those elements detached from the state were generally economically and socially marginal, and only very weak tendencies existed for them to merge into a force for change. Demands for inclusion arose only infrequently and unevenly, and then usually from constituencies which emerged or matured after independence.

SOME OBSERVATIONS ON CONTEMPORARY CIVIL SOCIETY FORMS

On the basis of these very rough comparative historical generalizations, a few observations will now be made about the present period. From the mid-1970s onwards and the onset of general economic difficulties for developmentalist states, interrelated changes in state-civil society relations occurred. A significant process of differentiation began to occur within 'estates', in which the connection between the state and the mass in each 'estate' was loosened or weakened (see below). It is important analytically to distinguish the content of this differentiation from the parallel process which occurred in Europe, and also from certain current populist interpretations of it.

In Europe the differentiation within and between estates, because of its base in extra-state dynamic capitalist growth, was simultaneously a process of formation of new, inclusive, economic institutions and new classes. In (formerly) developmentalist states, institution- and class-formation also continues, but the main trend is disintegrative. Following Ninsin's (1988) oblique criticism of Chazan, the current state-civil society differentiation has been primarily a consequence of *state contraction*, and largely under pressure from a crisis of state resources/revenues. Moreover, the content of this differentiation in developmentalist states is also specific. Mainly it has been less one where a separation between 'estates' as a whole and the state has occurred, and in which estates have separated from each other, and more one in which the mass in each 'estate' has been subject to a weakening integration. On the other hand, an elite in each 'estate' has normally retained some kind of foothold in the state. Hence the institutional differentiation which has occurred has been passive and centrifugal.

The other side of this centrifugal movement has been a transformation (and partial reversal) of the capitalist division of labour in the context of developmentalism's economic crisis. State-based proletarianization, peasantization and petty-bourgeois class formation have unravelled in fundamental ways. With regard to state-based proletarianization (and most clearly with reference to Uganda) Jamal and Weeks (1988), for example, note the phenomena of very severely falling wages and reduced formal sector job stability/security, a blurring of distinctions between urban and rural (the rise of urban farming), new patterns of circulation of household members between urban and rural areas and a blurring of distinctions between working-class and non working-class consumption patterns. Similar trends have been observed by other scholars (see Mustapha 1992 on Nigeria) with regard to the social disintegration of the territorial petty bourgeoisie. Contemporary studies noting depeasantization – at least other than in the sense of linear proletarianization – are also beginning to appear (see Booth 1993 on Tanzania, and Julin 1993 on Kenya).

A more analytical approach to these increasingly acknowledged trends would require a movement beyond the description of the phenomenon of declassing in terms of 'informalization' (or, more recently, 'deagrarization') to a theoretical and comparative empirical examination of its principal moments with regard to specific classes within specific countries and regions. Simultaneously new countervailing processes of class formation could be specified in this way. For example, proletarianization/deproletarianization could be decomposed into the moment of exploitation as such, or formal subsumption (labour as a commodity), the moment of

domination or real subsumption (labour power enriched and reproduced) and the moment of lack of security/competition between
workers (formation of an 'army' of the unemployed: see Balibar 1991). Peasantization/depeasantization could likewise be decomposed into the moments of production of agricultural
commodities, commodification of the household reproduction process, and constitution/reproduction of petty property (Gibbon and
Neocosmos 1985).

On the one hand, the state-led break-up of developmentalist
corporatism seems to have been accompanied by an increasingly
intense and anarchic level of competition for state resources
amongst the elites previously at the apex of each 'estate'. In
particular, an increase appears to have occurred in the level of
factional dispute between different 'fiefs' and in recourse to the
power of the personal or collective ruler in settling such disputes.
In the process, certain elite elements tended to become permanently
excluded. The significance of this last point is that in so far as the
formation of 'private' civil society has been modified through
processes of sub-elite exclusion, an important source of its politicization has tended to become driven by this part of the state's 'own'
'civil society'.

On the other hand the formation of civil society has become
mediated by complicated and contradictory processes at the level of
the division of labour. Only one example of this will be briefly
discussed. This is the interplay between declassing, 'de-stating' and
new processes of class formation. When viewed from the apex
the current economic situation in (post-) developmentalist states
can be characterized as one in which state monopoly capitalist
relations – mediated of course through the international division of
labour – are being at least partially transformed into private
monopoly capitalist relations. This corresponds to an intensified
privatization of the interests of the state elite as well as the
development of new sorts of relations between the state and state
elite on the one side and formally private capitals, both previously
linked to them and new, on the other. But when viewed from the
base, the same process of 'de-stating' has another aspect, namely
mass 'informalization'. As a result, the tendency for certain class
forces and social relations of a monopoly kind to become recon-
stituted in more or less modified forms in the formally private
sphere is accompanied by tendencies for other class forces and
monopoly relations to evaporate completely and for others again to

become recast, as non-monopoly relations arising out of an internal differentiation of those engaged in survival activities. This parallels, but extends, processes already well-established in the 'informal' sector during the dynamic period of developmentalism. (Normally it is also associated with a relocation of them towards extractive activities and commodity circulation.) To complicate matters further, the state sector by no means disappears completely and most households encompass social relations of a state monopoly, private monopoly and private non-monopoly kind.

At the level of civil society this becomes reflected both in the collapse of certain previously important institutions and the growth of new ones but perhaps more commonly by the subjection of pre-existing ones (including some which become detached from the state) to an ambivalent combination of new demands and identities. The latter point is most clearly illustrated in relation to the (re-)emergence of trade unions as key players on the African political stage, despite deproletarianization and the disintegration of the territorial petty bourgeoisie and despite their frequently close previous relations to the African state.

Some of the main trends and tendencies with regard to civil society in contemporary (post-)developmentalist states can thus be summed up as follows. First, an uneven process of disincorporation and internal disintegration of 'estates' and the accompanying un-ravelling of state monopoly capitalist relations and their division of labour means that the separation of state and civil society is not accompanied by the formation/re-emergence of large-scale power-ful entities with strong collectivist dimensions, either inside or outside civil society. This means that while the state is weaker than at any point since the end of colonialism, the mass of the popula-tion will probably remain outside civil society in its classical 'Western' forms and an unambiguous focus for its (and the state's) transformation will remain absent.

Second, those civil society organizations which 'survived' devel-opmentalism to play a role in the current period have probably done so through acquiring an increasing degree of autonomy *vis-à-vis* their original relation to the division of labour. In some cases what has occurred appears to be that they have established a new relation to entities produced in and through the developing division of labour, but other organizations have not and their future role is therefore likely to be unstable. Evidence exists of civil society organizations of this type enjoying a prominent role in

Africa during recent democratization struggles, but fading from the scene as soon as political parties were formed.

Third, in so far as a new rural civil society spontaneously unfolds from the new division of labour, it appears especially likely to be mainly organized or oriented around individualistic survival activities. Preliminary evidence (such as Kiondo 1994 on Tanzania) strongly suggests that the great majority of even explicitly 'civic' rural organizations emerging in the wake of the demise of developmentalism are predominantly an expression of resource-pooling in order to protect existing resources or attract further ones for group-specific benefits. Thus they tend to reproduce private and egoistical activity on a group scale. Neither, since their social/ideological basis is usually no longer the self-defining community, are they likely to be subject to 'infection' by contradictory social claims about what constitutes community interests.

Fourth, some evidence exists of the emergence or transformation of a few cooperative organizations, both in rural and urban areas, which are not merely of a resource-pooling kind and which have more contradictory relations to the state. These tend to be connected with the presence of (inevitably informalized) new kinds of non-monopoly accumulation and express the antagonism of such kinds of accumulation to monopoly forms. Current examples include small-scale miners' associations in Tanzania (see Chachage 1993).

Fifth, the combination of declassing and institutional dispersal and weakness in the post-developmentalist period means that civil society tends to be highly porous and open to 'external' forces and institutions, especially those which can locate themselves in relation to the traditions and discourses of newly maturing groups while simultaneously supplying resources for group benefits. Forces such as a socially-oriented 'fundamentalist' Islam can rapidly acquire a significant position, particularly with respect to previously disadvantaged groups, in situations where the state withdraws from social regulation and ideological control and the mass of the population simultaneously undergoes individualization. This tends to lend civil society an increasingly volatile character.

Sixth, a tendency can be identified in this conjuncture for politics nevertheless to remain mainly a preserve of the state and for opposition party politics to become mainly a preserve of those sections of 'estate' elites ejected from the state and seeking a way back into it. Given the still largely rural character of these societies, these elites are obliged to try to link up with the dominant spontaneous politics of civil society, which would appear to be a politics of resource allocation. On the other hand, states/state parties are usually strong enough to resist the civil society organizations which carry this politics. Moreover, as indicated, there are also tendencies for democratic politics expressing general interests to appear episodically and/or in scattered forms.

IMPLICATIONS FOR THE DEMOCRATIZATION PROCESS

Some implications for the democratization process will now be considered. Given external pressures, it is inevitable that state elites will feel obliged to seek or experiment with alternatives to developmentalist forms of political domination. These pressures will be strengthened by the detachment of certain institutions from the state and the episodic emergence of movements outside civil society. Efforts from above to reconstruct a developmentalist solution, even when a government firmly intends them, are meanwhile excluded by structural adjustment (see the interesting article on rural developmentalism in Ghana under Rawlings by Mikell 1989).

The *overall* result of the combination of the great extent of de-stating/exclusion/declassing which has occurred with the absence of a strong pole of politicization during this process is what Baylies and Szeftal (1992) have described with regard to Zambia as an impulse for transformation which is simultaneously 'popular but limited'. While a multiplication of areas of conflict develops, since their main source is a process of de-incorporation and unravelling, their momentum tends to be restricted.

There are certain ways in which this process can nevertheless become 'overdetermined', that is, transformed into something over and above the generation of episodic and fragmented pressures towards political liberalization'. While one can identify certain circumstances confirming the 'limited' aspect of the process, one can find others confirming and strengthening its 'popular' aspect. Moreover, these may be present simultaneously. For example, impulses towards change will be shaped by the presence/absence of particular 'vocabularies of revolt' (such as radical nationalism, Mahdism, 'Christian' and non-Christian spirit mediumship, and so on). Also important will be the presence/absence of sources of social tension, dislocation or unification arising outside the changing national state-society relationship (for example, as a result of the influx of citizens or non-citizens from other territories).

Possibly more profoundly, two other sets of overdetermining conditions can be identified. One of these sets concerns conditions at the level of state politics. Relevant here, for example, are efforts by the state to shift from political and economic modes of incorporating specific social groups to primarily administrative-repressive modes. Something like this very clearly occurred with trade unions in a number of African countries in the early 1990s, most obviously in Zambia, with the effect of inadvertently strengthening the liberalization process by placing the general issue of freedom of organization on the political agenda. But equally relevant are initiatives in the opposite direction, whether conscious or unconscious. According to Allen (1992) in Benin in 1990, for example, the state explicitly encouraged the organization of a national conference of dissenting forces, apparently in an effort to supply a framework for their (re-)incorporation. The result was rather to encourage their unity and ultimately to make the position of the authorities non-viable without liberalization. A kindred set of circumstances is described by Stepan (1985) with regard to Brazil in the early 1980s. Here, concerns amongst the ruling elite about the increasingly autonomous and therefore disruptive activity of the security apparatuses led to other elements of the elite leading a limited opening-up of the space for public debate, on the assumption that this would be occupied by a 'sideways' extension of the influence of semi-incorporated, 'responsible' forces. In fact, however, the result was the unanticipated occupation of this space by non-incorporated forces. This points to the more general significance of divisions within the state apparatuses, which in turn reflect the general nature of the ruling elite's self-organization.

A further set of overdetermining conditions refers to specific types of mutual interaction, attrition, deepening and so on which occur with respect to struggles by non-state forces in the context of de-incorporation. While the overall distribution of struggles by non-state forces in this situation is determined by the particular ways in which the state-society relation becomes loosened in respect of individual groups, the latter's responses may become linked through the emergence of a 'virtuous' mobilizatory circuit. The significance of such mobilizatory circuits is that they are associated with an enriched plebeian character and thus have further-reaching democratic implications. The absence of such circuits by contrast tends to be associated with a liberalization, the horizon of which is elections and the rule of law, but which is probably incapable of sustaining either in the longer term.

This chapter will conclude by sketching a 'mobilizatory circuit' in a post-developmentalist state. While Brazil in the early 1990s is far from being a genuinely democratic country, its transition from military rule in the 1980s had a partly plebeian basis absent in most other Latin American states, which left a mark on subsequent national politics and specifically on the 1988 democratic constitution. Indeed it is arguably the source of the probably unique (in Latin America) capacity of the Brazilian people peacefully to force the removal of their head of state other than through a national election, in 1993. On the other hand the impression left by the plebeian stamp should not be exaggerated or romanticized: Fernando Collor was after all only replaced by his vice-president, and the 1988 constitution was already being revised in 1993.

Political liberalization in Brazil took place during the 1980s in the wake of a coalescence of certain forces outside civil society, accompanied by a politicization of civil society itself. While the latter was partly influenced by the opening from above already described, it was also the result of changes inside civil society itself. These in turn were influenced by a combination of divisions within the Catholic Church, the self-organization on an unprecedented scale of semi-marginalized urban women and a temporarily rising economic conjuncture associated with an interlude of industrial male working-class formation.

The first two of these tendencies found expression in the up to 80 000 Communidades Eclesiales de Base (CEBs) formed in Brazil starting in the early 1970s. These small, decentralized and often temporary organizations were initially sponsored by the Catholic hierarchy as lay bodies aimed at responding to the shortage of priests and the growing influence of fundamentalist Protestantism amongst the urban poor. Later their leadership became identified with the socially-conscious middle-class Catholic left and their rank-and-file with women from the burgeoning urban slums (see Kowarick 1985; Vink 1985; Lehman 1990). Primarily 'cult' communities where the poor 'celebrated their faith and hope' (Vink 1985), many of the CEBs also took on a self-image of *representing* the poor. This was strengthened through the exclusion of 'cults' from the official Church and through their involvement with members' practical problems. On this basis, the problems became socialized, especially those problems concerning areas of former state provision (health, education) and regulation (such as land rights). The result was the emergence of a culture of resistance with strongly feminized elements.[1]

According to both Kowarick and Vink, struggles by the CEBs created a basis for a deepening of the movement of male industrial workers in the São Paulo area at the beginning of the 1980s. These coincided with an organized differentiation of the trade unions. Rank-and-file workers, some of them earlier active in the Church's own corporate organization for workers, organized first a set of local committees and later a new trade union federation (CUT), in response to the inability of the official federation (CGT) to accommodate the new workers and their demands. Later the CGT was also to increasingly detach itself from the state in order to maintain a base (Roxburgh 1989).

Stepan (1985) meanwhile strongly emphasizes the role of the independent press in these developments and certain later ones. These included the formation of an independent employers' organization with a non-statist ideology, via a newspaper-organized campaign and ballot. It also involved a promotion of the authority of the leader (Lula) of a new party, the Workers' Party: the first in Brazil to operate in a determinedly non-clientist way.[2] However, this party was primarily the effect of spontaneous political differentiation arising as a result of the cross-fertilization of the popular aspects of the civil society organizations described (compare the Leninist concept of a pre-existing party 'linking' popular struggles). On the other hand, and contrary to the formulations of the 'civil society'/social movements school, it proved to be the formation of this national party and its victory in various local elections which allowed the consolidation and development of the popular social movements themselves.

The Brazilian experience was an ambivalent one in many respects (as it remains), and it is obviously not immediately replicable elsewhere.[3] Clearly, it depended on a temporary economic boom, a split in the Catholic Church, high levels of female rural-urban migration, a large middle class which could sustain a serious independent press, and so on. It also bore the mark of a transition from a specifically military form of rule. In Africa the pattern is rather one of ongoing economic recession, relatively weak or apolitical churches, male-dominated migration patterns, a limited middle class and forms of civilian rule characterized by inter-elite factionalism. Yet there is no reason to exclude the possibility that 'mobilizatory circuits' can arise on bases other than the Brazilian ones. For example, should an economic upturn occur in Africa, feeding into increased accumulation from below and self-confidence for those forces identified with it, the implications could be far-reaching.

References

Allen, C. (1992), *Democratic Renewal in Africa: Two essays on Benin*, Occasional Paper No. 40 (Edinburgh: Centre for African Studies, University of Edinburgh).

Balibar, E. (1991), 'From class struggle to classless struggle', in E. Balibar, and I. Wallerstein (eds), *Race, Nation, Class* (London: Verso).

Baylies, C. and M. Szeftal (1992), 'The fall and rise of multiparty democracy in Zambia', *Review of African Political Economy*, No. 54.

Bernstein, H. (1990), 'Agricultural "modernization" the era of structural adjustment', *Journal of Peasant Studies*, Vol. 18, No. 1, pp. 3–35.

Booth, D. (1993), *Social, Economic and Cultural Change in Tanzania – A People-oriented Focus* (Stockholm: SIDA).

Chachage, C. (1995) 'The meek shall inherit the earth but not the mining rights: Small scale mining and accumulation in Tanzania' in P. Gibbon (ed.) *Liberalised Development in Tanzania* (Uppsala: SIAS).

Gibbon, P., Y. Bangura and A Ofstad (eds) (1992), *Authoritarianism, Democracy and Adjustment: The Politics of Economic Reform in Africa* (Uppsala: SIAS).

Gibbon, P. and M. Neocosmos (1985), 'Some problems in the political economy of "African socialism" ', in H. Bernstein, and B. Campbell (eds), *Contradictions of Accumulation in Africa* (London: Sage).

Hedlund, H. (ed.) (1988), *Cooperatives Revisited* (Uppsala: SIAS).

Jamal, V. and J. Weeks (1988), 'The vanishing rural-urban gap in Sub-Saharan Africa', *International Labour Review*, Vol. 127, No. 3 pp. 271–92.

Julin, E. (1993), *Structural Change in Rural Kenya*, Handelshögskolan vid Göteborgs Universitet, Ekonomiska Studier No. 41.

Kanyinga, K. (1993), 'The socio-political context of the growth of non-governmental organizations in Kenya', in P. Gibbon (ed.), *Social Change and Economic Reform in Africa* (Uppsala: SIAS).

Kiondo, A. (1994), 'The new politics of local development in Tanzania', in K., Kanyinga, A. Kiondo and P. Tidemand, *The New Local Level*

Politics in East Africa: Studies on Uganda, Tanzania and Kenya (Uppsala: SIAS), Research Report No. 95.

Kowarick, L. (1985), 'The pathways to encounter: reflections on the social struggle in São Paulo', in D. Slater (ed.), *New Social Movements and the State in Latin America* (Amsterdam: CEDLA).

Lehman, D. (1990), *Democracy and Development in Latin America: Economics, Politics and Religion in the Postwar Period* (Philadelphia: Temple Smith University Press).

Lubeck, P. (1985), 'Islamic protest under semi-industrial capitalism: Yan Tatsine explained', *Africa* vol. 55, pp. 369–89.

Mamdani, M. (1990), 'The social basis of constitutionalism in Africa', *Journal of Modern African Studies*, Vol. 28, No. 3 pp. 359–74.

Marx, K. (1843a, 1971), 'Critique of Hegel's Philosophy of Right', in *Early Texts* (Oxford: Basil Blackwell).

Marx, K. (1843b, 1971), 'On the Jewish question', in *Early Texts* (Oxford: Basil Blackwell).

Marx, K. (1844, 1971), 'Toward a critique of Hegel's Philosophy of Right: Introduction', in *Early Texts* (Oxford: Basil Blackwell).

Mikell, G. (1989), 'Peasant politicization and economic recuperation in Ghana: local and national dilemmas', *Journal of Modern African Studies*, Vol. 27, No. 3 pp. 455–78.

Mustapha, A.R. (1992), 'Structural adjustment and multiple modes of livelihood in Nigeria', in P., Gibbon, Y. Bangura and A. Ofstad (eds) (1992), *Authoritarianism, Democracy and Adjustment: The Politics of Economic Reform in Africa* (Uppsala: SIAS).

Ninsin, K. (1988), 'Three levels of state reordering: the structural aspects', in D. Rothchild, and N. Chazan (eds), *The Precarious Balance: State and Society in Africa* (Boulder, Col.: Westview).

O'Donnell, G. and P. Schmitter (1986), *Transitions from Authoritarian Rule: Tentative Conclusions about Uncertain Democracies* (Baltimore, Md: Johns Hopkins University Press).

Poulantzas, N. (1976), *Crisis of the Dictatorships* (London: Verso).

Raikes, P. (1992), 'The evolution of agricultural policy in East Africa', in Swedish University of Agricultural Sciences, International Rural Development Centre, 'Nordic workshop on peasant agricultural marketing in East Africa: proceedings, conclusions and recommendations'.

Roxburgh, I. (1989), 'Organized labour: a major victim of the debt crisis', in B. Stallings, and R. Kaufman (eds), *Debt and Democracy in Latin America* (Boulder, Col.: Westview).

Stepan, A. (1985), 'State power and the strength of civil society in the southern cone of Latin America', in P., Evans, D. Rueschemeyer and T. Skocpol (eds), *Bringing the State Back In* (Cambridge: Cambridge University Press).

Thompson, D. (1984), *The Chartists* (London: Temple Smith).

Törnquist, O. (1993), 'Popular politics of democratization: initial results on the importance of democratization for radical popular movements in Philippines and Kerala', paper presented to Nordic Conference on Social Movements in the Third World, Lund, August.

Vink, N. (1985), 'Base communities and urban social movements: a case study of the metalworkers' strike', in D. Slater (ed.), *New Social Movements and the State in Latin America* (Amsterdam: CEDLA).

Woodford-Berger, P. (1993), *Akan Female Linkages, Collective Identities and Political Ideology in Dormaa, Ghana* (Stockholm: Department of Social Anthropology, University of Stockholm), mimeo.

Notes

1. A useful comparison may be made between this situation and that in often more predominantly male African urban communities, especially where the latter are marginalized. The latter, when organized, sometimes adopt more violent and less 'social' forms. See Lubeck (1985) on the Yan Tatsine revolt in northern Nigeria in the early 1980s (an analysis which, however, does not mention the issue of gender, even though the movement was wholly male).

2. Anti-clientism as an ideology and practice is identified by Lehman (1990) with the weight of women-dominated organizations amongst popular forces in Brazil.

3. See Törnquist (1993) for an interesting discussion of various self-conscious attempts to replicate a similar chain of events in the Philippines.

Part II

Economy, Society and Political Development

6 Farmers' Movements and Agricultural Development in India[1]

Staffan Lindberg

Agricultural development and the emergence of a rural petty bourgeoisie (that is, the farmers) were central elements of the modernization process in most industrialized countries. The successful mobilization and organization of commercialized peasants and farmers was in particular vital to Western history (Esman and Uphoff 1984: 31). With the labour movement, producer oriented agrarian movements mobilized the majority of the population, and made them co-actors in the great social transformations which created the modern world (Olofsson 1988: 17). The significance of these movements can still be seen in the considerable political leverage that farmers have, despite their numerical weakness, on contemporary policies in Western Europe and North America.

Similar peasants' and farmers' movements appear to be developing in several parts of the Third World. Most famous, perhaps, are the new farmers' movements in India (Brass 1994), and in Mexico (Paré 1990). But there is also growing evidence of peasant collective action in this field in a number of other Latin American countries, as described by Schejtman in Chapter 7 of this volume. In Africa such organizations have emerged in, for example, Zimbabwe (Zinyama 1992) and Ghana (Songsore 1992).

In India, the new farmers' movements, or farmers' agitations as they are popularly called, seem to represent a break with the traditional peasant movements[2] which fought for land and better leasing arrangements. The new movements see the state and the urban industrial economy as the main enemy, while the traditional movements fought against landlords and the colonial state. Several questions can be raised in an analysis of these new movements.

• Are we witnessing a new phase in the development of Indian agrarian society?

- What is the class basis of these movements?
- Is there any resemblance to producer-oriented farmers' movements in Western Europe and the USA at corresponding stages of transition to an industrial society?
- How do the farmers orient themselves in the contemporary trend towards a liberal trade regime?

THE NEW FARMERS' MOVEMENTS IN INDIA

During the last 20 years the new farmers' movements have become one of the most important non-parliamentary political forces in India. In several states farmers have formed organizations to fight for better economic conditions in an increasingly commodified agricultural economy. The main target is the state and its intervention in the agrarian economy, supplying many of the inputs and regulating the markets. The farmers demand lower prices on inputs like seeds, fertilizers and pesticides, lower tariffs on electricity and water, lower taxes, and debt relief. Likewise they demand higher prices for their products of grains, cash-crops, vegetables, milk and so on. They argue that the terms of trade between industry and agriculture are increasingly developing in favour of industry against agriculture.

The movements, which started in Tamil Nadu and Punjab in the early 1970s, later spread to Karnataka, Maharashtra, Gujarat, Haryana, Uttar Pradesh and some regions in neighbouring states. Today the most important movements are Shetkari Sanghatana in Maharashtra, and the Bharatiya Kisan Union (BKU) in Western Uttar Pradesh. The movements in Punjab and Karnataka are also fairly strong. The movement in Tamil Nadu, which was very strong in the 1970s and early 1980s, has now become very weak (Nadkarni 1987; Brass 1994).[3]

The central message is the simple and powerful slogan: *Bharat against India! Bharat* is the indigenous name for India, with positive connotations, while *India* is the westernized name, symbolizing exploitation. They stand for the rural and the urban-industrial populations respectively. Sharad Joshi, leader of the farmers' movement in Maharashtra, has formulated this slogan and explains it in the following way: 'The real contradiction is not in the village, not between big peasants and small, not between landowners and landless, but between the agrarian population as a whole and the rest of the society' (interview, March 1989).

The new farmers' movements have had a strong influence on

Indian politics during the past decade. There are strong indications that these movements played an important role in the overthrow of Rajiv Gandhi's government in the 1989 general elections. In Uttar Pradesh and Haryana, for example, the BKU worked decisively for the National Front opposition, which won an almost complete victory over the Congress Party. The National Front government later tried to promulgate a new policy, involving the moratorium of debts of up to Rs10 000 and the preparation of a new liberal agricultural policy on subsidies and infrastructural support. The policy was only half completed when the government fell in early 1991. However, today almost all political parties have to reckon with the strength of the farmers' lobby, at least on the level of rhetoric. When the new Congress government tried to increase fertilizer prices by 40 per cent in July 1991, there was such a massive opposition from all political parties that the proposal had to be changed drastically.

BACKGROUND: CHANGING AGRICULTURE AND RURAL SOCIETY

The growth of the farmers' unions must first of all be seen against the background of agricultural development in India during the last three decades. One decisive watershed is the introduction of the so-called Green Revolution, which started in the mid-1960s. The new technology consists primarily of an application of a package of new hybrid seeds, chemical fertilizers and pesticides and was introduced in areas which had access to irrigation.

While overall gains in production were fairly slow in the late 1960s and the first part of the 1970s, agricultural development seems to have taken a more positive turn after that with a higher annual growth of output of food-grains than in the preceding decade. With wheat production already growing at a high rate, it is primarily gains in rice production that have added to the overall increase in growth rate (Sarma and Gandhi 1990: 20–1). This is so despite the fact that growth rates for crops like pulses and millets, mostly cultivated in dry rainfed areas, are still lagging behind. Thus, it would seem as if the Green Revolution has finally made it in India. At the given level of demand, India has become self-sufficient in food-grains.[4] There are, of course, important regional variations in the above-mentioned developments. Food-grain production has increased much more in the three northern states of

Punjab, Haryana and Uttar Pradesh than in other states (Sarma and Gandhi 1990: 21–2). Again, some regions within these other states have also experienced the same growth rate in food-grains or other crops.

At the same time there are also signs of an increasing integration of the rural and urban economies both in agricultural and industrial production. With the Green Revolution agriculture is becoming increasingly commodified. There is an increased demand for industrial products and the surplus created in agriculture is invested in small-scale industries and services. Rural labourers are also increasingly engaged in industries and services, either in their areas of residence or as migrant labour. This may be one of the main reasons for the impressive industrial growth in India during the 1980s and the early 1990s.

In contrast to the reports and studies of the 1960s and 1970s we now also have at least some evidence of decreasing poverty in rural areas. Official statistics show that in 1987/88 only 32 percent of the rural population lived below the poverty line,[5] against 40 percent in 1983/84 and 48 percent in 1977/78. An alternative estimate shows a change from 59 percent below the poverty line in 1970/71 to 51 percent in 1983/84 and 49 percent in 1987/88 (Minhas, Jain and Tendulka 1991). One should not overly rely on such figures, given the relative weakness of the official statistical data base in India. However, if one adds a number of other observations the picture becomes clearer. The Seventh round of the National Sample Survey (1987/88) reports increasing expenditure on consumer durables in all rural income classes.

Always criticized for not being efficient, for not doing enough, the Indian state has nevertheless played an important role in these transformations. State intervention in agricultural development has been massive: development of infrastructure (roads, electricity, irrigation, and so on); extension activities, supply of inputs, credit, and so on; public work programmes; special programmes for agricultural labourers and small farmers; and health and drinking water programmes. These large schemes have all played a role in the changes that are now becoming visible in the rural areas.

As far as agrarian relations of production are concerned the picture is less clear, and also varies a great deal between regions. To discuss that, however, a few words on my conception of class are necessary. The class analysis here and in the following is based on the theoretical and empirical analyses in Athreya, Djurfeldt and

Lindberg (1990, ch. 6). The main criterion is that of reproductive levels and appropriation of surplus from agricultural production. Poor peasants are defined as those peasants who cannot cover the grain requirements of the household from the income from its farm production. Middle peasants, on the other hand, comprise a range of peasant households, from those who can just about cover this requirement up to those households who are fully reproductive: that is, who are able to cover also the non-grain requirements of the household and the cash cost for production itself. Rich peasants are those households who can appropriate a surplus from the farm production, over and above the needs mentioned above. In contrast to capitalist farmers, however, rich peasants have to work on the land themselves, so income from their own labour is more important than from capital invested. There is also a considerable subsistence component in their production (Athreya, Djurfeldt and Lindberg 1990: 196–7).

Taking an overall perspective, one can say that there is evidence of a gradual strengthening of small to medium-sized capitalist farms, and of rich and middle peasant farms, which, however, depend on wage labour for all major operations. Land and tenancy reforms have had a very uneven impact, although in some regions strong peasant movements have managed with the help of urban allies to affect certain changes. More important, big landed property has been slowly disintegrating due to division of holdings between heirs, and in some cases because of selling of land in anticipation of land reforms. In this way some land has passed over to cultivating households. About one-third of all households is classified as agricultural labourers, and their land ownership is marginal, but there is no clear evidence of increased landlessness after the introduction of the Green Revolution (Athreya, Djurfeldt and Lindberg 1990: 125; Harriss 1992). Yet most rural areas still seem to be dominated by an elite of landlords, capitalist farmers and rich peasants, who control much of the land and the economy, and also dominate social and political institutions. It should also be noted that the character of this domination varies a great deal between a backward state like Bihar, and an advanced one like Punjab.

CLASS BASIS OF THE MOVEMENTS

The strong populist appeal of the new farmers' movements has led to the mobilization of the broad rural masses, but this does not mean that the movements equally represent the interest of all rural classes and strata. Behind the appeal there is a class basis of capitalist farmers in alliance with rich and middle peasants, who join the movements because of their precarious position in an increasingly commodified agricultural economy, in which prices on inputs and farm products are, to a large extent, politically determined via state intervention. Rural labourers and the majority of poor peasants, who earn their living mainly by wage labour, are only indirectly involved. To the extent that peasants and farmers gain, the basis for their demands for higher wages and better terms of employment expands.

Thus, the new farmers' movements represent a sharp break with 'traditional' peasant movements. This break can be summarized in the replacement of one slogan 'Land to the tiller!' by another 'Remunerative prices!' The traditional peasant movements are organized around the contradiction between landed and non-landed groups in a landlord-dominated agrarian society. Their demands vary from land reforms to rent reduction for tenants, and they typically organize land-hungry peasants, such as landless labourers, small tenants and poor peasants (Sen 1982).

'Renumerative prices!' articulates interests which are common to a commodity-producing peasantry, that is, peasants who are not only producing for the markets, but also using commodities bought on the market as inputs in their farming. The new movements, therefore, act on the issue of the price of agricultural produce and also on the price of inputs like fertilizers, electricity, and terms of credit from state-owned or state-sponsored financial institutions. Price formation is, to a large extent, influenced by the state, which thereby regulates the conditions of reproduction of the peasantry. The contradiction on which the 'new' farmers' movements act is therefore one *between the state and the peasantry*: it is the state which is seen as the main target of agitation, not the local landlords as in the traditional type of peasant movement.

The new farmers' movements are a strong indication of the structural transformation of Indian agriculture since independence. This transformation has shifted the political emphasis from the land question to a conflict over conditions of reproduction in a commodified agrarian economy. It has meant a change in the pattern of political alliances among the peasantry. In the 'traditional' peasant movements the middle peasants were allied with poor peasants and landless labourers, often playing a leading role. In the new movements, however, middle peasants are allied with rich peasants and capitalist farmers. How can that be?

The answer lies in the precarious situation of middle peasants in the agrarian economy after the introduction of the Green Revolution. This can be illustrated by data from a study, which I made together with Venkatesh Athreya and Göran Djurfeldt in Tiruchy District in Tamil Nadu, representing the two major ecotypes in Indian agriculture: a river irrigated cultivation system, and a dry, rainfed cultivation system respectively (Athreya, Djurfeldt and Lindberg 1990). In both areas, the level of commodification is high and has deeply affected the middle peasantry. As a result, the middle peasants (for a definition see the previous section) are divided. Only a minority of them, or less than 24 per cent, can reproduce themselves fully and autonomously thanks to their own labour power. Instead, the majority of them are pressed below this level and have to turn to non-farm sources for their reproduction. They are squeezed by market forces, made effective by the significant inroads of commodification both into consumption and into farm reproduction. In this process the middle peasantry has become more susceptible to unfavourable fluctuations in the prices paid for consumer goods and farm inputs, and in incomes from wage labour.

The class structure is fluid to some extent. Households oscillate between different levels of reproduction, and even between that of middle and rich peasants. This fluidity in the class structure underlines the role of the state in the formation of the agrarian class structure. Agricultural prices, both on output and inputs, are to a large extent administered prices. There is a political element hidden behind the 'invisible hand' of the market (Athreya, Djurfeldt and Lindberg 1990: 231–2). It is precisely the contradiction between the commodity-producing peasantry and the state, over policies affecting the terms of trade between agriculture and industry, which potentially unites the middle and rich peasantry with capitalist farmers in the new farmers' movements.

Poor peasants are less influenced by movements in the price of farm produce, since they are not commodity producers to any significant degree. However, the price of purchased inputs and of industrial consumer goods affects the real value of the wages they earn as agricultural labourers.

This is not to deny that the land question is still an important issue in many parts of rural India, only that its relative importance has decreased in the contemporary political opportunity structure.

It is in this context that middle peasants ask for higher prices on their produce rather than more land, a context that could again change with changing economic and political conjunctures. Moreover, the alliance forged between middle peasants and the upper levels of the agrarian class structure in the new farmers' movements is threatened by yet another contradiction. Middle peasants, to a large extent, complement their farm income with agricultural wage labour, which makes them at least potential allies of landless labourers and poor peasants in their struggle for higher wages against rich peasants and capitalist farmers (Athreya, Djurfeldt and Lindberg 1990: 315).

AGRARIANISM?

There are important historical parallels to what is now happening in Indian agrarian politics. During the second half the nineteenth century, in the midst of the industrialization and commodification of agriculture, producer-oriented farmers' movements in West Europe and North America came to replace earlier peasant movements and politics. Though it may be now almost forgotten by the contemporary social sciences, these movements represented important political and cultural forces in the modernization of these societies, ranging from 'agrarianism' in the USA to the various associations, cooperatives, and political parties in Europe.[6]

The most successful example of this type of development is perhaps to be found in Denmark. Denmark had an early and radical land reform in the late eighteenth century, which abolished the feudal land tenure system and created a class of independent peasants with 'family-sized farms'. At the same time a religious reform movement swept over the ethnically homogenous Danish countryside, forming the peasantry into a well-knit ideological community (Gundelach 1988). Olofsson (1988: 18) writes:

> the agrarian social movements in Scandinavia, most evident in the Danish case, were part of the emergence of a rural petty bourgeoisie, of peasants and farmers in possession of their land, successfully adapting to (an increasing) dependence on the market. The change in the market relations meant both a growing entanglement in the networks of the world market, mainly the English, and the growing internal Danish market, due to indus-

trialization and urbanization. This economic reorientation con-
curred with political modernization, with a protracted struggle
for parliamentarism and, later, democracy.

Towards the end of the nineteenth century in Denmark, the
farmers and the peasants built up an impressive array of strong,
efficient and encompassing organizations. The co-operative organizations in both production and distribution of agricultural
products formed the solid nucleus in the peasant movement. They
developed dairies as well as slaughterhouses; wholesale and marketing associations within the sphere of distribution, including
rurally based consumers' co-op; credit associations for mortgages
and loans as well as rural saving banks; a major political party –
the liberal Venstre party – representing the interest of the farmer
class; the people's high schools as an instrument for civic and
cultural training; a string of newspapers.

Though not perhaps developed to the same extreme extent anywhere else, the Danish example still epitomizes the development
during the late nineteenth and early twentieth century in many West
European countries and in parts of North America.

It is important not to romanticize this development. The continued viability of the family farm – the petty commodity-producing
farmer – at the expense of big estates must ultimately be interpreted
in terms of the political economy of industrial capitalist development and its relationship to the agrarian economy and society it
was interacting with. The Russian economist Chayanov (1966)
termed this form of capitalist penetration into agriculture as *vertical
concentration* in contrast to a horizontal one, in which big landed
property would expand at the expense of peasant farms. In vertical
concentration peasants become subordinate to capital, which, without taking over the land, 'begins to actively interfere in the
organization of production too, by laying down technical conditions, issuing seed and fertilizers, and determining rotation' (Djurfeldt 1981: 185). Capitalism also enters into primary processing of
agricultural raw material and, writes Chayanov:

> If to this we add in the most developed capitalist countries, such
> as those in North America, widely developed mortgage credit, the
> financing of farm circulating capital, and the dominant part
> played by capital invested in transport, elevators, irrigation, and
> other undertakings, then we have before us new ways in which

capitalism penetrates agriculture. These ways convert the farmers into a labour force working with other people's means of production. They convert agriculture, despite the evident scattered and independent nature of the small commodity producers, into an economic system concentrated in a series of the largest undertakings and, through them, entering the sphere controlled by the most advanced forms of finance capital. (Chayanov 1966: 262)

One explanation for this survival of the family farm is that it allows for surplus appropriation which is higher than what would be the case in horizontal concentration. 'In so far as family farms allow agribusiness to pump out the entire surplus value created in this sector, it increases the rate of profit for capital' (Djurfeldt 1981: 186).

As is well-known, vertical concentration often took a cooperative form, a process that 'goes much deeper than in its capitalist ones, since the peasant himself hands over to co-operative forms of concentration sectors of his farm that capitalism never succeeds in detaching from it in the course of their struggle' (Chayanov 1966: 264).

The historical development in Europe and North America has later been repeated in East Asia. Producer-oriented farmers' movements have played an important role in the development of agriculture and in politics in Japan after the Second World War and the land reforms carried out at that time. More recently still, in Taiwan, a similar process took place:

Agricultural modernization gave increased incomes and higher purchasing power to the rural population, thereby enabling it to form a market for industrial goods. The question is how this could happen when agriculture was being so heavily exploited at the same time. The answer lies in the increased productivity resulting from the restructuring of agriculture, chiefly because the land reform was accompanied by a series of institutional changes at the local, regional and national levels, which brought positive effects in terms of diffusion of technology, credits and infrastructure . . .

Perhaps the most important institutional change was the organization of the so-called Farmers' Associations at the bottom level. The removal of the landlords had left a lacuna with regard to land management and rural credit. If this problem had not been resolved, the land reform would not have been successful. A

Farmers' Association was an independent financial association with local management, which organized credit and marketing and helped with the introduction of new technology. (Gunnarsson 1992: 92–3)

There is also evidence from South Korea of the same process (Moore 1984). In all these cases, it seems, the organization of family farmers took place on the initiative of the state, but the thus formed farmers' movements have later developed into more autonomous political movements. Summarizing these experiences, Ling and Selden (1993: 9) write:

Farmers' associations in Japan, South Korea, and Taiwan are comprehensive cooperatives resting on the foundation of the family farm. These cooperatives not only provide a range of agricultural services, but also represent the political interests of farmers and negotiate with the state on their behalf. These associations, positioned between the state and rural households, are based in varying degrees on principles of voluntary participation, autonomy and democratic management. Indeed, democratic participation in rural cooperatives in these East Asian countries is a basis for protecting the interest of small farmers and a foundation for building a democratic polity.

Taken together these various experiences suggest that dynamic development of peasant agriculture needs strong organizations and cooperative institutions, or in short, the organization of peasants into autonomous movements (economic associations, cooperatives, political organizations, and so on) which address various development issues, press for more efficient administration, cheaper inputs and credit, a better infrastructure, and the diffusion of new knowledge. The state, on the other hand, must simultaneously be responsive to farmers' needs; that is, encouraging increased productivity via a combination of price incentives and institutional reforms so as to organize the conditions of production in an efficient way.

FROM AGITATION TO COOPERATION?

What are the possibilities that the new farmers' movements in India will develop in the same or similar ways as the most successful farmers' movements described above? Can they go from agitation to cooperation? Can they become organizations to effectively represent the interest of 'family farmers' in the Indian context?

Farmers' movements in India face a rather different historical situation from the early producer-oriented movements of late nineteenth- and early twentieth-century Europe, or even mid-twentieth-century East Asia. Most important, state intervention in agriculture and rural society is far more advanced. Backed and aided by a variety of international agencies, the Indian government has developed a very comprehensive system of extension and credit institutions, seed farms, and so on. Rural infrastructure – in the form of large irrigation projects, roads and power transmission – has also been built on an impressive scale. The opportunity, therefore, to organize around such projects, as happened in Europe and elsewhere, is not forthcoming to the same extent.

With agro-business industry the situation is similar. Large state corporations and private firms with strong international links to transnational corporations produce most of what is needed as inputs in Indian agriculture and also process some of its products. The structure is so developed that it is hardly conceivable that farmers' organizations could take over or control any sizeable part of it. It is only in fields not yet developed that farmers' organizations could perhaps make some inroads. In Punjab, for example, the farmers' movement is planning to set up a plywood factory, owned by farmers, to process eucalyptus wood grown on their farms.

However, there are still areas in which agriculture and rural society remain underdeveloped. Crop insurance is one such, and consumer cooperatives another. It would perhaps be easier to develop cooperatives since many rural areas are underserviced with well furnished shops of consumer articles and durables. Cooperative organizations need to be very well organized, however, in order to compete with merchants in market towns. There is need for a completely new conception of cooperatives in this respect, since earlier attempts in this direction have been heavily controlled, bureaucratized and corrupted by state administrations. Thus, the original idea of cooperation, autonomous of state and capitalist control, needs to be restored (Hatti and Rundquist 1993).

Another great opportunity structure seems to be in the field of alternative agricultural technology. There is today a great need to develop new small-scale irrigation techniques, dry crop cultivation, resource saving agriculture, and a less poisonous agricultural technique than that based on the extensive use of pesticides dumped in India by the multi-nationals. In all these fields state intervention is ineffective since it is based on large-scale bureaucratic organizations and linked to vested interests. Thus there is much room for local organizing, small irrigation associations, associations for bio-dynamic cultivation and so on.

In this context the development of the internal discussions and negotiations in the various farmers' movements may be crucial for the choices ahead. Since they are regionally specific movements, the outcome will also reflect this difference. For example, the ecological strategies that have been discussed in Maharashtra may be one such sign of variation. The discussion in the Shetkari Sanghatana on issues of alternative agricultural development gives a hint in this direction: small-scale and water-saving irrigation schemes, new water-sharing systems, new bio-technology, as well as rural industrialization (Omvedt 1991: 2289). This change from the 'one-point programme' of prices on farm products to what has been described by Sharad Joshi as a 'battle of production' may still be more of a dream than a real strategy (Omvedt 1992), but it certainly signifies a shift of emphasis and a profile which may have important bearings on the development of the agrarian economy as such.

Finally, farmers' movements may have an important role to play in the political changes now under way in India: the attempt to strengthen the democratic content of state institutions by making them more locally managed and accountable. The recent Panchayat reform to strengthen local government is a very important step in this direction and may provide a new political opportunity for the farmers' movements.

A decisive factor in the future development of the farmers' movements is what must be called the class struggle. Since the movements are formed out of an alliance between middle and rich peasants, one the one hand, and the elite of capitalist farmers and landlords on the other hand, there remains the question of whose interest will prevail in the movements. After all, the farmers' movements are (like all social movements) volatile social creations, which, depending on the outcome, potentially can serve both as promoters of a dynamic agrarian capitalism based on family farms, and, at the other extreme, as hindrances to an efficient implementation of such agricultural development. If the movements become dominated by an emerging agrarian bourgeoisie of capitalist farmers they may actually prevent the state from carrying out necessary institutional changes to further the cause of 'family farmers', such as improvements in agricultural taxation, new types of irrigation schemes, and further necessary land reforms in certain areas.

Landlordism of, say, the Latin American, German or Spanish type is hardly a problem in India. Big landlord and capitalist farms are fairly few and far between. Land reforms after independence, however ineffective, more or less did away with this type of landed property. The ones that are still there operate in niches and with special political protection, since their owners very often also occupy political positions. Their total production, however, is so small that they hardly matter in overall agricultural production. So the battle, as we have described it above, is between the local elite of smaller landlords and capitalist farmers and the large majority of rich and middle peasants. The outcome of this battle is an open affair, as far as one can tell. What speaks for the middle peasant-rich peasant alliance is what has been called the 'numbers game': that is, the fact that they represent such a vast group of powerful patrons to be relied upon when mobilizing the rural vote in elections.

Of equal importance in this regard are the policies of the Indian state and international capital which, by setting terms and conditions for the development of the agrarian economy, may determine the way in which peasants/farmers can be mobilized in the future. In fact, it is the interplay between these forces and the various farmers' movements that in the end will determine the outcome. These processes and forces are not bound *a priori* to favour the interest of capitalist farmers alone. Other outcomes are possible. If, for example, middle peasants-cum-family farmers can achieve a strong influence in these movements, this would possibly put pressure on the Indian state to pursue policies more friendly to small and intermediate producers. This in turn could facilitate a scenario of agrarian development not unlike that of Western Europe and parts of the USA, where family farming and its vertical concentration under state agencies, cooperative institutions, and agro-industrial capital have become the dominant features.

If the emerging class of middle and rich peasants as manifested in the new farmers' movements, can bargain successfully with 'the components of the predominantly urban organized economy and society', they may become the 'hegemonic agrarian class' in India (Rudolph and Rudolph 1987: 342). In this scenario, state policy could then further strengthen the position of these sections of the peasantry *vis-à-vis* other agrarian classes. States do not just react to classes, they may also have a strong impact on class formation itself:

> while states can be shown to be shaped, produced, and determined by class interests and action, they have also produced class structures, transformed them or made them disappear, as when a bourgeoisie or a peasantry has been created by deliberate state policy . . . Both of the possible routes of determination must be considered. (Shanin 1982: 316)[7]

RESPONSE TO GATT

The development of the new farmers' movements in India is particularly interesting in the context of the contemporary phase of economic globalization, dominated by neo-liberal precepts. Classical farmers' movements in the West typically developed as a response to disputes over customs tariffs to protect domestic agriculture from the competition of imported grains from the new world (Gerschenkron 1966). Two main types of movement emerged: some movements came to stand for protection, while others were for open competition, seizing whatever comparative advantage could be developed, in which farmers' cooperative movements sometimes were decisive.

This scenario now seems to be repeated in India. The recently concluded Uruguay round of GATT (General Agreement on Tariffs and Trade) has divided the farmers' movements into two camps.

As is well known, world trade in agriculture is highly distorted. A number of studies have recently shown the character of this distortion. Summarizing these studies, Gulati and Sharma (1994: 1857) state that they:

> reveal that direct and indirect subsidies, which flow to the agricultural sector, manifest themselves into distorted world prices of agricultural commodities. These distorted world prices, in turn, result into a situation of deceptive comparative advantage that leads to inefficient use of world resources, which ultimately leads to efficiency and welfare losses around the world. Therefore, the underlying philosophy of the GATT treaty is to correct these distortions.

Despite being mainly pushed by the developed countries, especially by West European and US interests, the GATT agreement nevertheless promises increased opportunities for the export of agricultural produce from developing countries over the next ten years. GATT stipulates that subsidies to farmers, if higher than 10 per cent of the total value of agricultural produce, should be significantly reduced over a period of six and ten years for developed and developing countries respectively. Likewise the agreement calls for reducing direct export subsidies to various commodities. Restrictions on imports should also be removed, although important exemptions are allowed in case of, for example, problems with balance of payments. It is generally understood that this agreement will favour increased exports from developing countries, while both total production and export from developed countries will be reduced.

Other, more general, GATT regulations also affect agriculture: GATT provisions that 'governments must provide protection to seed-breeders, either through patents or any other way they like' (Jain 1993: 55). Finally, the general treaty also provides for more liberal rules for foreign investments in all fields, which in the case of India will mean opening up for big transnational agri-business.

A common reaction to the treaty among many intellectuals is one of severe criticism: 'The GATT deal has set the seal on a new world trade order in which the interest of the world's poorest countries and people have been sacrificed to the self-interest of northern governments, and to powerful transnational companies' (Watkins 1994: 60).

In India, the debate around the so-called Dunkel draft[8] and recently concluded GATT agreement and its implications for agriculture has led to a deep split in the farmers' movements. In fact, the movements and its intellectuals have become sharply divided between a protectionist and a liberal position.

On the protectionist side, we find the Karnataka Rajya Ryota Sangha led by M.D. Nanjundaswamy and the BKU of Uttar Pradesh led by Mahendra Singh Tikait, which, together with allied factions of farmers' movements of other states, have staged a series of protest demonstrations. Their arguments have been developed by some well-known intellectuals from the environmentalist movement, notably Vandana Shiva, who has travelled worldwide to protest against GATT and its implications. On 2 October 1993, shortly before the final GATT agreement, this was manifested by a big demonstration in Bangalore with more than 100 000 participants, representing not only Karnataka, but also participants from other parts of India, and radical environmentalist movements in Europe and the USA (Rane 1993).

GATT is viewed by this faction as being extremely adverse to the interest of Third World peasants and farmers. The general argument is that GATT does not sufficiently remove the subsidies and other policies of the developed countries which allows them to dump their surplus of agricultural produce on the world market, while it forces developing countries to reduce restrictions on agricultural imports and cut down on their present level of subsidization. It is also claimed that GATT provides for increased penetration of transnational agri-business in Third World agriculture, in controlling seeds by the extension of Western patent laws, and by providing room for their increased sale of other inputs, as well as for contract farming, processing of agricultural produce, and so on. This, in combination with the threat of privatization of banks and the possibility that peasants and farmers will lose their lands to these banks and companies, makes for very bleak prospects, it is claimed. GATT regulations are also interpreted as an obligation to apply Western (read US) patent laws on seeds, and an opportunity for Western transnational agri-business to patent seeds developed in India which are not presently covered by such patents. Indian farmers would then be forced to pay royalties not only when they purchase these seeds, but also when re-sowing them in subsequent years. To supply such seeds to friends or neighbours would also be forbidden (Shiva 1992).

In 1994, this anti-GATT position has been spreading to the whole political opposition in India, from the left to the right. It has, for example, become a major issue in Hindu fundamentalist agitations (Agha 1994), which draw on the picture painted by Vandana Shiva and some influential leaders in the farmers' movements: 'The anti-Dunkel movement will bring the focus back to emotional nationalism which is our political ground', says K.N. Govindacharya, General Secretary of the Bharatiya Janata Party (Agha 1994: 29).

The most outspoken approval of the GATT agreement comes from Sharad Joshi, the leader of Shetkari Sanghatana in Maharashtra, who since the beginning of the 1990s has moved towards a more liberal position on the future of agricultural development. He holds that farmers must become entrepreneurs on a free market, rather than subsidized peasants in a state-regulated agricultural economy with low and artificial prices. Recently his Sanghatana has promoted projects like Shetkari Solvent (India) Limited and Pawan Proteins India Limited, with farmers as shareholders. GATT offers, he claims, great potential for the export of fruits, vegetables and other agricultural products, in which India has a comparative advantage:

> The Indian primary producer is generally in a position of comparative advantage in the international market despite fragmentation of land, low capital formation and sustained State repression. The advantage is sizable in fruit, cotton, some foodgrains and health-foods. That is the reason why many industrial houses are turning increasingly to the export of agricultural produce for meeting their requirements of foreign exchange. The middle-layer farmer is quietly confident of being able to compete in the international markets if only the Government kept its cotton-picking hands off. (Joshi 1993: 4)

On the patent issue Joshi simply declares: 'What's wrong with Dunkel? I prefer to pay royalty for good quality seeds rather than pick up bad subsidized ones' (Rattanani 1994: 19).

The pro-GATT faction claims that to a large extent the anti-GATT position taken by the other faction of the farmers' movements is based on a rather superficial reading of GATT and of insufficient knowledge of the agricultural economy in India. When it comes to subsidies, for example, it is clear that Indian agriculture suffers from a negative subsidy: that is, agriculture is being taxed rather than supported, primarily via price policies. Prices on Indian crops are generally lower than they are in the international markets (Joshi 1993; Omvedt 1993; Sanotra 1994).

What is the reality behind this debate? What are the implications for Indian agriculture and its farming population?

Despite widespread protests, it seems India will have to adhere to its agreement in the Uruguay round and join the World Trade Organisation which will oversee the workings of the agreement. The alternative is not very attractive. India would have to negotiate separate trade treaties with the 124 countries that have signed the agreement so far.

Looking at the implications for India, GATT actually carries quite a few prospects for boosting agricultural production and employment and thereby generating a dynamic growth situation. A recent analysis maintains that:

India stands to gain rather than lose from trade liberalization by the GATT members. The domestic support levels in India are negative in most of the agricultural commodities studied here, which is in sharp contrast to the support levels prevailing in the developed countries of the world . . . Diverse agro-climatic conditions in India and the existing differentials in actual and potential yields, all augur well for exports of agricultural commodities . . . The analysis also reveals that future export items will be fish and fish preparations, cereals like rice and wheat, tea and tobacco, fruits, vegetables and their processed items. (Gulati and Sharma 1994: 1861)

Despite fears to the contrary, the seed patent issue is also most likely to be settled in favour of Indian farmers, or, as one recent report states:

Under GATT, the Government will have to decide on the seed patenting issue. Given the options, India has decided against it and is evolving its own *sui generis* system to protect both farmers' and researchers' rights. The Agricultural Ministry is working on the draft bill, to be called the Plant Varieties Bill. (Rekhi 1994: 66–7)

What is also clear, however, is that the present policies of the Indian Government are not supportive to export of agricultural products. The trade is thoroughly regulated and controlled, and many experts doubt that it will be easy to change this institutional set-up (Rekhi 1994). In this respect, therefore, farmers' organizations could play a positive role by pressing for an export promotion policy which deregulates the market, improves transport and storage facilities, and promotes research on suitable products and also pushes up productivity. Could they also on their own organize at least part of the exports, develop satisfactory and competitive product standards and supervision of these, and encourage, but also control, linkages between farmers and processing industries through contracts, they would follow in the footsteps of some of the more successful farmers' movements of the developed world.

CONCLUSION

Contemporary mobilization of farmers in India still lacks the organizational breadth of its predecessors in more developed countries. They are more prone to agitation and political manoeuvres than to self-organization in terms of, for example, service, credit, insurance or marketing cooperatives. The reason for this may be the vastly more complex situation facing contemporary farmers' movements in the Third World. In addition to the problems of generating farm incomes in a state-controlled agrarian economy, they also face environmental issues and a complex international economic context. State intervention is also much more pronounced than at the corresponding stages of the development of farmers' movements in the West. The dominance of the state over markets for inputs and farm produce is probably the main reason why the new farmers' movements have taken a political rather than an economic form. However, opportunities exist to develop broad and family farm-based movements, which could fulfil similar roles to those performed by such movements in Western Europe and parts of the USA.

However, as we have seen above, several crucial issues remain to be resolved. The dominance of the interests of what has been called 'family farmers' (that is, middle and rich peasants) is far from certain in the new farmers' movements. Depending on an ensemble of political and economic factors, other class forces may come to prevail. Another crucial question is if the farmers' movements can develop a more sophisticated view on foreign policy in the field of agriculture to take advantage of possible export markets, in which India undoubtedly would have considerable comparative advantages if the rules of GATT were to be followed.

References

Agha, Z. (1994), 'The Opposition: Damning Dunkel', *India Today*, 15 April, pp. 27–30.

Anderson, A. C. (1946), 'Agrarianism in Politics', in J. S. Roucek (ed.), *Twentieth Century Political Thought* (New York: Philosophical Library), pp. 197–218.

Athreya, V., G. Djurfeldt and S. Lindberg (1990), *Barriers Broken: Production Relations and Agrarian Change in Tamil Nadu* (New Delhi: Sage).

Brass, T. (ed.) (1994), Special Issue on New Farmers' Movements in India, *The Journal of Peasant Studies*, Vol. 21, Nos 3–4.

Chayanov, A. V. (1966), *The Theory of Peasant Economy* (Homewood, Ill.: Richard D. Irwin).

Cleary, M. C. (1989), *Peasants, Politicians and Producers: The Organisation of Agriculture in France since 1918* (Cambridge: Cambridge University Press).

Dhanagare, D. N. (1990), 'Shetkari Sanghatana: The Farmers' Movement in Maharashtra – Background and Ideology', *Social Action*, Vol. 40, No. 4, pp. 347–69.

Dhanagare, D. N. (1991), 'An Apoliticist Populism: A Case Study of B.K.U.', in K. L. Sharma and D. Gupta (eds), *Country-Town Nexus* (Jaipur: Rawat Publications), pp. 104–22.

Djurfeldt, G. (1981), 'What Happened to the Agrarian Bourgeoisie and Rural Proletariat under Monopoly Capitalism? Some Hypotheses Derived from the Classics of Marxism on the Agrarian Question', *Acta Sociologica*, Vol. 24, No. 3, pp. 167–91.

Economic Survey 1990–91 (New Delhi: Government of India, Ministry of Finance).

Esman, M. J. and N. T. Uphoff (1984), *Local Organizations: Intermediaries in Rural Development* (Ithaca, NY, and London: Cornell University Press).

Flores, X. (1970), *Agricultural Organization and Development* (Geneva: ILO).

Gerschenkron, A. (1966), *Bread and Democracy in Germany* (New York: Harold Fertig).

Gulati, A. and A. Sharma (1994), 'Agriculture under GATT: What it holds for India', *Economic and Political Weekly*, Vol. 29, No. 29, pp. 1857–63.

Gundelach, P. (1988), *Sociale bevaegelser og samfundsaendringer: Nye sociala grupperinger og deres organisationsformer ved overgangen til aendrede samfundstyper* (Social movements and social change: New social groupings and their organisational forms in the transition to new social formations) (Aarhus: Politica).

Gunnarsson, C. (1992), 'Economic and demographic transition in East Asia: Economic modernisation vs family planning in Taiwan', in M. Hammarskjöld, B. Egerö and S. Lindberg (eds), *Population and the Development Crises in the South* (Lund: Programme on Population and Development in Poor Countries), pp. 81–101.

Gupta, D. (1988), 'Country-Town Nexus and Agrarian Mobilization: Bharatiya Kisan Union as an Instance', *Economic and Political Weekly*, Vol. 23, No. 51, pp. 2688–96.

Gupta, D. (1991), 'The Country-Town Nexus and Agrarian Mobilisation: Situating the Farmers' Movement in West U.P.', in K. L. Sharma and D. Gupta (eds), *Country-Town Nexus* (Jaipur: Rawat Publications), pp. 74–103.

Gupta, D. (1992), 'Peasant Unionism in Uttar Pradesh: Against the Rural Mentàlity Thesis', *Journal of Contemporary Asia*, Vol. 22, No. 2, pp. 155–68.

Harriss, J. (1992), 'Does the "Depressor" still work? Agrarian Structure and Development in India: A Review of Evidence and Argument', *The Journal of Peasant Studies*, Vol. 19, No. 2, pp. 189–227.

Hatti, N. and F.-M. Rundquist (1993), 'Co-operatives as Instruments of Rural Development – the Case of India', *Journal für Entwicklungspolitik*, Vol. 9, No. 4, pp. 383–97.

Jain, S. (1993), 'Dunkel Draft: Seeds of Discontent', *India Today*, 30 November, pp. 54–6.

Joshi, S. (1993), *Farmers and Dunkel DFA* (Draft Final Act Embodying the Results of the Uruguay Round of Multilateral Trade Negotiations) (Pune, Ambethan), mimeo.

Köll, A. M. (1992), 'Peasant Movements and Democracy: In Eastern Europe in the early 20th century,' in L. Rudebeck (ed.), *When Democracy Makes Sense* (Uppsala: AKUT, Working Group for the Study of Development Strategies), pp. 179–99.

Lindberg, S. (1994), 'New Farmers' Movements in India as Structural Response and Collective Identity Formation: the Cases of Shetkari Sanghatana and BKU', *The Journal of Peasant Studies*, Vol. 21, Nos 3–4, pp. 95–125.

Lindberg, S. (1995), 'Farmers' Movements and Cultural Nationalism in India: An Ambiguous Relationship', *Theory and Society*, Vol. 24, No. 6, pp. 837–68.

Ling, Z. and M. Selden (1993), 'Agricultural Cooperation and the Family Farm in China', *Bulletin of Concerned Asian Scholars,* Vol. 25, No. 3, pp. 3–12.

Minhas, B. S., L. R. Jain and S. C. Tendulka (1991), 'Declining Incidence of Poverty in the 1980's: Evidence versus artifacts', *Economic and Political Weekly*, Vol. 26, Nos. 27–8, pp. 1673–82.

Moore, M. (1984), 'Mobilization and Disillusion in Rural Korea: The Saemul Movement in Retrospect', *Pacific Affairs*, Vol. 57, No. 4, pp. 577–98.

Nadkarni, M.V. (1987), *Farmers' Movements in India* (New Delhi: Allied).

Olofsson, G. (1988), 'After the Working-class Movement? An essay on What's "New" and What's "Social" in the New Social Movements', *Acta Sociologica*, Vol. 31, No. 1, pp. 15–34.

Omvedt, G. (1991), 'Shetkari Sanghatana's New Direction', *Economic and Political Weekly*, 5 October.

Omvedt, G. (1992), 'Interview with Sharad Joshi', Unpublished ms.

Omvedt, G. (1993), 'The Dunkel Draft and American Imperialism', in *Frontier*, 15 May, pp. 4–7, and 22 May, pp. 3–7.

Omvedt, G. (1994), *Reinventing Revolution: New Social Movements and the Socialist Tradition in India* (Armonk, NY: M. E. Sharpe).

Österud, Ö. (1978), *Agrarian Structure and Peasant Politics in Scandinavia* (Oslo: Universitetsforlaget).

Paré, L. (1990), 'The Challenge of Rural Democratisation in Mexico', in J. Fox (ed.), *The Challenge of Rural Democratisation: Perspectives from Latin America and the Philippines* (London: Frank Cass), pp. 79–96.

Rane, W. (1993), 'Farmers' Rally against GATT Proposals', *Economic and Political Weekly*, Vol. 28, No. 4, p. 2391.

Rattanani, L. (1994), 'Sharad Joshi. Knowing his Onions', *India Today*, 15 January, p. 19.

Rekhi, S. (1994), 'GATT. Shifting Systems', *India Today*, 31 July, pp. 66–7.

Rudolph, L. I. and S. H. Rudolph (1987), *In Pursuit of Lakshmi: The Political Economy of the Indian State* (Bombay: Orient Longman).

Sahasrabudhey, S. (ed.) (1989), *Peasant Movements in Modern India* (Allahabad: Chugh Publications).

Sanotra, H. S. (1994), 'Anti-GATT Movement: Spreading waves of confusion', *India Today*, 15 May, pp. 50–3.

Sarma, J.S. and V. P. Gandhi (1990), *Production and Consumption of Foodgrains in India: Implications of Accelerated Economic Growth and Poverty Alleviation* (Washington, DC: International Food Policy Research Institute).

Sen, S. (1982), *Peasant Movements in India* (Calcutta: K.P. Bagchi).

Shanin, T. (1982), 'Class, States and Revolution: Substitutes and Realities', in H. Alavi and T. Shanin (eds), *Introduction to the Sociology of Developing Societies* (London: Macmillan), pp. 308–31.

Shannon, F. A. (1957), *American Farmers' Movements* (Princeton, NJ: van Nostrand).

Shiva, V. (1992), 'Will liberalised agriculture benefit farmers or TNCs?', *The Observer*, 13 February.

Songsore, J. (1992), 'The Co-operative Credit Union Movement in North-Western Ghana: Development or Agent of Incorporation?', in D.R.F. Taylor and F. Mackenzie (eds), *Development From Within: Survival in Rural Africa* (London: Routledge), pp. 82–101.

Sorokin, P. A., Zimmerman, C. C., and Galpin, C. J. (eds) (1930), *A Systematic Source Book of Rural Sociology* (Minneapolis: University of Minnesota Press).

Watkins, K. (1994), 'Briefings: GATT: a Victory for the North', *Review of African Political Economy*, No. 59, pp. 60–6.

Wright, G. (1964), *Rural Revolution in France: The Peasantry in the Twentieth Century* (Stanford, Calif.: Stanford University Press).

Zinyama, L. M. (1992), 'Local Farmer Organizations and Rural Development in Zimbabwe', in D.R.F. Taylor and F. Mackenzie (eds), *Development From Within: Survival in Rural Africa* (London: Routledge), pp. 33–57.

Notes

1. This chapter is based on a research project on 'The New Peasant Movements in India' at the Department of Sociology, University of Lund. It has received financial support from SAREC, Stockholm and from the Nordic Institute of Asian Studies, Copenhagen.

2. The use of the terms 'peasant' and 'farmer' here may be slightly confusing to a reader unacquainted with Indian studies. Ideally 'farmer' signifies a fully commercialized agricultural producer, while 'peasant' stands for agricultural producers, who are to varying degrees producing for subsistence. In India, since most agricultural producers still retain many subsistence features including extensive use of family labour, they are usually called peasants. On the other hand, the new peasant movements in India are commonly referred to as farmers' movements, indicating that they are organizations catering to commercial aspects of agriculture.

3. Other works on the new farmers' movements are Dhanagare (1990 and 1991), Gupta (1988, 1991 and 1992), Lindberg (1994 and 1995), Omvedt (1994), and Sahasrabudhey (1989).

4. See *Economic Survey 1990–1991* and earlier for these long-term trends in Indian agriculture.

5. The poverty line was defined as Rs15 per person per month in 1960–61 prices.

6. For this type of agrarian politics or agrarianism see, for example, Sorokin, Zimmerman and Galpin (1930) and Gerschenkron (1966). For a contemporary world-wide survey see Esman and Uphoff (1984), and Flores (1970). For agrarian politics in the USA see, for example, Anderson (1946) and Shannon (1957). For France see Wright (1964) and Cleary (1989). For Scandinavia see Österud (1978). For agrarian politics in Eastern Europe before the Second World War see Köll (1992).

7. It is important to stress that these varieties are here conceived of within a framework of a more or less state guided capitalist market economy, which moreover to a large extent is dominated by international capital. The point stressed here is that there is room for variations, not only in form but also in content. We are not dealing with the desirability of one form or the other, but rather with the actual potentialities. It is my conviction that these variations may have important bearings on the future for poor peasants and agricul-

tural labourers, and also beyond the present limitations of capitalist market economies, whether there be a kind of socialist market economy or something else.

8. The Uruguay Round of the GATT negotiations, which began in 1986, and was finally concluded with an agreement in April 1994, has in India all along been referred to as the Dunkel draft, named after the GATT Director-General Arthur Dunkel.

7 Peasants and Structural Adjustment in Latin America

Alexander Schejtman

This chapter is an attempt to examine the relations between stabilization and structural adjustment policies (SAPs) and peasant collective action.

In the first part, an attempt is made to present, in a very stylized form, the process of change of the agrarian structure in order to stress both the long-standing nature of the tensions between the peasant economy and capitalist agriculture and the highly heterogenous nature of the peasant sector, since the impact of SAP varies according to the different conditions of the peasantry.

In the second part, I try to emphasize that SAPs will imply a radical transformation of the 'rules of the game' beyond the specific policies or the options for shock or gradual treatment adopted in each country. This means a transition from one pattern of accumulation and mode of regulation of the economies to another, whose precise characteristics are still in the making.

In the next part, a very simple typology of peasant mobilizations is considered, and some illustrative cases of the main types are presented, stressing the implicit or explicit contents of strategic demands and identity-related demands in most of them.

Finally, in the concluding part, an attempt is made to consider what is really new in the new peasant movements and what of this newness derives from the implementation of SAPs.

HACIENDA AND PEASANT ECONOMY

If one had to choose a single factor determining the pattern of social and economic development in most Latin American countries, it is not an exaggeration to say that it would be the peculiar characteristics of the process of agrarian change: that is, the

126

establishment of the hacienda system and its peasant periphery as it evolved from the agrarian structures established during the colonial period and was consolidated towards the middle of the nineteenth century.

In fact, the distribution of power; the patterns of accumulation; the patterns of income distribution and consumption; the biased nature of technological change and the inability of this structure to foster entrepreneurial capabilities; these have a had a lasting effect on the behaviour of social actors.

Patterns of agrarian change: a stylized version

In order to depict in a very schematic form the different pathways of change experienced by the hacienda system we can follow Baraona's proposal and conceptualize it as a complex structure, composed of two kinds of productive units: the landlord's enterprise and the internal and external peasant economies, the former receiving access to land and other productive perquisites against an obligation to work in the landlords' enterprise (Baraona 1965: Schejtman 1970).

In Figure 7.1, this basic pattern of land occupation corresponds to square E, which we might call a traditional hacienda. Stimulated by the dynamics of internal and external demand for its products, different processes of change took place, depending on:

(a) the productive potential of the land involved;
(b) the entrepreneurial skill of the landlord;
(c) its access to capital and the degree of internal or external pressure from an organized peasantry.

The path leading from E to B to C and eventually to X corresponds to the process of modernization of the landlord's enterprise at the expense of the peasant economy due to contradictions in the use of land, water and work force, which in the last stage (X) leads to the eventual disintegration of the peasant economy, the proletarization of the peasants involved and the transformation of the hacienda into a capitalist enterprise *tout court*; in this case the labour force is paid entirely in cash. It is a process that took nearly one century and affected mainly estates in irrigated and highly productive areas, facing dynamic demands for their products.

Some estates remained in conditions characterized by points B or C in Figure 7.1 even during the middle of the present century.

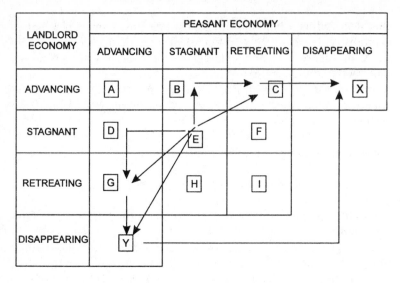

Figure 7.1   Paths of change of the hacienda system

When the landlords' enterprise lacked capital for its own expansion and there was a demand for labour-intensive products, a path from E to D to G, under internal share-cropping, was very often selected. This allowed the growth of the peasant economy, but in conditions of subordination that inhibited the development of entrepreneurial skills among the peasants. The transition from E to Y or G to Y was normally a consequence of land reform, particularly the most radical ones (with the exception, of course, of those cases in which the estates became government or collective enterprises).

As we shall mention later, a path from Y to X corresponds either to processes of counterreform (as in Chile, 1974) or to the development of a dynamic land market in conditions in which the peasants are unable to exploit their valuable land by themselves. To an extent, this might be the case of changes induced by the recent reforms in article 27 of the Mexican Constitution.

Parallel to the transition from hacienda either to capitalist enterprise or to a peasant economy, the agrarian structure witnessed a process of sub-division in non-hacienda lands, like those in peasant or indigenous communities and those received through the land reform processes.

As a result of these changes, the agrarian structure has been characterized as a bimodal one, constituted by a small segment of capitalist enterprises, with different degrees of modernization (B, C, X in Figure 7.1) and a larger segment of peasant or family units with various degrees of differentiation. This structure characterized the social landscape of the agricultural areas of most Latin American countries until the process of structural adjustment started.

Some Implications of Agrarian Bimodality

Economies where agrarian structures in the early phases of industrialization were characterized by the presence of vast numbers of small farmers witnessed the development of a massive demand for simple production and consumption goods. This stimulated the emergence of an industrial sector geared towards the satisfaction of this demand and this in turn generated new demands for food and agricultural inputs. A 'virtuous circle' of reciprocal demands was created which allowed for the gradual sophistication of patterns of consumption and production techniques. One consequence was the emergence of large numbers of entrepreneurs. Furthermore, the agricultural techniques developed during this process were appropriate for most of the of agricultural producers because of the homogenous character of the agrarian structure.

In contrast, the demand by a small minority for luxury consumption goods and for the capital goods used in the process of modernization had to be satisfied by imports, and the demand for simple goods from an impoverished peasantry was not enough to stimulate the development of mass production of consumption goods and agricultural implements. This situation was, however, modified by the policies of ISI.

The existence of bimodal structures creates complex obstacles to the wide diffusion of technical progress which constitutes a necessary condition for the development of economic structures capable of generating growth with equity.[1] In homogenous structures, a feasible technological option (that is, one that is coherent with the relative endowment of productive resources) is relevant for the majority of the agricultural units. In a bimodal structure, given a set of relative prices, an option which is feasible for the modern agricultural enterprises will not, in all probability, be a good one for the family farms.

The Contrast between Peasant and Capitalist Agriculture

It can be argued, both from an empirical and a theoretical point of view, that, in a context of bimodality, there are important differences in the criteria guiding the decisions about what to produce, how to produce (that is, the kind of technique to be used) and about the destination of the product (market or self-consumption) between capitalist and peasant agriculture. These differences, which are summarized in Table 7.1, are extremely relevant for analysing the differential impact of adjustment policies and for the design of a development strategy for the agricultural sector.[2]

As we know, in capitalist agriculture there is a clear separation between capital and labour, and as a result, profit, wages and even rent are objective expressions of the relations between owners of means of production, land owners and sellers of labour. Hence, the principal criterion used to determine what, how, and how much to produce is the level of expected profits and/or the rate of accumulation. In these units, the relations between agents are regulated by the laws of the market. There is no place for exchange based on reciprocity or, in other words, for considerations of community and kinship. Production is exclusively market-oriented so that decisions on what and how to produce are completely unrelated to what the producers and their families consume. Considerations of risk and uncertainty arise strictly in terms of probabilities, in the sense that they are internalized in the decision-making process, as ratios between expected profit and the probabilities associated with each level of expected profits.

Very often the peasant sector is treated as homogenous, whereas in fact it is composed of very different types of producers, whose only common trait is the family nature of the work force and the close relationship between production and consumption. As my study on the Mexican case reveals, one can distinguish, considering their productive potential, between those whose potential output is not even enough to satisfy their basic food consumption requirements (sub-subsistence units) and those at the other extreme who are able to accumulate a surplus above the conditions of simple reproduction and even to begin to increase the amount of hired labour (transitional units).[3]

The capitalist sector, as I mentioned earlier, is also very heterogenous in most countries, with some highly modernized and capital intensive enterprises, along with more traditional extensive large states.

Table 7.1   The contrast between peasant agriculture and capitalist agriculture

	Peasant agriculture	*Capitalist agriculture*
Purpose of production	Reproduction of the producers and the production unit	Maximization of the rate of profit and capital accumulation
Origin of the labour force	Basically the family and, on occasion, reciprocated loans from other units; exceptionally, marginal quantities of wage labour	Wage labour
Commitment of the head to the labour force	Absolute	Non-existent, apart from legal requirements
Technology	Very labour-intensive; low intensity of capital and purchased inputs	Greater capital intensity per labour unit and higher proportion of purchased inputs in the value of the final product
Destination of the product and origin of inputs	The market, in part	The market
Criterion for intensification of labour	Maximum total product, even at the cost of a fall in the average product. Limit: marginal product = 0	Marginal productivity wage
Risk and uncertainty	Assessment not based on probabilities; 'survival algorithm'	Internalization based on probabilities, in search of rates of profit proportional to risk
Nature of the labour force	Makes use of non-transferable or marginal labour	Uses only transferable labour on the basis of skills
Components of net income or product	Indivisible family product or income, realized partially in kind	Wages, rent and profit, exclusively in the form of money

Source: Schejtman (1980), p. 119.

Needless to say, the impact of the crisis and of the adjustment policies is different for each group.

STRUCTURAL ADJUSTMENT: RADICAL CHANGES IN THE RULES OF THE GAME

Although it was the oil shock of 1974 and the external debt problems that generated the tensions of the 1980s, leading to the International Monetary Fund/World Bank recommendations to stabilize and adjust the economies, these problems only highlighted the crisis of the pattern of development that characterized both the industrial economies and those in the Latin American region since the great depression of the 1930s.

Objectives and General Implications of SAP

As we already know, huge budget and foreign account deficits and the heavy burden of external indebtedness resulted in enhanced ability of the multilateral finance and development institutions to 'persuade' Latin American governments to implement SAPs.

SAP has two interrelated objectives: a macro-economic one geared to correct internal (that is, inflation) and external imbalances through reductions in aggregate demand (reduction of government expenditure, contraction of the money supply, high interest rates, and so on) and a micro-economic objective, whose proclaimed aim is to correct inefficiencies in resource allocation, which means changing relative prices or, as it is usually said, 'putting prices right'; in particular, wages, interest rates and the exchange rate.

For these purposes, a policy of trade liberalization, of devaluation, privatization of public enterprises, elimination of price intervention (subsidies, controls, and so on) have been applied with more or less consistency throughout the region, in some places, where political conditions allowed, as shock treatment, in others, more gradually. These options were not necessarily related to the degree of authoritarianism (Tironi and Lagos 1991).

SAP must be understood as a radical process of change in the functioning of the economies, initiating a transition from one 'regime of accumulation' to another, in the sense that the rules which governed the distribution and re-allocation of the social product are suffering important changes together with a change in the 'mode of regulation' since 'the set of institutional forms, systems and explicit or implicit rules which insure the compatibility of behavior within an accumulation regime' are also changing. (Lipieds 1984, quoted by Tironi and Lagos 1991: 35).

Although this process is mainly manifest in the more mature industrial economies (Britain is, of course, a case in point) many of its main traits are also characteristic of the transition in Latin America from what is called the 'peripheral Fordism' of the ISI period to new forms of accumulation and regulation which are in the making.

The Impact of Crisis and Adjustment Policies on Output, Income and Employment

ECLAC (Economic Commission for Latin America and the Caribbean, also known as CEPAL) has coined the expression of the 'lost decade' (referring to the 1980s) in order to illustrate the serious set-backs in the levels of income, output and employment (see Figure 7.2). In fact, at the end of the decade, the real per capita product was equivalent to the one the countries had 10, 13 and even

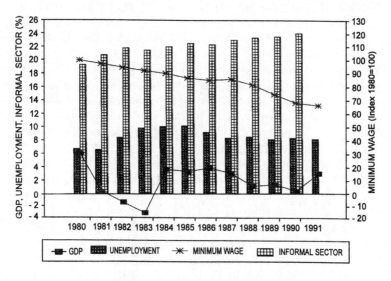

Source: PREALC (1992).
Figure 7.2   GDP, unemployment, wages, informal sector
(1980–1991)

more years ago; per capita GDP fell, for the region as a whole, by 8.3 per cent and there was a steep decline in the level of investment, from nearly 23 per cent of GDP at the beginning of the decade to slightly more than 16 per cent at the end.

The level of employment declined drastically and so did the level of wages; part of the decline in employment was absorbed by the so called 'informal sector' at very low levels of productivity. Furthermore, according to PREALC (1987) wages decreased most in badly paid jobs. Unemployment levels were also higher in the lower income strata.

A study made by ECLAC and UNDP (CEPAL/PNUD 1990) on the levels of poverty and indigence (using the methodology of the so called 'poverty line') indicated that, whereas between 1970 and 1980, there was a decrease in the percentage of households below the poverty line from 40 to 35 per cent, they increased during the 1980s to 37 per cent.[4] On the other hand, households below the indigence levels were 19 per cent, 15 per cent and 17 per cent, respectively, in the above mentioned periods. In other words, the absolute number of poor households rose at an annual rate of 1 per cent during the 1970s and at a rate of more than 3 per cent during the 1980s. However, behind these averages there are large differences among countries (see Figure 7.3).

The proportion of poor households is much higher in the rural than in the urban sector, and in the small urban areas as compared with the metropolis. At the beginning of the 1980s the absolute number of poor households was 5 per cent higher in rural than in urban areas, even though rural population was only one-third of

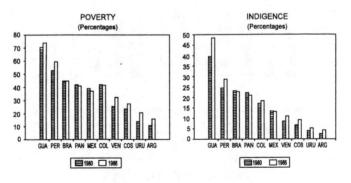

Source: CEPAL/PNUD (1991).
Figure 7.3 Poverty and indigence

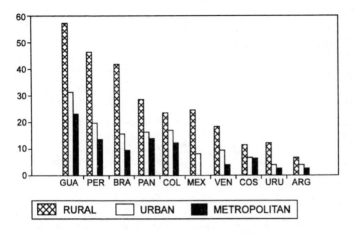

Source: CEPAL/PNUD (1991).
Figure 7.4   Rural and urban levels of indigence (percentages)

the total. During the 1980s, this situation was reversed since the number of urban poor increased at twice the rate of the increase of the urban population (42 per cent and 20 per cent respectively), whereas the numbers of rural poor increased at the same rate as the rural population. Nevertheless the absolute number of destitute persons is still higher in the rural areas (see Figure 7.4).

The Impact on the Peasantry

As mentioned earlier, the peasant sector is highly differentiated and therefore the impact of adjustment policies depends on the particular relation of the peasants to the market, both as producers and consumers and as labourers. For those in the surplus or transitional category, devoted to the production of exportable commodities, the level of employment and income tended to increase even when they were subordinated to agro-industrial or commercial enterprises (see Figure 7.5). For those devoted to non-tradable basic foods, the impact was ambiguous because, although importable substitutes became more expensive, internal demand decreased. For instance, in Bolivia these factors have resulted in a decline in the real price and quantity of agricultural products, particularly affecting peasant production. A price index of agricultural products declined by 29 per cent between the beginning of the 1980s and the end of 1988, relative to overall consumer prices. From 1985 to 1988, total

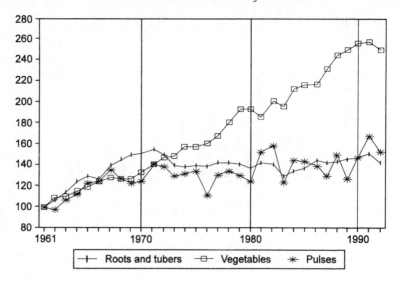

Source: FAO (1994).

Figure 7.5 Small agricultural producers' output, main products index (1961 = 100)

agricultural production volume fell by 17 per cent and remained 15 per cent below the 1980–85 average in 1988 (World Bank 1990; Healy 1991).

For sub-subsistence workers and, in general, for those who depend on work outside the family farm, the situation has worsened in those areas devoted to non-tradable goods and has improved in those where production for export has increased, at least in terms of family income, since a demand for women's work has developed. The number of this kind of units tended to decrease during boom periods and increase in slack periods (De Janvry and Sadoulet 1988).

Peasant Movements or Peasant Struggles

A vast literature has been produced during the 1970s and particularly during the 1980s in relation to what has been loosely called 'social movements': the majority of these studies has focused on popular struggles in the urban areas, where the main forms of protest are demands for basic services and housing, and mobilizations against food price increases.

Wolf has argued that to some extent, the frustration:

> with the record of self proclaimed Vanguard Parties and cen-
> trally-manipulated populist mass organizations . . . gave place to
> this new focus on the various forms of popular protest against
> domination by central authorities. The expectation was that these
> national popular movements would be capable of replacing
> traditional styles of party politics and state bureaucratic authori-
> tarianism or paternalism by autonomous and spontaneous popu-
> lar participation. The course of such a transformation could not
> be specified in advance, but the hopes expressed showed some
> ambivalence between the gaining of control of the State and the
> freeing of civil society from dependence on the State. It seems
> unlikely that the participationist utopia can become reality, but
> the vigor and diversity of social movements add to the indetermi-
> nacy of the future. From one point of view such vigor is the only
> real guarantee of advances toward greater equity. From another,
> it introduces a threat of complete ungovernability of the national
> societies. (Wolf 1991: 21)

Concepts and Approaches

There seems to be no agreement among social scientists as to when
a social struggle reaches the condition of a social movement
(Escobar and Alvarez 1992); Touraine (1987: 175), for instance
maintains that a social movement 'is an organized action by one
social category against another for the control of the central
resources of a given type of society', and distinguishes them from a
confrontation as a 'more limited conflict directed towards a change
in the distribution of goods, influence or authority within the
organized social system, without the willingness or capacity to
transform the "social relations of production".[5]

Generally speaking, the analysis of peasants' collective actions
has emphasized either strategy or identity, the former stressing the
struggle for productive resources or, more precisely, for the peasants' control of the production process, and the latter stressing
social recognition of their specific identity. Although the Anglo-
Saxon literature tends to emphasize the strategy approach and the
French literature tends to emphasize the identity approach, most
analyses of concrete Latin American cases include explicitly or
implicitly both dimensions.[6]

A TYPOLOGY OF PEASANT MOBILIZATIONS[7]

As we mentioned earlier, the peasants are a highly heterogenous group and because of this, the nature of their demands varies. We could think of a combination of at least two criteria by which to classify peasants' mobilizations: the nature of the demands and the nature of the obstacles to organization. In relation to the first criterion, a distinction has to be made between demands as producers and demands as wage workers; and, in relation to the second, the degree of dispersion and the degree of social homogeneity, and the existence of communication infrastructure and the ability to commit resources to organizing.

Surplus and Transitional Peasants

In general terms, the demands of this category are for the control of their process of production and of the surplus: that is, demands for better prices, credit, marketing institutions and infrastructure, property titles, sub-divisions, and so on. This type of producers is usually able to finance, at least partly, the organization concerned, communicate effectively with others and the public, and so on. Some examples of this kind of mobilization follow.

The coca-leaf growers of Chapare (Cochabamba, Bolivia)

This group of peasants organized themselves through a network of unions to fight against programmes and legislation that threatened to limit the area of coca-growing and to introduce cash crop alternatives:

> early in the 1980s, the Chapare 'sindicatos' proved themselves to be audacious agrarian reformers. In 1983, under the protection of a Center-Left governing political coalition..., the Chapare 'sindicatos' carried out a mini-land reform in their area. Local sindicatos organized, in a rapid, ad hoc manner, the invasion of land owned by professionals, government employees, military officials, and commercial groups. Dozens of properties, generally ranging from 100–1,000 hectares, were carved up, either in toto or in part, by the peasant reformers . . . This extensive amount of underutilized land became, therefore, a prime target for takeover by sindicato-led peasants who were, at one and the same time,

fleeing the drought-ridden highlands and seeking to cash in on
the rising coca-leaf-related income. (Healy 1991: 92–3)

In the defence of their trade, the peasants were able to invoke
cultural, nationalistic and popular consumption values, because:

> For several thousand years, the coca leaf has been an essential
> part of rural lifestyle (medicinal, ritual, social) for the indigenous
> majority in various regions of the Andes. This enables the
> Chapare federations to make the case that coca is synonymous
> with Andean culture and that eradication by foreign powers will
> destroy their way of life and cultural heritage. This cultural
> perspective has enabled them to attract support from traditional
> coca-chewing (as opposed to producing) regions. (Healy 1991: 93)

For a large proportion of indigenous people coca chewing is
customary.

The organizational capabilities of the peasants transcended their
specific 'sindicatos' and were able to play a major role at the
Central Obrera Boliviana (the national workers' organization)
where the power of the miners' federation was eroded when the
mines were closed by a Government decree in 1985, and more than
90 per cent of the workers were laid off.

It is interesting to point out the contrast between the implications
of the coca trade in Bolivia and Colombia. In Bolivia it led to the
strengthening of the democratic participation of organized peasants, whereas in Colombia the drug traffickers purchased more than
two million hectares of land (roughly 10 per cent of the country's
total agriculture area). They assumed the leadership of the alliances
between the land owners and the military:

> during 1988 and the first half of 1989 there were 62 massacres of
> peasants, most of which took place in the main areas of mafia
> influence. Furthermore, the purchase of land by the traffickers
> has affected the regional peasant economies both because of the
> purchases themselves and because of the high increase in land
> prices. (Zamosc 1990a: 69–70)

The coalition of ejidos of the Yaqui Valley

This coalition of collective *ejidos* of the Yaqui and Mayo Valley in

Northern Mexico, after abandoning the officially sponsored CNC (Confederación Nacional Campesina, or National Peasants' Confederation), initiated a prolonged struggle for land reform in the highly productive lands of Sonora. The struggle culminated with the expropriation of 75 000 hectares at the end of the more or less populist government of Echeverría. The coalition was able to organize its own credit unions, crop insurance schemes, marketing programmes and even housing projects against the active opposition of the officially sponsored CNC and of the official Bank of Rural Credit (Banco de Credito Rural: Gordillo 1988).

The National Association of Small Plot Owners (ANAPA)

ANAPA was created in 1985 in Peru, in the context of the subdivision of the agrarian cooperatives created by the land reform. Although at the beginning it received the sponsorship of the organization of agricultural entrepreneurs, it later changed its allegiance towards the larger peasant national organizations. Their demands pertained to credit, prices and the distribution of water, and they organized to challenge a presidential decree that insists on the flexibility of land markets, stating that 'it allows the entrance of private enterprise to the countryside which is against the Constitution and the interests of small producers and landless peasants' (Conclusion of the 3rd National Convention of ANAPA: Monge 1989).

The tobacco and fique cultivators in Southern Santander, Colombia

A regional peasant union of some 50 000 peasant families, specializing in tobacco and a hard fibre, felt it was threatened by the competition of synthetic fibres and in the varieties of tobacco it was able to produce so:

> in January 1984 . . . a meeting of 40,000 peasants and sharecroppers decided that a hundred and sixty delegates will go to the regional capital and demand negotiations on tobacco and fiber prices, cooperative marketing systems, crop diversification programs and land for the sharecroppers. The group seized the government building in Bucaramanga and declared that they would not leave without a pledge signed by the President or the Minister of Agriculture.

After 4 days of negotiations the peasants obtained an agreement signed by the Minister of Agriculture. In their struggle they avoided any attempt by the politicians to capitalize on their problems and 'told journalists that, instead of begging favors, the people should fight with dignity for their own development' (Zamosc 1990b: 47–54).

These cases, which illustrate the many struggles throughout the region by peasants who are basically small producers of marketable goods, should be interpreted as attempts to defend the viability of a free or autonomous peasant economy and develop it further.

Land Deficit Peasants

The central demand of this group of peasants who depend largely, but not exclusively, on their income as agricultural producers is, of course, land enough to be able to develop a viable peasant economy. Some examples of this kind of struggle follow.

The rubber tappers in Acre in the Amazon Basin

In 1975–76, the rubber tappers in Acre began to resist the felling by the land-owners of the rubber trees on which their livelihood depended. Their action linked up with an increased national and international environmental consciousness and this generated support for the rubber tappers from the press, the national confederation of agricultural workers and the church, thereby broadening the conflict. Chico Mendes, one of the leaders of the movement, was brutally murdered in 1988, creating world-wide political repercussions.

> The initially defensive character of the movement became a fundamental political problem for the rubber tappers; they needed to move beyond a pure 'stalemate'. In a qualitative leap, in 1985 the Rubber Tapper's Movement proposed the creation of land reservations for rubber extraction, and built a broad alliance among rubber tappers and the indigenous nations of the Amazon forest. The proposal was elaborated and adopted at the First Congress of Rubber Tappers held in Brasilia, which brought together movement leadership from many regions of the Amazon, and led to the creation of the national Council of Rubber Tappers. The idea of the extractive reserves became a broad proposal for an agrarian reform for the forest. (Grzybowski 1990: 31)

The civil strike of Sarare peasants in Colombia

After being isolated from the rest of the country by the collapse of a bridge, Sarare peasants organized a strike, together with teachers, employees, and workers. Ten thousand peasants occupied six towns and organized an unarmed civil guard of 2000 peasants to maintain order and to paralyse drilling operations in the major oil deposit discovered in the 1980s in Sarare. After seven days of striking they rejected a low level commission and asked for a ministerial commitment for their demands, which they finally obtained when the Minister of Government and Public Works signed an agreement satisfying most demands. The civil strike of Sarare promoted links with other popular organizations (Zamosc 1990b 47–8).

The 'Coordinadora Nacional Plan de Ayala' (CNPA) in Mexico

The CNPA, after succeeding in eliminating government agents trying to control their movement, established a struggle platform containing demands for 'the legal recognition of long standing indigenous rights, the distribution of land that exceeded the legal limits of private property, the communal right to control and defend natural resources, agricultural production, marketing and consumption subsidies, rural organizations and the preservation of popular culture' (Paré, 1990: 85). The CNPA included many organizations of indigenous origin and considered the struggle to preserve or reclaim land as part and parcel of the struggle to preserve language and culture. According to Paré, CNPA first adopted the slogan 'Today we fight for land, tomorrow for power' and in reaction to the imprisonment of the leaders in 1982, they changed their slogan to 'Today we fight for land and for power'.

Rural Workers

In this category, which is not necessarily a clear cut one, we include landless or near landless peasants who work as temporary workers, and workers migrating from one place to another as well as permanent workers in large agricultural and agro-industrial rural enterprises.

Some workers within this group (particularly the near landless but also some landless peasants) have a stronger identity with the condition of producer than that of wage worker in a strict sense, even though most of their income is derived from this latter condition.

The Committee of Peasant Unity (CUC) in Guatemala

Created in 1988, the CUC was defined from the beginning as an organization that took as an example the struggles of the urban working classes, and was able to organize at the beginning of the 1980s one of the largest strikes ever registered, which covered 40 sugar mills and 70 large estates, and mobilized about 80 000 men and women in the middle of intense repression and harassment. The strike was publicly announced by the press three months before it began: 'the cane and cotton cutters are preparing themselves for the battle for better wages'. The strike was successful because it resulted in a significant increase in wages. However, the price was high for some of the participants. In a massacre in January 1980, at the Mexican Embassy, five members of the CUC were killed, among them two of its founders (Bran 1985).

The struggle of the 'Bóias Frias' and of the landless rural workers

Agricultural workers, living in the peripheries of the cities of the sugar cane and orange growing regions of São Paulo, began to organize first to challenge the state and demand better urban services. Changes in the working conditions in the sugar and orange plantations gave rise in 1984 to a movement for demands for better wages and working conditions. Through this movement these workers 'elaborated an identity as sugar cane workers and orange growing workers' and 'due to the greater freedom of organizing guaranteed by the new constitution, the unions of rural wage labourers in São Paulo have broken with the official state-level federation and with CONTAG (National Confederation of Agricultural Workers) and have created their own Federation of Agricultural Wage Laborers' (Grzybowski 1990: 34).

The movement of the landless rural workers had as their objective the struggle for land and for agrarian reform and was able to organize large-scale land occupations. These 'involved collective resistance against the aggression of the landowners and the police . . . they exerted pressure on the state to expropriate land and distribute it to the landless'. The Movement of Landless Rural Workers was able to organize, between January and June of 1989, 42 land occupations in 15 states, mobilizing 10 000 families. In spite of its strength and ability to organize this massive mobilization, the movement has been unable to broaden its social base and develop alternative tactics and political alliances.

The Ethnic Content

In many, if not most, of the struggles involving indigenous communities, and particularly in those of the first two categories considered above, the struggles had very often an ethnic content merged with the demands for the viability of peasant agriculture. As an illustration of the different forms that movements with this content can acquire, we will look at the Indigenous Authorities Movement in Colombia (IAMC), and the *rondas campesinas* in Peru.

The IAMC

Before the emergence of this movement in the Cauca region a peculiar structure of land tenancy and institutional organization prevailed. Large haciendas with tenants or *terrajeros* coexisted side by side with *resguardos* (Indian community lands). The Cabildo de Indígenas (Indigenous Council) governed community lands, and the municipal authority was the local link with a central government. The authority of both was eroded by the hacienda's power.

The Cauca region witnessed many years of an increasing pressure by *terrajeros* and indigenous community members on hacienda lands. In this context, the IAMC emerged. A process of land seizures by the communities took place which was increasingly manifested as land recoveries that were reincorporated as community lands under the authority of the Cabildo. 'These struggles over land were carried out among the most vicious and bloody repression . . . the communities defended themselves by demonstrating massively in villages and municipalities, appealing to the *modern* national government against the *colonial* regional power' (Findji 1992: 105).

It was in the context of the land reform process that the specific nature of the land claims by indigenous people became apparent, expressing themselves as struggles for territory as against struggles for land, particularly during the last decade.

Originally the land reform model of *family units* implied the reenactment of the republic's long-standing policy of parceling out resguardos. The indigenous struggle however halted [this plan] and was replaced [by INCORA: Columbian Institute for Land Reform] ... by the modern concept of *community enterprise* based on the model of producers' cooperatives . . . A significant sector of the indigenous movement refused to accept INCORA's enterprises defending instead [the organization] of community enterprises under Cabildo jurisdiction. (Findji 1992: 107–8).

These fights by the Guambianos people generated an increasing consciousness of ethnicity, and in a Conference to evaluate 15 years of struggle 'the Guambianos proclaimed before the entire world their *principal rights* and the Cabildos of Guambia solemnly entered, carrying their authority symbols. The Guambia flag, especially created for the occasion was hoisted.' And their communications to the public began to be preceded with the following phrase: 'from the Guambiano people to the Colombian people' (Findji 1992: 111).

A price for the lands recovered by the Guambianos was paid by INCORA to the former owners as a part of the land reform procedures and was supposed to be repaid by the beneficiaries to INCORA. However, since Guambianos considered these lands as recovered they were not willing to pay for them. This impasse was solved by the Council of State ruling that 'law 89 (of 1980 . . . recognizes the existence of Indigenous Cabildos as autonomous forms of government in the resguardos . . . a special function of indigenous resguardos . . . is to protect and recover the vernacular indigenous properties . . . therefore, the Cabildos are Public Law entities of a special nature . . . according to the precepts of Law 89' (Decision of 16 November 1983). In 1982, the indigenous authorities invited the President to a meeting held on a recovered hacienda, Santiago, 'Guambiano territory'. This implied the legitimation of the recovery and a decision was made to suppress a law based on the national security doctrine that was unanimously rejected by the indigenous people (Bejarano 1985).

The peasant patrols (rondas campesinas) of Northern Peru

In 1974 in the village of Cuyumalca, Province of Chota, the first *ronda* was formed as a vigilante group against rustling which had proliferated in the Andean villages of Northern Peru. Its creation was both a result of the increasing thefts and of the incompetence and corrupt nature of the local police and judiciary. These patrols began to spread throughout the Northern mountains since they represented an efficient alternative to the established authorities.

After their legitimacy was widely accepted by the peasants, they began to broaden their sphere of action to include cases of disputes about land, family, and so on. 'By the late 80s many rondas were adjudicating a tremendous volume of cases. The committee in Puras, Canal, addressed 138 conflicts in 14 different village assemblies . . . In Chota, there was at least one ronda meeting each week during 1990 . . . and peasants presented more than a hundred cases a month for arbitration' (Starn 1992: 99).

The punishments imposed by the patrols were different from those prescribed by the law. They included flogging, the obligation to do community work or the offender being ridiculed in front of the community. In some cases, although very few, even the death penalty was imposed.

The peasant patrols established very formal procedures for their activities. A general assembly elected a steering committee composed of a president, a secretary and a treasurer. The proceedings of the meetings are recorded and the verdicts in the trials are written, signed and stamped with the patrol's seal. The *rondas* are organized in sub-regional and regional federations.

Although left-wing and centrist political parties have tried to coopt the patrols, most of them maintain their autonomy. Beyond acting as a combination of police and court the patrols also took initiatives to construct schools, polyclinics, roads, and so on in the villages.

Local governments showed mixed reactions to the patrols, ranging from official authorization to outright repression. In 1986, the APRA (Ariaya Popular Revducianaria Americana) government issued an executive decree which legalized the patrols, but required the peasants to register their patrols with the local civic authorities. Although the law strengthened the *ronda* movement against the police and the judges, most patrols have simply ignored the registration requirement (Huamaní, Moscoso and Urteaga 1988).

CONCLUSIONS

The New Mode of Accumulation and Regulation

It is still not clear what is going to be the new 'style of development' of the Latin American countries that have been implementing SAPs, and although we can conceive that we are in a transition from something it is not easy to define where this transition is taking us. We do, however, see in the recent peasant mobilizations new actors and new demands: the landless or tenants or share-croppers demanding land for themselves, the small-holders fighting for the control of the conditions of production and the wage workers fighting for better wages and conditions of work.

Although the implications of the SAPs are still in the making, among those measures that have already affected the position of the peasantry in the larger economy we can mention: the opening of the market for land, the increased flexibility of the labour market, trade liberalization and a reduction in the role of the government.

The elimination of the various restrictions that limited the purchase of land, derived from the different land reforms, are being implemented throughout the region in different forms that range from the Chilean case, in which there are no restrictions, to the case of Mexico where the article 27 of the Constitution that prohibited the sale or rental of *ejido* lands has been reformed, allowing the association of private entrepreneurs with the *ejidatarios* and putting minor restrictions on the sale of *ejido* parcels.

Many indebted peasants have been resorting to the sale of their plots, as happened with thousands of land beneficiaries in Chile and with Colombian peasants in the cocaine areas, who were tempted by the high increases of the value of land in the more productive areas.

In relation to the labour market, many laws protecting the conditions of work and the level of wages are being reformulated through the euphemism of 'flexibilization', making it easier to dispose not only of redundant workers but also of those who accumulated rights according to former laws. On the other hand, the process of replacing permanent workers with transitory and migrant labourers has accelerated. All this has also debilitated the unions and the peasant organizations.

Trade liberalization has opened the agricultural sector to foreign competition, seriously affecting those activities that have no (short-term) comparative advantages. This has produced an increased polarization within both capitalist and peasant agriculture, depending on the kind of products in which these producers specialized.

Linkages between agro-industry and small producers of export crops have been created or strengthened, increasing, (in many cases) the levels of income and productivity, whereas producers for the internal market of non-competitive crops have seen their incomes deteriorate.

Public expenditure has been reduced, which meant that subsidies, public investment, and social expenditure declined and official marketing institutions and those in the technical assistance area either disappeared or were privatized; agricultural credit was reduced and interest rates increased, and so on. Although all these measures affected agricultural producers in general, the non-competitive ones or those in a marginal situation were hardest hit. Furthermore, since most rural development programmes were drastically reduced or concentrated on the more viable units, peasants in marginal areas had to depend more on wage income than in the recent past.

The Main Implications of the SAPs

Among those changes in the role of the government and in the functioning of the economy that have induced changes in the conditions of peasant organization and mobilization the following can be mentioned:

(a) the ability of the governments to control or coopt peasant organizations has weakened, and many new and/or splinter groups from the government controlled unions have been emerging as autonomous representatives of more particular interests, either by locality, product or ethnic condition;

(b) in some places where the development of autonomous organizations has not been very strong and because of the weakening of the government, traditional clientist relations with local bosses (*caciques*) have been strengthened;

(c) in many countries the process of differentiation among the peasants has been accelerated, increasing the gap between surplus and transitional producers in high productivity areas and landless and near landless peasants who, at least during the first phases of SAP, have seen their levels of employment and income deteriorate, with serious implications for their nutritional conditions.

Another new element is that the pressure for land reform and its presence in political platforms has lost the importance it had in the post-war period. This might be due to the extreme political and social tensions produced by the land reform processes of the 1960s and 1970s. Further, the decline of the relative weight of the rural population through urbanization and migration has reduced the validity 'of the argument that land reform was the only way of preventing revolutionary upheavals fuelled by rural poverty and discontent' (Wolf 1991). Lastly, the numbers of wage workers have been increasing faster than the numbers of small-holders.

It seems that the elements of identity in peasant mobilizations are much more explicit than they were in the past. Particularly, among the indigenous populations, 'another important aspect of the struggles is the way in which they foster the development of a critical consciousness vis-à-vis traditional politics. For the peasants, mobilization is a moment of truth ... [implying] a frontal critic of clientism ... [giving] expression to an implicit project that seeks the extension of citizenship in the countryside' (Zamosc 1990a: 55).

Although it is undeniable that most of the peasant mobilizations have political significance, they are very rarely geared towards changing the relations of power in society. Whenever the peasants tried to go beyond the local or ethnic nature of the struggle, the autonomy of the movement was lost. It is precisely because of this that some social scientists speak about peasant mobilization and not about a peasant movement: 'because of the absence of an organic agent that would impart coherence and a sense of political direction to the sprinkling of agrarian struggles' (Zamosc 1990a: 55).

The emergence of a plurality of social actors – indigenous people, women, ecologists, and so on whose demands for recognition or social identity are not necessarily geared towards a change in the power structure – constitutes a challenge for the political process, if the recent wave of democratization in the region is to be deepened, or even sustained in the difficult conditions imposed by SAPs.

References

Baraona, R. (1965), 'Una tipología de haciendas de la sierra ecuatoriana', in O. Delgado (ed.), *Reformas agrarias en América Latina* (Mexico City: Fondo de Cultura Económica).

Bejarano, J.A. (1985), 'Campesinado, luchas agrarias e historia social de Colombia: notas para un balance historiográfico', in O. Delgado (ed.), *Reformas agrarias en América Latina* (Mexico City: Fondo de Cultura Económica).

Bran, A. (1985), 'Guatemala, organizaciones populares y lucha de clases en el campo: Notas para su estudio', in P. Gonzales Casanova (ed.), *Historia política de los campesinos latinoamericanos*, No. 2 (Mexico City: Siglo XXI).

Calderón, F. and Dandler, J. (1965), *Movimientos campesinos y etnicidad* (La Paz: Cered).

CEPAL (1990), *Changing Production Patterns with Social Equity*, LC/G.1601-P (Santiago: CEPAL).

CEPAL/PNUD (1990), *Magnitud de la pobreza en América Latina en los anos ochenta*, División de Estadísticas y Proyecciones (CEPAL) y Proyecto Regional para la Superación de la Pobreza (PNUD-RLA/86/004), April.

De Janvry, A. and Sadoulet, E. (1988), *Investment Strategies to Combat Rural Poverty: A Proposal for Latin America*, Working Paper No. 459 (Department of Agricultural and Resource Economics and Division of Agriculture and Natural Resources, Bervereg University of California), April.

Dirven, M. (1993), 'Integración y desintegración social rural', *CEPAL Review*, No. 51, Separata, December.

Escobar, A. and Alvarez S.E. (1992), *The Making of Social Movements in Latin America: Identity, Strategy and Democracy* (Boulder, Col.: Westview).

FAO (1994), *AGROSTAT* (Agricultural Statistics Database), V.3.0, Rome, FAO

Findji, M.T. (1992), 'The Indigenous Authorities Movement', in A. Escobar and S.E. Alvarez (eds), *The Making of Social Movements in Latin America: Identity, Strategy and Democracy* (Boulder Col.: Westview).

Fox, J. (1990), 'Editor's introduction: The challenge of rural democratisation: perspectives from Latin America and the Philippines', *The Journal of Development Studies*, Vol. 26, No. 4, (July) pp. 1–18.

Gordillo, G. (1988), *Campesinos al asalto del cielo: De la expropiación estatal a la apropiación campesina* (Mexico City: Siglo XXI).

Grzybowski, C. (1990), 'Rural workers' movements and democratisation in Brasil: The challenge of rural democratisation: perspectives from Latin America and the Philippines', *The Journal of Development Studies*, Vol. 26, No. 4, pp. 19–43.

Healy, K. (1991), 'Political ascent of Bolivia's peasant coca leaf producers', *The Journal of Interamerican Studies and World Affairs*, Vol. 33, No. 1, pp. 88–121.

Huamaní, G., M. Moscoso and P. Urteaga (1988), 'Rondas campesinas de Cajamarca: La construcción de una alternativa', *Debate Agrario*, 3, CEPES (Centro de Estudios Sociales), Lima, July-September.

Mathews, J. (1989), *Age of Democracy: The Politics of Post-fordism*, (Oxford: Oxford University Press).

Monge, C. (1989), 'Las demandas de los gremios campesinos en los 80', *Debate Agrario*, 5, Lima, January-March.

Paré, L. (1990), 'The challenges of rural democratisation in Mexico', *The Journal of Development Studies*, Vol. 26, No. 4 (July), pp. 83–7.

PREALC (1987), *El empleo urbano: diagnóstico y desafíos de los noventa* (Santiago de Chile: PREALC).

Rello, F. (1987), *Burguesía, campesinos y Estado en Mexico: el conflicto agrario de 1976*, Programa de Participación (Geneva: UNRISD).

Schejtman, A. (1970), Hacienda and peasant economy in Central Chile, B. Litt. Thesis, Oxford University.

Schejtman, A. (1980), 'Economía campesina: lógica interna, articulación y persistencia', in C. Wilber (ed.), *The Political Economy of Development and Underdevelopment* (New York: Random House) pp. 274–98.

Starn, O. (1992), 'The making of collective identities', in A. Escobar and S.E. Alvarez (eds), *Political Economy and Economic Development in Latin America* (Boulder, Col.:Westview).

Tironi, E. and Lagos R.A. (1991), 'The social actors and structural adjustment', *CEPAL Review*, No. 44 (August), p. 35.

Touraine, A. (1987), *Actores sociales y sistemas políticos en América Latina* (Santiago de Chile: PREALC).

Wolf, M. (1991), 'The prospect for equity', *CEPAL Review*, No. 44 (August), p. 21.

World Bank (1990), *World Development Report* (Oxford: Oxford University Press).

Zamosc, L. (1986), *The Agrarian Question and the Peasant Movement in Columbia: Struggles of the National Peasant Association 1967–1981* (Cambridge: Cambridge University Press).

Zamosc, L. (1990a), 'The political crisis and the prospects for rural democracy in Colombia: The challenge of rural democratisation: perspectives from Latin America and the Philippines', *The Journal of Development Studies*, Vol. 26, No. 4, pp. 44–78.

Zamosc, L. (1990b), 'Luchas campesinas y reforma agraria: un análisis comparado de la Sierra ecuatoriana y la Costa Atlántica colombiana', *Agricultura y Sociedad*, No. 56 (July-September). pp. 201–79

Notes

1. The relationships between technical progress, competitiveness and growth with equity are developed with some detail in CEPAL (1990: 61–153).

2. Detailed analysis of the contrast between the peasant and the capitalist agricultural enterprises are developed in Schejtman (1980).

3. Census data tend to underestimate the degree of differentiation of the small producers and because of that to overestimate their productive potential. In the Mexican case, 66% of the considered units were beyond the possibility of satisfying through agricultural production their basic food needs, even if they employed known technological alternatives for their main crop (maize).

4. In terms of people those figures were 47, 41 and 43 per cent respectively, since the average number of children per household among the poor is higher than the national average.

5. According to this, the only mobilizations which qualify as social movements are such major upheavals as Zapata's rebellion in Mexico, the Ucureña conflict in Bolivia that led to the expulsion of the latifundists from the valley of Cochabamba before the land reform of 1952, the Mapuche movement in southern Chile during the Allende government and, to a lesser extent, the rebellion in the valley of La Concepción in Cuzco, Peru, in the early 1960s, led by Hugo Blanco, a Trotskyist militant.

6. Dirven (1993). See also Zamosc (1986, 1990a, 1990b), Calderón and Dandler (1965), Healy (1991), Huamaní, Moscoso and Urteaga (1988), Paré (1990), Rello (1987), Gordillo (1988), Grzybowski (1990) and Fox (1990).

7. This is a very rough approximation to the diversity of peasants' demands and mobilizations because it is not always easy to avoid the overlapping of demands and types of struggle due to the ambivalent and changing nature of the peasants vis-à-vis society in general and the market in particular.

8 Institutions, Interest Groups and Economic Policies in Southern Africa

Tor Skålnes[1]

Students of economic liberalization in developing countries frequently argue that state autonomy is necessary to bring it about, because organized interests tend to favour a protectionist status quo. In Africa, however, policies designed to distance authorities from organized lobbying have usually been self-defeating because they have encouraged rather than discouraged particularism and therefore obstructed rational, flexible policy-making (Sandbrook 1985; Callaghy 1988). However, in Zimbabwe and South Africa organized groups are strong enough to influence national policies effectively. Such groups pay heed to national requirements and long-term considerations and often favour liberalization. The theory of societal corporatism helps explain why.

Within the field of the political economy of development, theories of policy-making now almost invariably stress the role interest groups play to maintain a protectionist status quo, while 'state autonomy' is given pride of place in explanations of liberalization. State autonomy, in this literature, connotes the ability of a government to ignore pressures from domestic groups and classes.[2] Consequently, the current processes of political liberalization and democratization in Africa and elsewhere are seen as likely to reduce governmental enthusiasm for market-based economic reform. In other words, aid donors are considered fundamentally mistaken in their new-found belief that more open political systems will lead to sustained economic reform and better economic management.

Underpinning the view that the free play of interest group politics will only serve to stall necessary economic reforms are two fundamental assumptions: (a) that losses resulting from policy change are often certain and immediately felt while benefits are usually uncertain and, at best, long term; and (b) that losers are often spatially concentrated and well organized while winners are frequently dispersed and badly organized. Since people must be expected to follow their own narrow and short-term interests to the exclusion of broader and more long-term considerations, this bodes ill for reform. Among Africanists, it has become commonplace to argue with Robert Bates that farmers and rural dwellers in general must be expected to constitute the main beneficiaries of reform while industrialists, bureaucrats, urban workers and consumers bear the brunt of adjustment (Bates 1981, compare Bates 1989). Farmers, however, are often remotely located, have difficulty communicating with each other and the government, and are rarely represented by strong organizations. They are therefore unreliable political allies for a government wishing to implement change in the face of vocal and organized protests from urban constituents.[3]

In a few African countries, however, this logic is defied by the existence of strong, well-organized urban groups which argue for liberalization. In Zimbabwe, a long-protected manufacturing sector represented a major domestic political influence behind the recent adoption of a World Bank-sponsored structural adjustment programme, while in South Africa trade unions and industrialists alike find cause to argue for greater export orientation under a fairly liberal trade regime. A possible explanation is suggested by the literature concerned with societal corporatism as practised in Western Europe. This literature contains comparative evidence to suggest that interest groups, under certain institutional and political circumstances, regularly adopt positions and attitudes which reflect a willingness to take into account long-term considerations of national economic growth and well-being in addition to the narrow, short-term interests of their members.[4] Under such circumstances, compromises over economic reform may be easier to fashion, and beneficial consequences result both for the legitimacy of market-oriented economic policies and for the sustainability of liberal politics in the longer run.

In Zimbabwe, where a form of societal corporatism was already long established and entrenched at independence, a dialogue between the government and powerful societal groups was continued. The particular institutional form of interest group politics in Zimbabwe provides a major basis for understanding the government's economic policies and ability to embark on adjustment in the 1990s. In South Africa, too, associations based on economic interests are well entrenched. In contradistinction to Zimbabwe, however, not only business and farmers' associations, but labour unions as well, are well organized and politically influential. Not coincidentally, an intense debate is currently being conducted in South Africa concerning the possibility for capital and labour to reach some kind of *modus vivendi* over economic policy under majority rule.

INTEREST GROUPS AND ECONOMIC EFFICIENCY

Some years ago, Mancur Olson developed a much-debated theory of how interest groups undermine the public values of efficiency and growth due to their narrow interest in issues of redistribution (Olson 1982). According to this theory, the extent of the formation of 'distributional coalitions', which seek to capture a larger share of the 'economic pie' for their members rather than promote more efficient production, correlates negatively with the rate of economic growth. However, evidence suggests that this relationship does not hold up in comparisons among developed countries. The European countries in which interest groups have been most influential in economic policy-making have ranked among the most successful growth-achievers in the post-war period (Rogowski 1983). Indeed, it has been argued that such societal-corporatist systems have managed their way through economic crises while holding both unemployment and inflation at comparatively low levels. Thus important distributional goals and competitiveness have been promoted at the same time (Cameron 1984). This has been achieved through government-mediated compromises between labour and employers in which unions have agreed to moderate wage rises, reduce strike activity and accept productivity-enhancing technological change in return for redistributive social policies and countercyclical demand management.

In Africa, authoritarian rulers have generally attempted to weaken or suppress organizations based on broadly defined interests, such as those of sectors and classes. The means for doing so have ranged from outright repression to cooption by use of threats and inducements. In this way, African governments have denied themselves access to information needed for the formulation of public policy and for correcting past mistakes. Rather than building sufficient consensus around a shared view of the general interest, African military and one-party regimes have relied on fluid, narrow and often rather localized bases of support.

Soon after independence, African rulers generally moved to ban rival parties and also to restrict the effectiveness of 'functional' representation: in other words, the representation of class-based and sectoral interest groups. Erstwhile voluntary associations were often constrained to act within a 'state-corporatist' framework whereby they became affiliated with the single party, their leadership hand-picked and controlled from above, and their organizational bases nominally secured by the granting of representational monopoly on the principle of 'one interest, one organization'.[5] The contents and forms of interest articulation and demand-making were strictly controlled by governments.

Taking the rhetoric of African leaders at face value, state corporatism may be said to have constituted an attempt by the authorities to distance policy-making institutions from the demands and pressures of societal groups in the interest of national development: in other words, to increase state autonomy. However, efforts to enhance government discretion in policy-making often led to the very result which it was ostensibly meant to avoid.

In Zambia, for instance, lobbying by business associations in the 1960s and 1970s for modifications to governmental economic policies was attempted with singular lack of success. However, individual firms and businessmen were often effective in gaining limited favours (Beveridge and Oberschall 1979: 268–9). While interest group politics failed, fragmented forms of interest articulation prevailed. The making of tight rules and restrictions encouraged activity to seek exemptions from those rules. As administrative discretion increased, policy became fragmented and political corruption ubiquitous. This pattern, as any student of Africa knows, is hardly confined to Zambia.

Indeed, the pattern outlined above has been so prevalent in Africa that several observers have detected in it the basic feature of the continent's political economy. In early statements, Richard Sklar, following Gaetano Mosca, noted the rise to power in Nigeria of a new 'political class'. Access to political power rather than control of productive assets became the primary means for class formation and consolidation (Sklar 1965, 1979). Various authors have expanded upon this aspect of African political economies and its economically and politically destructive consequences. Thomas Callaghy, Richard Joseph and Larry Diamond employ Max Weber's concepts of 'patrimonialism' or 'prebendalism' to analyse features of African political economy such as personalist political authority, a blurred distinction between the public and the private domain, and economic policies – foreign exchange controls, licensing arrangements, and so on – used to confer favours on particular individuals (Diamond 1987; Joseph 1987; Callaghy 1988).[6]

In Africa, therefore, state corporatism served to create a cloak behind which political leaders could pursue their own narrow interests. Rather than serving to align private aspirations with national goals, they have served to encourage narrow and localized pressure-group politics while suppressing sectoral and class-based conflicts. The irrelevance of state-corporatist structures, in other words, encouraged a different kind of interest group politics which exacerbated the problem of narrowness and undermined possibilities for enhancing economic efficiency.

In Zimbabwe and South Africa, on the other hand, organizations representing sectors and classes have been able to compete more openly. Hence, both the possibility and the need exists to create institutions within which real bargaining can take place between such associations and the government. The result, it will be argued, is a greater realization on the part of domestic political actors of the need to follow policies of increasing world-market orientation.

INTEREST GROUPS IN ZIMBABWE

Low levels of economic development, only partial penetration of markets, highly dispersed rural populations living in relatively self-contained communities, and consequent lack of the functional specialization that gives rise to the sectoral and class conflicts typical of thoroughly modernized countries make African populations susceptible to the kind of informal, patron-client politics described above. However, several African societies had been sufficiently transformed at independence so as to exhibit a degree of sectoral and class conflict and the organizational forms that go with such conflicts. Farmers created independent rural cooperatives to further their own interests in the marketplace; workers combined in labour unions; businessmen formed associations in order to influence public policy. That such interest groups were deemed important is underscored by the sustained attempts to coopt or suppress them. Governmental repression contributes heavily to explaining the relative absence of large, organized, interest groups in Africa.

This is underscored by the experience of Zimbabwe, where interest groups have been able to maintain a high degree of autonomy from government. European-dominated organizations, such as those representing industry, commercial agriculture, mining and commerce, have a history dating back to the first half of this century. Africans, however, were to a large extent hampered by repressive legislation prior to 1980. On the coming of independence, however, voluntary associations representing African workers and farmers immediately tried to establish themselves.

A number of African countries are relatively small in size and population and exhibit unitary systems characterized by centralized national decision-making. In Europe, countries exhibiting such traits have sometimes developed elaborate structures for bargaining between inclusive and centralized economic interest groups. Such government-interest group collaboration takes place in Zimbabwe as well, and has a history dating back to the 1930s. However, authoritarian government attitudes and policies have served to limit participation, especially of labour. This is as true for post-independence as for pre-independence times.

Nevertheless, Zimbabwean interest groups have considerable experience of trying to influence governmental policy. The case of Zimbabwe illustrates the point that the existence of broad-based, inclusive and nationally organized interest groups may be crucial to the effectuation of necessary, macro-economic, policy change.

I have presented my interpretation of the politics of Zimbabwean economic policy-making elsewhere, and only a brief synopsis will be provided here (Skålnes 1993, 1995). In 1965, the white minority regime of Ian Smith's Rhodesian Front made a Unilateral Declaration of Independence from Great Britain in order to halt the process of political inclusion of the African majority then under way. As a result, the country was subjected to international economic sanctions, sanctions which necessitated the application of a host of economic controls including import licensing and foreign exchange rationing. The manufacturing sector, represented by the Association of Rhodesian Industries (ARnI) – known as the Confederation of Zimbabwe Industries (CZI) after 1980 – had demanded such restrictive practices since the late 1950s, but it was the political decision to 'go it alone' in 1965 rather than political pressure by ARnI which made it imperative to launch a programme of ISI. For a few years until the mid-1970s, ISI seemed to be generally successful as the economy grew by 7–8 per cent annually and an increasing number of manufactured goods were produced locally. In the agricultural sector, too, diversification away from tobacco and into crops such as wheat, cotton and soyabeans occurred at a rapid rate. Import substitution policies were, rather remarkably, accompanied by fairly orthodox fiscal and monetary policies, but around 1975 the pressures upon the economy intensified due to guerrilla war, and the government began to resort to deficit financing.

After the establishment of majority rule in 1980, the pressures upon government finances increased rather than abated, as Robert Mugabe's Zimbabwe African National Union-Patriotic Front (ZANU-PF) government responded to pressures for increased social services for the majority of the population. Throughout the 1980s, the central government budget deficit amounted to (on average) 10 per cent of GDP. Such large deficits created inflationary pressures. In response, the government resorted to ever stricter price controls. In the first few years of independence, the ZANU (PF) government also let the real exchange rate appreciate, and removed export subsidies. When crisis struck in 1982, partly due to falling prices for Zimbabwe's products on the world market, exports had already stagnated while imports had escalated. An International Monetary Fund-sponsored stabilization programme was embarked upon in late 1982, and brought with it a devaluation of the Zimbabwean dollar, subsidy cuts on controlled consumer goods, public expenditure restraint and significantly increased levels of taxation. However, no trade liberalization occurred. Instead, the government reinstated export subsidies in the hope that these, together with devaluation, would stimulate exports.

Initially, there was little demand for trade liberalization in Zimbabwe, apart from the calls made by the Commercial Farmers' Union since 1983 for the exemption of a few very specific imports from the general procedures. The manufacturing sector was quite happy to maintain its operations behind protective barriers, and lobby instead for the progressive extension of export subsidies to help expand production. What a happy situation it would have been had secondary industry been able to hold on to the captive domestic market while at the same time being able to excel in foreign markets by means of export incentives! Yet despite such incentives, by the end of the 1980s manufactured exports had hardly reconquered the heights which they had reached in the immediate aftermath of the lifting of sanctions almost a decade earlier.

Towards the end of the first decade of independence, it became increasingly obvious that government capacity for managing the economy was severely constrained. Government budget deficits remained very high and drained the private sector of investible resources. Repayment of foreign debt commanded a large share of foreign exchange earnings, reducing the amount of productive inputs which could be imported. Inflation was consistently above 10 per cent despite price controls and even perennial price and wage freezes. Private sector productive equipment became gradually more obsolete. Although the government did recognize that high official budget deficits were a central cause of the economy's sluggish long-run performance, it failed to take adequate measures. As the World Bank stepped up its pressures upon the government to have the economy liberalized, the CZI undertook to alter radically its long-standing position on the issue of trade liberalization.

The manufacturing sector in Zimbabwe contains a number of companies which are actually or potentially (given a proper set of incentives) competitive on external markets, and a range of companies which are not. The CZI organizes both types of company. Indeed, the organization is very broadly based and includes most industrial enterprises in the country. Not surprisingly, the Confederation lobbied for many years for the retention of import licensing, coupled with the provision of export incentives. The interesting aspect of the CZI's change of heart in the late 1980s, therefore, is the extent to which the organization carried with it the bulk of its membership as it started, around 1987, to lobby for gradual trade liberalization. Together with the World Bank, and with the support of more 'natural' free-traders such as the commercial farmers, the mining houses and commercial operators, the CZI secured, in 1990, the adoption of the Economic Structural Adjustment Programme (ESAP).

The details of the ESAP will not be outlined here, save to mention that it was originally planned as a five-year exercise after which the average level of tariffs was to be reduced to around 30 per cent while the system of import quotas, foreign exchange rationing and export subsidies was supposed to be dismantled. Simultaneously, a scaling back of the government budget deficit to about 5 per cent of GDP was envisaged. ESAP was adopted over the strong resistance of many Cabinet ministers, officials in the various economic ministries, as well as the Zimbabwe Congress of Trade Unions

(ZCTU). The adjustment programme ran into trouble due to a severe drought in 1992, government reluctance or inability to reduce public spending rapidly enough, and some vacillation on key matters such as the real exchange rate and monetary policy. Yet as drought receded, the government moved swiftly on 1 January 1994 to completely abolish import licences and foreign exchange controls one year ahead of schedule, while devaluing the currency by 17 per cent.[7] During 1995, reducing the public deficit and privatizing parastatal companies proved to be intractable problems and the cause of much donor dissatisfaction.

The adoption of more market-oriented policies in Zimbabwe came in part as the result of the lobbying efforts of the CZI and other firmly-entrenched interest groups in Zimbabwe, and in part as the consequence of pressures by a few government officials and by the World Bank. Over the last six or seven years, some Zimbabwean interest groups have become ever more tightly integrated in the policy-making process. These groups include the vast majority of the potential members in their sectors, command significant shares of the country's economic resources, and in general enjoy the support of their members as autonomous spokesmen for their interests. Increasing government cooperation with these organizations is tantamount to the strengthening of a system of societal corporatism in the country.

In Zimbabwe, however, such societal corporatism effectively excludes labour. Since the adoption of ESAP, the government has become increasingly heavy-handed in its dealings with the ZCTU, which has always been a weak voice for the interests of workers. In South Africa, in contrast, labour unions are unusually strong. In that country, a future majority-based government will probably not be in a position to ignore labour demands to the extent that has been possible in Zimbabwe. Therefore, South Africa may be seen as a test case for whether a societal corporatism with labour can take hold on the African continent in these times of global pressures for the opening up of economies.

THE CASE OF SOUTH AFRICA

Parallel to the negotiations about South Africa's transition to democracy, discussions were conducted between labour unions, business associations and the government about setting up a tripartite body for the deliberation of future economic policy. In November 1992, the National Economic Forum (NEF) was created, whose task it was to chart common ground on issues such as employment creation, tariffs and exchange rates, and reorganization of the public sector. In addition, a number of other fora have been created, focusing on issues such as housing and electricity. There are also several regional fora on economic issues. Here, however, we will deal only with the NEF, which was undoubtedly the most important. In 1995, the NEF and other negotiating fora were merged into the National Development and Labour Council (NEDLAC).

The very idea of setting up such a forum implies that the actors believe that common understanding and compromise is possible. Indeed, a notable movement away from extreme positions has taken place in South Africa since the legalization of the African National Congress (ANC) in 1990. A major reason is the perception that apartheid's legacy has been doubly negative: not only is there extreme inequality and deprivation but also long-lasting economic stagnation, falling investment levels and deteriorating export performance. In the minds of a growing number among the political elite, the challenge is, therefore, to effect a proper set of policies for both redistribution and growth. This necessitates an accommodation with foreign capital and international financial institutions, as well as with the domestic private sector. South Africa seems an unlikely territory for the construction of an effective societal corporatism given the country's history of racial domination, extreme exploitation and the consequent political and ideological polarization of the community, but the ANC and its trade union ally, the Congress of South African Trade Unions (COSATU), have bent and revised earlier dogma on statist socialism. Bargaining with private economic power-holders has therefore become possible.

In fact, COSATU has been at the forefront of trying to develop realistic industrial and trade policies for the liberation movement and was certainly the key force behind the establishment of the NEF. Indeed, when COSATU made creating the NEF one of its central demands, it was not only in the knowledge that the then National Party government would otherwise impose larger doses of its economic medicine without consulting labour, but also apparently out of fear that 'unilateral restructuring' of the economy could be a real possibility under an ANC-dominated administration as well. Therefore, COSATU jealously guarded its organizational autonomy from the ANC, and wanted to see structures put in place which guaranteed labour unions a permanent place at the bargaining table. COSATU wanted the NEF to become a true bargaining forum whose decisions it would be difficult for Parliament not to ratify. The previous National Party government, many employers and several ANC officials were sceptical of according the NEF such strong powers (*Race Relations Survey*: 324–7). However, it proved difficult for the presently ANC-dominated government to treat the NEF, and its successor NEDLAC, as mere advisory bodies in the face of strong COSATU and business demands for strengthening these bodies, and given ANC rhetoric about developing a 'participatory' democracy that involves civil society in decision-making beyond the mere act of voting every five years (Patel 1993: 59).

As we have seen, the expectation is that a rather encompassing organization such as COSATU would tend to take a fairly broad and long-term view of economic matters as opposed to being concerned exclusively with its own members' short-term benefits. Such a broad perspective is reflected, for instance, in the words of the deputy general secretary of the COSATU-affiliated Southern African Clothing and Textile Workers Union, Ebrahim Patel:

[COSATU has been] absorbing the lessons from the decline of trade unions elsewhere in the world – unless the movement addressed the needs of the broader society at the same time as that of its constituency, it would become isolated, deemed no more than the voice of another special interest group ... [COSATU also] accepted that international trade liberalization would fundamentally restructure the South African economy. (Patel 1993: 3)

The union federation's concern with economic efficiency can also be gleaned from more concrete policy statements calling for stepped-up production of manufactured goods which meet the needs of the poor and are 'comparable in terms of price and quality with international standards. In this way, local production will not need to be protected with tariffs. This will also make the economy competitive in international trade' (COSATU 1992: 73). COSATU is extremely anxious to debate with employers a way of restructuring the large South African, mostly inward-oriented, manufacturing sector in such a way that cheaper goods can be produced while real wages and jobs can be defended. Increased productivity is the key to the success of this strategy. Several unionists recognize the importance of reduced strike activity and of wage restraint, which could be traded for increased social welfare provision by the state and greater willingness on the part of industry owners to allow for worker participation in the management of firms.

In April 1993, COSATU's Industrial Strategy Project (ISP) presented some preliminary results of its research into manufacturing sector restructuring. Although this is not a policy statement attributable to COSATU as such, some of the points raised are quite interesting to the extent that they reveal the thinking of at least some labour leaders. Reporting on a World Bank document on the trade regime in South Africa, the COSATU/ISP group noted that although the level of overall South African tariffs is not very high, the dispersion of such tariffs is. Furthermore, export subsidies have only very ineffectively countered the anti-export bias of the system, and at a high cost to the Treasury. The ISP group supported this analysis by the World Bank and agreed with its primary recommendations that South Africa must become more outward-oriented by rationalizing its tariff system and providing exporters with automatic access to inputs at world prices. After this has been achieved, overall levels of protection should be lowered in a gradual manner so as to avoid loss of industrial capacity. However, some selective protection should continue, while trade in basic wage goods – the producers of which have benefited from particularly high trade barriers in the past – should be liberalized immediately to make them more affordable to the poor (Joffe, Kaplan, Kaplinsky and Lewis 1993).

Much of the ISP's analysis and suggestions was incorporated into the report *Making Democracy Work* by the ANC's Macro-Economic Research Group (MERG 1993). A carefully prepared, 300-page document, the MERG report covers most economic sectors as well as general macro-economic and trade policy. Recommendations on tariffs are generally cautious, as are suggestions on export subsidies. But exceedingly high tariffs should be down-sized, and lobbying by individual firms discouraged through the introduction of more uniform tariffs. After a grace period of five to eight years, South Africa should meet GATT requirements. Significantly, exchange rate management should be flexible, according to the report, and aim at maintaining the real effective rate; that is, the South African rand should be allowed to slide so as to make up for a higher domestic than international inflation rate, which would help promote manufactured exports. The MERG group envisages no controls on profit remittances by foreigners (but continued restrictions on capital transfers abroad by domestic residents), and wants to promote foreign investment. The report also expresses a growing consensus in the liberation movement elite that, above all, fiscal and monetary discipline has to be maintained. Therefore, a moderate budget deficit is envisaged (the World Bank view is cited that a deficit amounting to 6 per cent of GDP could be sustained) along with a moderate inflation level (not to exceed 8 per cent), while real interest rates should be kept positive but low. Despite ambitious public housing, education and health programmes, total government expenditure need not rise very much as a proportion of GDP, the MERG report says, and could actually fall slightly in the medium run.

Judging from the MERG report, ANC economists have absorbed many of the lessons taught by those development scholars who have recently emphasized the need for an activist state that works with the markets rather than against them. The MERG group's emphasis on the need to increase manufactured exports, maintain a competitive exchange rate, rationalize tariffs, ensure fiscal prudence and avoid high inflation corresponds well with major 'lessons' from the East Asian experience.[8]

MERG thinking, however, differs from the previous government's more neo-liberal approach which gave greater priority to reducing inflation, privatizing state-owned industries and creating more flexibility in the labour market. The private/public ownership issue has been a particularly thorny one for the liberation movement.

For a long time, nationalization of 'the commanding heights' of the economy was central to the liberation movement's programme of redistribution. As recently as February 1990, Nelson Mandela maintained that 'the nationalization of the mines, banks and monopoly industry is the policy of the ANC and a change or modification of our views in this regard is inconceivable'.[9] Nevertheless, a more flexible position was soon adopted. After a March 1992 meeting, COSATU came up with the following unexceptional candidates for full state control: education, health, posts and telecommunications, electricity supply, water provision, public transport and steel. State takeovers in other sectors would be contemplated, but only after 'consultation and negotiation'. A much more useful suggestion, given the oligopolist structure of South African industry, is to formulate anti-trust policies in the interest of increased competition and efficiency (*Race Relations Survey* 1993: 330–1).

The MERG report says that 'the decision on whether an enterprise should be publicly or privately owned should be made on a case-by-case basis' (MERG 1993: 273), although the gist of the report's argument is in favour of state-owned enterprises, which are seen as able to increase investment and promote efficiency if only politicians will refrain from interfering in their operations. The report also contains a commitment to renationalize recently privatized enterprises but stresses that foreign investors should be given a firm guarantee that their assets will not be taken over by the government. Much more controversially, *Making Democracy Work* proposes the 'creation of a state mineral marketing auditors office, and the national marketing of certain minerals, such as is already done for gold', on the assumption that this would eliminate transfer pricing and reduce commissions paid for the handling of exports (MERG 1993: 220). Unsurprisingly, this suggestion drew adverse criticism from the private sector, prompting the ANC's Paul Jourdan to deny that the ANC would nationalize mining companies or impose mineral marketing boards.[10]

Arguably, this confusion is the result of the leadership in the ANC, COSATU and the South African Communist Party (SACP) trying to tread a fine line between assuring foreign investors and the domestic private sector on the one hand, and staying in touch with its militant constituency on the other. But it is not just a case of trying to bridge a growing division between the top leaders and the rank-and-file, for the rank-and-file itself may be increasingly divided. In July 1993, two constituent COSATU unions, the National Union of Metalworkers of South Africa (NUMSA) and the South African Clothing and Textiles Workers' Union (SACTWU) held their congresses. While 59 per cent of NUMSA congress delegates voted in favour of a resolution supporting 'nationalization without compensation' (with 41 per cent voting against), the econmic policy statement adopted by the SACTWU conference recognized that in practice nationalization could not take place without compensation, and that such compensation would be 'beyond the resources of a democratic state'. Even more tellingly, the SACTWU document went on to argue that 'the inefficiencies associated with state-owned enterprises elsewhere in the world would be difficult to avoid. The goal of greater economic democracy in state-owned enterprises has been elusive elsewhere, and no concrete proposals have been advanced to suggest that we can achieve these.'[11] Much of the discussion above has centred on the contents of reports prepared by academics affiliated to (or at least sympathetic to) COSATU and the ANC. However, the recommendations contained in those reports do not represent the views of intellectuals alone. In fact, extensive consultation took place with the members of the various organizations making up the democratic movement. Indeed, the reports have been used in the simultaneous preparation of a joint Reconstruction and Development Programme (RDP) by the ANC, COSATU and the South African National Civics Organization, under the coordination of former COSATU general secretary Jay Naidoo. The RDP went through six drafts and was extensively discussed at various meetings and conferences of the democratic movement.

Debates on the RDP drafts revealed three main issues of contention: macro-economic stability, nationalization, and cooperation with business. At COSATU's special congress in September 1993, for example, delegates from several union affiliates voiced the opinion that an overly firm stress on macro-economic stability could block significant redistribution. It was also felt that 'nationalization of strategic sectors should be included' and that relations with business would not always be cooperative.[12] Significantly, however, few voices were apparently raised against the document's emphasis on lower tariffs and greater world-market orientation.

Judging from the final text, however, it appears that critics have made little headway in pressuring the ANC and COSATU to adopt more 'radical' positions on government expenditure, nationalization and relations with business. The RDP emphasizes the provision of basic needs such as housing, health and education for all 'without compromising the interests of future generations' and states that 'the present level of borrowing by government is around 6 per cent of GDP. The RDP does not propose increasing this debt burden. As the economy starts to grow, the debt burden [should] gradually decline.'[13] Rather, existing resources will be reallocated so as to increase public investment and reduce wasteful government consumption. On nationalization, the RDP suggest that the

> democratic government . . . consider . . . increasing the public sector in strategic areas through, for example, nationalization, purchasing shares in companies, establishing new public corporations or joint ventures with the private sector, and . . . *reducing*

the public sector in certain areas in ways that will enhance efficiency, advance affirmative action and empower the histori-cally disadvantaged. (emphasis added)[14]

Furthermore, the document reaffirms the need for the future democratic government to commit itself to formulating economic policy in cooperation with civil society, including trade unions and business associations.

From the left, COSATU has been severely criticized for its moderate stance on the above issues and for cooperating so closely with the 'nationalist' ANC rather than pushing more narrowly 'working-class' demands. Grave doubts have been raised that CO-SATU can actually ensure member compliance with policies of world-market orientation, combined of course with increased social security and welfare provision, the traditional formula applied in small European countries wishing to reduce social tension while nevertheless pursuing growth-oriented policies (Katzenstein 1985). But it is difficult at present to judge the overall political strength of militancy on the shop floor. The recurrent election of a large number of SACP members to positions within COSATU is no longer the measure of support for hard-boiled confrontation that it used to be, given the fact that the SACP has itself become almost as divided between 'moderates' and 'radicals' as has the ANC.

Greater centralization of power is perhaps inevitable if com-promises between labour, capital and the state are to be hammered out and made to stick: complaints are heard that associations are too fragmented as it is now. On the side of business, a number of organizations exist that to some degree compete with each other, and some of which reportedly have rather little capacity to ensure that agreements reached can be made binding on constituent firms. Among these organizations are the South African Chamber of Business, the Afrikaanse Handelsinstituut, the South African Con-sultative Committee on Labour Affairs, the Chamber of Mines, and several others. On the side of workers, COSATU may be the largest union federation with its 1.2 million members, the National African Congress of Trade Unions and the Federation of South African Labour Unions being next largest with around 250 000 members each. But the federation itself is only a coordinating organ for the constituent unions, such as the powerful National Union of Miners and the NUMSA. Both a centralization of power within COSATU and, at minimum, a greater degree of coordination with the National African Congress of Trade Unions and the Federation of South African Labour Unions may be necessary if bargaining is to be effective. Some people in the ANC and COSATU hoped that the NEF (and now NEDLAC) would provide an incentive for the strengthening of both employer and worker organizations (for example, Mboweni 1992: 28). If such strengthening materializes, it will serve as yet another illustration of our contention that government and political institutions have an important, independent effect upon the nature and character of associations of economic interest.

CONCLUSION

Numerous scholars have argued that state autonomy is necessary for the successful pursuit of economic liberalization and export-led growth. It is probably fair to say that the popularity of this argument rests, at present, on a certain reading of a few exemplary cases, most prominently those of South Korea, Taiwan, Singapore and Hong Kong in East Asia and Ghana in Africa. However, in the last two or three years, a greater number of cases have been analysed and we therefore have a larger set from which to draw inferences. The effect has been to undermine the general validity of the earlier 'conventional wisdom'. Some specialists on South-East Asia, for instance, note that there has been considerable government-business cooperation in the design and implementation of world market-oriented policies in Thailand and Malaysia (Doner 1991; Laothamatas 1992). Indeed, the World Bank notes in its recent assessment of the 'East Asian miracle' that such cooperation has been a notable feature of policy-making in the paradigmatic Asian success stories as well, and consequently state autonomy has been unduly emphasized (World Bank 1993: 157–89).

The main purpose of this chapter was to demonstrate that interest groups can under certain circumstances – depending on the strength of their organizations, the size of their memberships, and the nature of the political institutions set up to deal with their demands – adopt long-term views on the nature of members' self-interest and therefore flexible positions on matters of economic policy. The recent experience of Zimbabwe and – in a fledgeling way – South Africa indicates that policy flexibility and a movement towards greater world-market integration can be promoted within the framework of societal corporatism, sometimes with, sometimes without, labour. The significance of this becomes clear if developments in Zimbabwe and South Africa are viewed against the background of earlier experiences elsewhere in Africa, where governments have attempted to suppress the free expression of economic demands, ostensibly in order to promote the 'national interest'. Generally, this mode of creating state autonomy has proved self-defeating.

The argument for state autonomy as a requisite for economic liberalization in Africa may seem compelling to many of those who identify past policies of protectionism with urban bias and see little hope that the dispersed peasant beneficiaries of present policy changes can provide organized support for market-oriented governments. It is therefore of particular interest to note, in the cases of Zimbabwe and South Africa, the urban origins of the most vocal and organized political pressures for liberalization.

If state autonomy were indeed necessary for liberalizing reforms, the current opening-up of political systems around the developing world would represent a retrogressive step in cases where autocrats have made some initial moves to adjust their economies structurally unless, of course, some domestic support could be belatedly drummed up. Along such lines, Joan Nelson has stressed the need, if structural adjustment is to be sustained in the medium and long run, for more active government solicitation of political support from reform beneficiaries after an (in her view) inevitable period of autocratic policy-making in the early stages of reform (Nelson 1993). In the African context, however, the risks inherent in such a political strategy are hinted at by the failure of Ghana's Jerry Rawlings to secure the support of local traders and cocoa farmers even after a decade of successful economic reform (Herbst 1993). While it is too early to pronounce any final judgement, a strategy whereby local interest groups are invited to take part in discussions and negotiations at the outset of reform, as in Zimbabwe and South Africa, may prove to be a wise choice, at least where such interest groups are represented by broadly-based and inclusive organizations.

References

Amsden, A.H. (1985), 'The State and Taiwan's Economic Development', in P.B. Evans, D. Rueschemeyer and T. Skocpol (eds), *Bringing the State Back In* (Cambridge: Cambridge University Press), pp. 78–106.

Bates, R.H. (1981), *Markets and States in Tropical Africa* (Berkeley and Los Angeles: University of California Press).

Bates, R.H. (1989), *Beyond the Miracle of the Market: the Political Economy of Agrarian Development in Kenya* (Cambridge: Cambridge University Press).

Beveridge, A.A. and A.R. Oberschall (1979), *African Businessmen and Development in Zambia* (Princeton, NJ: Princeton University Press).

Callaghy, T.M. (1988), 'The State and the Development of Capitalism in Africa: Theoretical, Historical, and Comparative Reflections', in D. Rothchild and N. Chazan (eds), *The Precarious Balance* (Boulder, Col.: Westview) pp. 67–99.

Callaghy, T.M. (1990), 'Lost between State and Market: The Politics of Economic Adjustment in Ghana, Zambia, and Nigeria', in J.M. Nelson (ed.), *Economic Crisis and Policy Choice: The Politics of Adjustment in the Third World* (Princeton: Princeton University Press), pp. 257–319.

Cameron, D.R. (1984), 'Social Democracy, Corporatism, Labour Quiescence and the Representation of Economic Interest in Advanced Capitalist Society', in J.H. Goldthorpe (ed.), *Order and Conflict in Contemporary Capitalism* (Oxford: Clarendon Press) pp. 143–78.

COSATU (1992), Handbook for Shop Stewards, *Our Political Economy: Understanding the Problems* (Pretoria: COSATU).

Deyo, F.C. (ed.) (1987), *The Political Economy of the New Asian Industrialism* (London: Cornell University Press).

Diamond, L. (1987), 'Class Formation in the Swollen African State', *The Journal of Modern African Studies*, Vol. 25, No. 4, pp. 567–96.

Doner, R.F. (1991), 'Approaches to the Politics of Economic Growth in Southeast Asia', *The Journal of Asian Studies*, Vol. 50, No. 4, pp. 818–49.

Gereffi, G. and D.L. Wyman (eds) (1990), *Manufacturing Miracles: Paths of Industrialization in Latin America and East Asia* (Princeton, NJ: Princeton University Press).

Haggard, S. (1990), *Pathways from the Periphery* (London: Cornell University Press).

Herbst, J. (1993), *The Politics of Reform in Ghana, 1982–1991* (Berkeley and Los Angeles: University of California Press).

Jenkins, R (1991), 'The Political Economy of Industrialization: A Comparison of Latin American and East Asian Newly Industrializing Countries', *Development and Change*, Vol. 22, (April), pp. 197–231.

Joffe, A., D. Kaplan, R. Kaplinsky and D. Lewis (1993), 'Meeting the Global Challenge: A Framework for Industrial Revival in South Africa', paper prepared for IDASA meeting, 27–30 April.

Joseph, R.A. (1987), *Democracy and Prebendal Politics in Nigeria* (Cambridge: Cambridge University Press).

Katzenstein, P. (1985), *Small States in World Markets* (Ithaca, NY: Cornell University Press).

Kaufman, R.R. (1985), 'Democratic and Authoritarian Responses to the Debt Issue: Argentina, Brazil, Mexico', *International Organization*, Vol. 39, No. 3, pp. 473–503.

Kentridge, M. (1993), *Turning the Tanker: The Economic Debate in South Africa*, Social Contract Series, Report no. 32 (Johannesburg: Centre for Policy Studies).

Laothamatas, A. (1992), *Business Associations and the New Political Economy of Thailand: From Bureaucratic Polity to Liberal Corporatism* (Boulder, Col.: Westview).

Lembruch, G. (1984), 'Concertation and the Structure of Corporatist Networks', in J.H. Goldthorpe (ed.), *Order and Conflict in Contemporary Capitalism* (Oxford: Clarendon Press), pp. 60–80.

Mboweni, T. (1992), 'The Role of the Trade Union Movement in the Future of South Africa', *South African Labour Bulletin*, Vol. 16, No. 8, pp. 24–9.

MERG (1993), *Making Democracy Work: A Framework for Macro-Economic Policy in South Africa. A Report to Members of the Democratic Movement of South Africa from the Macroeconomic Research Group* (Bellville: Centre for Development Studies).

Nelson, J.M. (1993), 'The Politics of Economic Transformation: Is Third World Experience Relevant in Eastern Europe?', *World Politics*, Vol. 45, No. 3, pp. 433–63.

Nyang'oro, J.E. (1989), 'State Corporatism in Tanzania', in J.E. Nyang'oro and T.M. Shaw (eds), *Corporatism in Africa* (Boulder, Col.: Westview), pp. 67–82.

Olson, M. (1982), *The Rise and Decline of Nations* (New Haven, Coun., and London: Yale University Press).

Patel, E. (1993) 'New Institutions of Decision-Making', in E. Patel (ed.), *Engine of Development? South Africa's National Economic Forum* (Kenwyn: Juta), pp. 1–16.

Race Relations Survey 1992/93 (Johannesburg: South African Institute of Race Relations).

Remmer, K.L. (1986), 'The Politics of Economic Stabilization: IMF Standby Programs in Latin America, 1954–1984', *Comparative Politics*, Vol. 19, No. 1, pp. 1–24.

Robinson, P.T. (1992), 'Grassroots Legitimation of Military Governance in Burkina Faso and Niger: The Core Contradictions', in G. Hydén and

M. Bratton (eds), *Governance and Politics in Africa* (Boulder, Col., and London: Lynne Rienner), pp. 143–65.

Rogowski, R. (1983), 'Structure, Growth, and Power: Three Rationalist Accounts', *International Organization*, Vol. 37, No. 4, pp. 713–38.

Sachs, J.D. (1989), 'Introduction', in J.D. Sachs (ed.), *Developing Country Debt and Economic Performance*, Vol. 1, (London: The University of Chicago Press), pp. 1–35.

Sandbrook, R. with J. Barker (1985), *The Politics of Africa's Economic Stagnation* (Cambridge: Cambridge University Press).

Schmitter, P.C. (1974), 'Still the Century of Corporatism?', *Review of Politics*, 36 (January), pp. 85–131.

Skålnes, T. (1993), 'The State, Interest Groups and Structural Adjustment in Zimbabwe', *The Journal of Development Studies*, Vol. 29, No. 3, pp. 401–28.

Skålnes, T. (1995), *The Politics of Economic Reform in Zimbabwe: Continuity and Change in Development* (London: Macmillan).

Skidmore, T.E. (1977), 'The Politics of Economic Stabilization in Postwar Latin America', in J.M. Malloy (ed.), *Authoritarianism and Corporatism in Latin America* (Pittsburgh: University of Pittsburgh Press), pp. 149–90.

Sklar, R.L. (1979), 'The Nature of Class Domination in Africa', *The Journal of Modern African Studies*, Vol. 17, No. 4, pp. 531–52.

Sklar, R.L. (1965), 'Contradictions in the Nigerian Political System', *The Journal of Modern African Studies*, Vol. 3, No. 2, pp. 201–13.

Truman, D.B. (1951), *The Governmental Process* (New York: Alfred A. Knopf).

Whitaker, C.S. (1991), 'Doctrines of Development and Precepts of the State: the World Bank and the Fifth Iteration of the African Case', in R.L. Sklar and C.S. Whitaker, *African Politics and Problems in Development* (London: Lynne Rienner), pp. 333–53.

World Bank (1993), *The East Asian Miracle: Economic Growth and Public Policy* (Oxford: Oxford University Press).

Notes

1. The author wishes to thank the Research Council of Norway for funding this research. Helpful comments were received from Peter Gibbon, Alhadi Khalaf, Atul Kohli, Guillermo O'Donnell, Phil Raikes, Lise Rakner, Richard Sandbrook, Richard Sklar, and Arne Tostensen.

2. Several studies have proclaimed a causal link between political authoritarianism and orthodox policies of macro-economic stabilisation (such as Skidmore 1977). Later, authoritarianism was depicted as a necessary condition for fully-fledged structural adjustment (Kaufman 1985). The collapse of authoritarian regimes in Latin America and the economic chaos that many of them left behind led, however, to a reconsideration of these issues in the late 1980s (Remmer 1986). At the same time, however, certain highly repressive East Asian regimes continued to achieve rapid economic growth. Rhys Jenkins explains Latin American stagnation and East Asian success in terms of the alleged greater autonomy of the latter regimes (Jenkins 1991), and the suppression of societal demands is seen as a fundamental reason why growth rates have been so high by other writers, such as Amsden (1985), Haggard (1990) and Deyo (1987).

3. Joseph (1987) and Diamond (1987) are highly sceptical of democratization in the context of clientelist politics, and predict that competitive party systems will only exacerbate the tendency to disperse the resources of the state. Thomas Callaghy regards Ghana as the only successful African case of structural adjustment, and believes that economic restructuring can only come about after a *coup d'état* whereupon a military regime cuts off all links to societal groups (Callaghy 1990). C.S. Whitaker is one of a relatively small group of academics who see democratic legitimacy as a necessary condition for the establishment of the political authority and trust needed to counter 'rent-seeking' by individuals and groups (Whitaker 1991).

4. The literature on forms of interest group intermediation is large. Philippe C. Schmitter introduced the concept 'societal corporatism', and contrasted it with both 'pluralism' and 'state corporatism' (1974). For later conceptual discussions, see, for instance, Lembruch (1984).

5. In Tanzania, for instance, the ruling Tanganyika African National Union moved in the early 1960s to outlaw the independent Tanganyika Federation of Labour and the autonomous farmers' cooperatives and to form party-affiliated labour and cooperative movements, as well as students', women's, youth and even parents' organisations (see Nyang'oro 1989). Structures for the regimentation of all interests in society perceived as legitimate by the regime were erected in Ghana in the late 1950s and early 1960s, under President Kwame Nkrumah. However, African leaders have differed in the extent to which they have used state corporatism as a strategy for enhanced political control and inclusion. Sometimes they have failed. In the late 1980s, for example, the Zambian trade-union movement became a centre for the opposition, and in Burkina Faso the trade union movement has proved difficult to incorporate within pseudo-democratic 'participatory' institutions (Robinson 1992).

6. Democracy, in the form of multi-party electoral competition, may not automatically represent an antidote to patron-client politics. In

fact, as both Diamond and Joseph argue, a competitive party system might exacerbate the destructive features of distributive politics by creating a need for the construction of much larger clienteles (Diamond 1987; Joseph 1987). Clientelist networks, by facilitating the aggregation of localized demands into vertical structures, feed on the same 'territorial' principle as constitutes the basis for popular assemblies and legislatures. Local demands must of course be reflected in democratic processes, and some degree of clientism and log-rolling is unavoidable even in modern, advanced countries. Therefore, institutions for the functional representation of interests, interests that may cross-cut localities and aggregate demands by encouraging the creation of broader interest groups, may be needed to moderate the excesses of localized, clientelist demand-making.

7. *The Herald* (Harare), 1 January, 1994, p. 1.

8. Briefly, that the form rather than the extent of state intervention is the crucial issue. This is well illustrated by the experience of the East Asian 'newly industrializing countries'. The governments of South Korea, Taiwan and Singapore have actively intervened through credit controls, the setting-up of public manufacturing enterprises and so on. Import control has also been used to shield some products from competition on the domestic market. However, outward orientation led to a strong exposure to competition even in cases where the domestic market was oligopolized (see Gereffi and Wyman 1990; Haggard 1990). East Asian governments set export targets for firms and channelled investment towards them, and supported local firms through active exchange rate management (Sachs 1989). Thus, while East Asian economies have been far from open and the governments far from non-interventionist, the world market orientation of these countries did have a highly disciplining effect on key government policies as well as on the strategic decisions of individual firms.

9. Quoted in Kentridge (1993: 3).

10. As reported in the *Financial Mail*, 11 February, 1994, p. 38.

11. *South African Labour Bulletin*, Vol. 17, No. 4 (July/August 1993), pp. 17–18.

12. *South African Labour Bulletin*, Vol. 17, No. 5 (September/October 1993), p. 23.

13. *Reconstruction and Development Programme*, 6th Draft, 13 January 1994, p. 59.

14. *Reconstruction and Development Programme*, 6th Draft, 13 January 1994, p. 35.

9 Structural Adjustment and Democratization in Zimbabwe

Lloyd M. Sachikonye

In 1990, Zimbabwe launched a five-year Economic Structural Adjustment Policy (ESAP) substantially financed by the World Bank, International Monetary Fund and Western donor countries. The economic reform measures contained in the ESAP programme coincided with a phase of political liberalization which culminated in a formal renunciation of the one-party state concept by the ruling ZANU-PF party in early 1991. It is important to understand the conjunctural context of these twin processes of economic and political liberalization. In this chapter, I explore the pressures for economic liberalization, outline the major elements in ESAP and assess the impact of adjustment on the process of political liberalization, and, more broadly, the impact on the democratization process. I also consider whether economic liberalization in the form of structural adjustment is conducive or obstructive to political liberalization. The chapter will outline briefly two contending perspectives on the relationship between economic reform and democratization.

STRUCTURAL ADJUSTMENT AND POLITICAL LIBERALIZATION

Structural adjustment involves both 'stabilization', which often entails devaluation and substantial cut-backs of public expenditure and 'adjustment', which seeks to transform economic structures and institutions through varying doses of deregulation, privatization, reduction of allegedly oversized public bureaucracies and the institution of 'realistic' prices to stimulate greater efficiency and productivity, especially in export production (Mosley, Harrigan and Toye 1991).

'Political liberalization' has been defined as a process of political change controlled from the top down, as a means of preserving most of the status quo. It has been argued that: 'it is a game elites play to manage the granting of very carefully selected concessions. It is a cosmetic exercise and does not install the fundamentals of democratization' (Qadir, Clapham and Gills 1993: 416–17). At the same time, however, it is acknowledged that political liberalization may sometimes lead to a deeper process of democratization, if the impetus for change escapes from elite control to encompass broader social forces and its purpose is transformed from the preservation of interests to genuine reform (Qadir, Clapham and Gills 1993). Thus, political liberalization is a necessary but insufficient condition for a definitive process of democratization. In our evaluation of the political liberalization process in Zimbabwe, the limitations on democratization will become plain.

Let us briefly outline two contending perspectives on the linkages between political liberalization and economic development. The collapse of the socialist model in Eastern Europe has been interpreted in some quarters as a confirmation of liberal economic theory which argues that 'undemocratic' socialist states were unable to produce sustained economic growth, and that their political structures prevented economic change (Leftwich 1993: 609). According to this perspective, economic mismanagement, stagnation and decline flowed directly from the absence of democratic and popular participation. Political liberalization, it is argued, is a necessary condition for both economic liberalization and growth (Leftwich 1993).

This perspective has been challenged by another which observes that most major post-1960 'success' stories of economic growth in the developing world, Brazil, South Korea, Taiwan, Thailand and Indonesia, 'have not occurred under conditions remotely approximating continuous and stable democracy: quite the opposite. Even in the developmentally successful democratic societies – such as Botswana, Malaysia and Singapore – de facto one-party rule has been the norm for 30 years' (Leftwich 1993: 613).

On the contrary, no examples of sustained growth in the developing world have occurred under conditions of uncompromising economic liberalism, whether democratic or not:

from Costa Rica to China and from Botswana to Thailand, the state has played an active role in influencing economic behaviour and has often had a significant material stake in the economy itself. Crucially, then, it has not been regime type but the kind and character of the state and its associated politics that have been decisive in influencing developmental performance . . . In short, the combination of democratic politics and economic liberalism has rarely been associated with the critical early breakthroughs from agrarianism to industrialism, now or in the past. (Leftwich 1993: 614)

This intense debate on the linkage between liberal market economy and political liberalization forms the immediate background to the national discourse on adjustment and democracy in Zimbabwe. I now spell out the main elements of economic reform (as encapsulated in ESAP) before I assess their political ramifications.

THE MAIN ELEMENTS OF ZIMBABWE'S ESAP

The pressures which the Zimbabwe economy encountered in the second half of the 1980s were considerable. They were related to a rising budget deficit, ballooning government expenditure, mediocre export performance, low investment and high unemployment. The budget deficit was in excess of 10 per cent of GDP during much of the 1980s. Real GDP growth between 1980 and 1990 at 3 per cent per annum only matched the population growth rate. Investment was barely adequate to maintain, let alone increase, the capital stock. Private sector investment stagnated at 10 per cent of GDP in the 1980s (International Bank for Reconstruction and Development, or IBRD 1992: 1). The tightly regulated business environment with controls on investment, labour conditions and pricing, and the aforementioned unsustainable fiscal deficits were acknowledged as deterrents to potential investors (Zimbabwe Government 1991). Export growth at 3.4 per cent per annum between 1980 and 1989, coupled with debt repayments which reached a peak of 34 per cent of export earnings in 1987, severely constrained the growth of imports.

Thus the growth which had occurred in the 1980s rested on a fragile basis given the structural weaknesses built into the economy. This assessment of Zimbabwe's shaky economic performance was not confined to the Zimbabwe Government and the major international financial institutions. Independent analysts observed that the economy had reached crisis conditions and that therefore its restructuring had become unavoidable. The restructuring of the manufacturing sector, for instance, had become imperative if it was to generate jobs and foreign exchange on a significant scale (Riddell 1990). If such restructuring did not occur, the long-term overall growth rate of the economy would be low or negative, resulting in a downward spiral of investment and growth, of exports and employment (Riddell 1990).

In sum, Zimbabwean economic policies in the 1980s could not lead in the medium and long term to a sustainable industrial transition such as had occurred in the newly industrialized countries in Asia (Stoneman and Cliffe 1989: 60), and a consensus started to emerge towards the end of the 1980s that substantial reforms were needed to cure the malaise of the Zimbabwean economy. Although the diagnosis was not contested, there were sharp differences about the correct prescription. I return below to the political context of those divergences over economic reform.

Zimbabwe was required by the World Bank and the International Monetary Fund to meet specific conditions before financial inflows could be released. These conditions centred on budget deficit reduction, fiscal and monetary policy reforms, trade liberalization, public enterprise reforms (including privatization), and the deregulation of investment, labour and price controls (Zimbabwe Government 1991). These were, by any standards, far-reaching structural reform measures. Their premises were deliberately based on optimistic projections of the outcome of the 5–year ESAP programme from 1991 to 1995. These included a forecast 5 per cent annual growth rate from 1991 to 1995; reduction of the budget deficit to 5 per cent of GDP by 1995; the decline of the external current account deficit to 4 per cent of GDP and of the debt service ratio to 20 per cent, both by 1995. Furthermore, direct subsidies and transfers to public services would be reduced from about Z$629 million in 1991 to a maximum of Z$40 million by 1995.

The economic reform programme included a phased process of trade liberalization to move away from a state-administered foreign exchange allocation system to a market-based one. This would ensure that, with the exception of a few goods to be excluded only on the grounds of defence, safety or overwhelming public interest, all items would be importable on the Open General Import Licence (OGIL) system by 1995 (Zimbabwe Government 1991). These measures would contribute to greater investment inflows which were projected to rise to 25 per cent of GDP by 1995. GDP and consumption per capita were expected to rise by 2 per cent during the same period. Finally, the reform programme was expected to contribute to a reduction of the current high unemployment level of well over 30 per cent as it was anticipated that 100 000 new jobs would be created in the formal sector in the period 1992–95 (IBRD 1992: iii).

PHASES OF ESAP

Certain observations about the outcome of Zimbabwe's ESAP are now possible. They are necessarily provisional but it is unlikely that the remaining short phase will significantly change the present general trends in the economy. In this section, I briefly outline the phases through which the economic reforms have gone before discussing their outcome at some length.

Four phases through which ESAP has been implemented can be identified. The first phase lasted from October 1990 to mid-1991. It was a phase characterized by the implementation of trade liberalization in a context of pronounced optimism in both government and private sector circles. The basis of the optimism lay in the assumption that as trade liberalization unfolded and more commodities were placed under the OGIL, levels of capacity utilization and product quality would improve significantly. In particular, the textile and chemical sub-sectors geared up towards improved levels of capacity utilization because they were set to benefit immediately from the placing of their inputs on OGIL. This business optimism received a boost from the pledges amounting to US$700 million to finance ESAP by international financial institutions and Western donors at a consultative meeting in Paris.

The second phase which lasted from mid-1991 to December 1991 witnessed emerging divisions within the bourgeoisie and mounting criticism with respect to the economic reforms. The divisions centred on the concept of adjustment itself and the sequencing of the implementation process. The major business lobby, the CZI, for example, questioned the wisdom of stringent monetary measures when other factors in the economic equation – the investment and import factors – had not yet been sufficiently addressed. The increased cost of finance, in the absence of expanded access to foreign exchange for import and investment purposes, translated into trebled interest rates (pegged at 40 per cent) and a high inflation rate (of 46 per cent) in 1992. The non-exporting firms were disadvantaged by ESAP, argued the CZI, which asserted that these firms were an important link in the production cycle, and that therefore deliberate efforts were required to assist them to face up to the challenges posed by the reforms. Finally, the substantial increases in charges for their goods and services by what the CZI termed 'monopolistic parastatals' seriously jeopardized the performance of the private sector. It was somewhat ironic that the decried price increases were a consequence of the deregulation process so strongly championed originally by organizations such as the CZI itself.

A major recession and drought marked the third phase of the economic reforms in 1992. Instead of spurring growth, the aforementioned monetary measures undermined it to the extent of creating conditions for a domestic recession. Some new investment projects were shelved because of escalating costs of imported equipment. Capacity underutilization was a major indicator of the recession. The Central Statistical Office estimated that, in the last quarter of 1992, some 89 per cent of manufacturing firms were operating below capacity.

The recession was also characterized by the collapse of the domestic market as inflation and falling incomes eroded real incomes so most consumers could not afford much more than basic commodities. For example, clothing and other retail sectors plummeted in 1992 by 35 per cent and 50 per cent respectively. This was the background of substantial dismissals totalling an estimated 20 000 workers, which further diluted demand.

However, a major exogenous factor which compounded the recession was the severe drought of 1992. It crippled agriculture, the output of which fell by about 40 per cent, sending shock-waves throughout the economy. Food imports placed tremendous pressure on government finances. Drought-related imports amounted to an estimated US$323 million in 1992 and US$152 million in 1993 (Moyana 1992).

The fourth phase of ESAP covers the first half of 1993. As the recession deepened, demands became more strident that government should reduce its money market borrowing because its expenditure was already excessive. In particular, the private sector was extremely critical towards what it perceived to be contradictory policies: tight monetary measures largely aimed at the private sector and profligacy by the government. The accumulated public debt of

Z$16 billion cost nearly Z$3.6 billion in interest and capital repayments in 1992 (First Merchant Bank 1992).

This substantial government expenditure was also an object of attack by opposition parties. The Democratic Party and the Forum Party of Zimbabwe were particularly scathing about the excessive size of both the cabinet and government bureaucracy. In their view, the austerity measures induced by ESAP were being disproportionately borne by almost all sectors except by the ZANU-PF government leadership and its protégés in the state bureaucracy and the parastatals (Democratic Party 1991; Forum Party of Zimbabwe 1993). Thus the criticism of government profligacy was almost universal, ranging from the international financial institutions themselves to the domestic private sector and the opposition parties. This is the broad context in which disillusionment with ESAP sparked demands for its revision in some quarters and its scrapping in others. Those demands did not emanate solely from the traditional opponents of the programme within the labour movement and sectors of non-exporting firms. For example, a leading bank, the Standard Chartered Bank, called for the abandonment of the targets stipulated by the International Monetary Fund, stressing that if this was not done, economic growth was unlikely to match the 3 per cent population growth rate.

The current phase which began in mid-1993 is one in which the economy began to recover following a good agricultural season. An estimated 2 per cent increase in agricultural output was recorded in 1993 following a decrease of 8 per cent in 1992. Cautious optimism greeted the expectation of a 4 per cent increase in 1994. In addition, basic indicators pointed to the slowing down of inflation and lower interest rates. Inflation was estimated to have fallen from 46 per cent per annum in December 1992 to 21 per cent in January 1994. The Reserve Bank's overnight lending rate was reduced from 39 per cent in early 1993 to 28 per cent in December 1993.[1] A number of manufacturing sub-sectors – textiles and ginning, clothing and footwear – registered a significant up-turn (First Merchant Bank, 1993).

However, the drop in interest rates and the inflation rate must be set against continued substantial losses by parastatals during this phase. Those losses are projected to increase to Z$822 million in 1993–94 (IBRD 1992: 9). From the viewpoint of the international financial institutions, parastatals' performance has failed to meet expectations:

the progress until now has mainly consisted of the introduction of financial measures in the form of tariff increases and price adjustments to reduce operating losses. But the point is being rapidly reached where such increases are becoming a constraint on growth and affect the competitive position of Zimbabwe's economy. (IBRD 1992: 9)

Thus the parastatals look set to remain ESAP's Achilles heel. Finally, the modest signs of an upturn referred to above need to be viewed against the substantial retrenchments which have occurred to date. The decline in formal sector employment has been considerable: one estimate is that in early 1994 less than 12 per cent of the total work force was employed in the sector compared with 15 per cent in 1980. The employment creation targets of ESAP will therefore not be met.

THE OUTCOME OF ESAP

The outcome of ESAP reforms by mid-1994 appeared profoundly ambiguous and mixed. It remained uncertain whether the recovery which began in 1993 will be sustained. This assessment of ESAP's outcome is supported by data from a field study on the impact of adjustment on industry and labour (Sachikonye 1994). The findings relate to industrial restructuring, labour relations and the social implications of adjustment.

First, on a positive note, the evidence from a survey of 20 firms from manufacturing, agro-industrial and parastatal sectors shows that large firms and corporations have taken advantage of ESAP to undertake extensive re-tooling to improve productive capacity and product quality. There have been comparatively large investments in new equipment in such sectors as textiles and clothing, paper and packaging, chemicals and steel. Further, approximately 46 per cent of the sampled work force received training in 1991–3 for varying periods. In my view, extensive re-tooling and the increased emphasis on the training of company work forces represent a restructuring process. This process does not relate to change in ownership and control of the firms, but to the reorganization of production to maximize capacity, productivity and competitiveness.

Brief examples of this industrial restructuring process follow. Textile companies invested Z$1 billion in new equipment between

1990 and mid-1993, Z$229 million was spent on plant modernization in paper manufacturing and packaging, and the iron and steel corporation, ZISCO, embarked on a Z$1.5 billion modernization programme. There were also significant infrastructural investments in the dairy, railway and telecommunications sub-sectors. From the stand-point of industry in general, a major advantage conferred by ESAP were the confidence-building measures which made acquisition of new equipment a feasible, if not indispensable, strategy. The context of economic liberalization provided a boost to industry through changes in investment, trade and labour regimes.

At the same time, however, some ESAP measures (as I observed above) have presented significant constraints on the restructuring firms, but especially on medium and small-scale firms. I observed that the investment rush by firms had resulted in huge financial exposures as interest rates soared above 40 per cent in 1992 and 1993. The response of the firms was either the postponement or shelving of certain projects, and the restructuring of debt through rights issues.

Second, the most significant development under ESAP concerning labour relations was the deregulation of post-independence controls. This deregulation process was aimed at increasing the flexibility of management in 'hiring and firing' workers, which increased management control over workers at the workplaces. Under ESAP, a work regime is emerging which is accompanied by stricter supervision and increased workload. In our survey, approximately 70 per cent of sampled workers confirmed that the work process had been intensified under ESAP. There was a pervasive feeling of employment insecurity in the context of deregulation of labour controls, especially the dismantling of job security safeguards. But as the effects of ESAP have revealed themselves, the response amongst workers in certain sectors has been one of growing restiveness, if not militancy, as the increasing number of strikes in the second half and first quarter of 1994 suggests. The more notable of the strikes were those by telecommunications workers, bank and university workers and medical doctors.

Third, we need to consider (albeit briefly) the broader social implications of ESAP as they relate to dismissals and an emerging social consumption crisis. The cumulative evidence on dismissals suggest that the previous estimate of 50 000 during the 5-year reform programme was likely to be superseded by 1995. Field findings tended to confirm that the burden of dismissals had been borne by contract workers, the 'unskilled' and 'semi-skilled'. Out of the dismissed workers sampled, 89 per cent belonged to the un-skilled and semi-skilled categories. A little over a third had been employed for six years or more but, although the principle of 'last in and first out' seems to have been generally followed, it was the unskilled, semi-skilled and contract workers who were regarded as dispensable and easy to replace if an economic upturn occurred.

Finally, price inflation and the removal of subsidies on basic commodities under ESAP in the context of low wage increases created conditions for a social reproduction crisis. Whilst of the sampled workers, 65 per cent could afford to purchase bread, 52 per cent some milk and 47 per cent some beef on a regular basis, the picture was getting bleaker for the remainder. Workers had been forced to reduce their food intake since ESAP began; some com-plained of weakness and loss of weight and others of headaches and dizziness at work due to lack of food. Survey findings also pointed to a diminishing access by working-class households to such social services as health and education. Approximately 10.7 per cent of sampled workers had withdrawn one or more of their children from school owing to inability to pay fees. Remittances to rural areas in the form of agricultural inputs, food parcels or cash seemed to be on a downward trend as 49 per cent of sampled workers remitted only Z$100 or less and 24 per cent remitted nothing in 1992. ESAP appeared to be succeeding in dislocating extended family networks and urban-rural linkages. Given the important role of such net-works in the livelihood of rural families, this trend points towards a major social crisis.

POLITICAL LIBERALIZATION IN THE CONTEXT OF ESAP

Comparatively speaking, Zimbabwe attained its independence rela-tively late (in 1980), about 20 years after most African states gained theirs. The international context was becoming much less conducive to the authoritarian thesis that the one-party state system could be a suitable model for developing countries such as Zimbabwe. Thus, although most of Zimbabwe's neighbours such as Zambia, Mozam-bique and Angola had installed one-party states, there was no immediate pressure to follow suit. In any case, the division of the nationalist movement into two factions, the Zimbabwe African

National Union (ZANU) and the Zimbabwe African People's Union (ZAPU) – both of which drew on substantial but regionally-based support – precluded the institution of a one-party state as a viable model. However, following the merger of the two parties into ZANU-PF in 1987, the one-party state question was placed on the agenda. The landslide victory of the merged ZANU-PF party (which won 147 out of 150 seats in Parliament) in the 1990 elections provided fresh impetus to the demands for a one-party state amongst party loyalists. But both the external and domestic environments had now become decidedly hostile to the one-party state concept due to the collapse of the model in Eastern Europe and concerted challenges against it elsewhere in Africa. At the launch of ESAP in 1990, Zimbabwe was formally a multi-party state; and although no political conditionalities were defined, to institute a one-party state would have derailed Western support for the economic reforms.

It is against this background that we assess Zimbabwe's experience in forging political pluralism. Indeed, the debate in Zimbabwe has been almost exclusively centred on political pluralism rather than on the broader question of democratization (Mandaza and Sachikonye 1991). As just observed, there was much animated discussion on the negative attributes of the one-party state concept in 1990 when the ruling ZANU-PF signalled a wish to overturn the multi-party system operative since independence. Yet the debate did not proceed beyond the advocacy of a competitive multi-party system. It was simply assumed that democracy would be ushered in, if there were no obstacles to the formation of political parties, if access to the state-controlled media was ensured and freedom of assembly was guaranteed, for example. The debate did not consider the general parameters of democratization. Questions about workplace democracy, about human and civil rights, and about the autonomy of civil society institutions, such as universities and trade unions, were rarely raised. The relationship between the Zimbabwean state and civil society did not become an object for serious reflection. The social content of multi-party democracy itself was not questioned; the 'political kingdom' based on pluralism was viewed as a panacea for national problems.

The absence of a vigorous theorization of what democratization would politically and economically entail in Zimbabwe contributed to the tendency to reduce, or equate, democracy to political pluralism. It was not difficult for ZANU-PF to accommodate the principle of pluralism. It did not represent a significant departure from the political system installed at independence; some would argue that it merely represented continuity. This process of continuity entailed a grudging tolerance of opposition parties but in a context of pronounced state authoritarianism.

Our argument is that although the principle of political pluralism was reaffirmed following the one-party state debate, authoritarian practices continue to be in vogue, undermining the possibilities of a substantive democratization process. As we have observed, in the Zimbabwean context, political pluralism has been confined to the formation of parties and their participation in the electoral process. It has not been extended to include reasonably fair access to state-owned radio, television and newspapers or the access of opposition parties to state funding (from which ZANU-PF has received Z$50 million to date). Thus, although there is a theoretical commitment to multi-partyism, in practice ZANU-PF imposes structural constraints on opposition parties. State security organs are manipulated to intimidate opposition candidates and frustrate their political mobilization campaigns. Clearly, the political system is not open and free despite the constitutional commitment to pluralism. Authoritarian tendencies are explicit in the harassment of opposition politicians, critical journalists, trade unionists and students. Pluralism in practice continues to be undermined.

The authoritarianism which underlay its political practices was replicated by the ZANU-PF government in the design and implementation of economic reform. There was no prior national debate on the pros and cons of ESAP, and neither was a concerted effort attempted to build a broad consensus for it. For example, the labour movement and the peasant organizations were completely marginalized in the design of ESAP. This was so despite the substantial negative effects, especially dismissals and cuts in real wages, which labour would sustain. Thus the economic liberalization programme represents a top-down approach to reform. The major players are the Zimbabwe state and certain, but not all, fractions of the domestic bourgeoisie on the one hand, and international finance capital and Western donor countries on the other. No wide or popular participation in the formulation of the far-reaching economic reforms occurred.

This is the background against which opposition parties have attacked the ESAP reforms. In their view, the economic crisis which made ESAP necessary was the outcome of ZANU-PF's mismanagement, particularly its failure to curb government expenditure which was inflated by an enormous cabinet and rampant nepotism in the parastatals. According to the opposition ZANU-NDONGA party: 'anyone who believes that ESAP is the answer to the problems in this country should have his head re-examined because ESAP is being administered by precisely the same group that led us to this [economic] mess' (Ndabaningi Sithole as quoted in *The People's Voice*, April 1992).

The opposition movement therefore blames the ZANU-PF government for the unpopular austerity measures enshrined in ESAP. However, none of the opposition parties has so far developed a coherent economic policy alternative to ESAP. Indeed, they broadly support a capitalist development path via economic liberalization. Although they promise 'a better deal' for employer interests, for labour, consumers and investors, their policy manifestos are short on specifics. To that extent, the opposition's critique of ESAP is of limited utility and therefore not very convincing to the electorate, if recent by-elections won by ZANU-PF are a reliable indicator.

HEGEMONIC CRISIS AND ADJUSTMENT

As I have observed above, the immediate effects of ESAP on wages, incomes, and on living standards more generally have been disastrous to date. Even though the hardships arising from the austerity measures were predicted, those on whom they have been inflicted see in them evidence that ESAP is neither justified nor likely to result in a successful outcome. This is the context in which the ZANU-PF government has launched a major publicity 'blitz' to project a more positive image for ESAP. The 'blitz' has harnessed the contributions of party cadres, ministers, parliamentarians and the government information service to reassure a restive public opinion that the social and economic pain caused by ESAP would soon fade.

The expectation was that propaganda would succeed in moulding public opinion back in favour of the programme, thus creating conditions for its legitimation. This was, of course, a naive and condescending perspective; the negative image of ESAP has proved rather enduring despite the campaign in the state-controlled press, on radio and television. Attempts to exploit the existence of a minuscule Social Development Fund as a major solution in relieving the economic distress of the unemployed and lower-income workers and other vulnerable social groups have not fared better.

As the capacity of the ZANU-PF government to meet the basic material expectations of the populace has dwindled, its hegemonic hold has weakened in spite of its parliamentary majority. The labour movement, an important constituent element of civil society, has strongly resisted cooption by the state and the conflict between the government and the unions has been accentuated by the unions' uncompromising opposition to ESAP. The labour movement has censured ESAP as basically an anti-labour programme because rising unemployment, wage cut-backs and deregulated price increases have substantially undermined living standards. It has challenged the ZANU-PF government to debate the outcome of ESAP so far and continues to call for the negotiation of a social contract with all the interested parties with a stake in economic reform. As a consequence, the government has seen its dominance, if not credibility, in the debate on ESAP become increasingly tenuous.

Due to its criticism of ESAP and its demands for democratization as opposed to authoritarian political practices, the labour movement has been increasingly viewed as a potential political focus of organized opposition. This view has been encouraged by some of the statements made by the movements' leadership in the ZCTU to the effect that ZCTU intended to increase its political weight through construction of a broad coalition of various social interests including cooperatives, the intelligentsia and consumer groups. Stressing the limitations of adhering to a workerist agenda, the ZCTU Secretary-General has observed the need for such a broad coalition in order to weaken further ZANU-PF's slipping hegemonic hold:

> there is a great potential to expand our constituency of consensus. Demonstrations are becoming chronic in Zimbabwe as the nation's economic fortunes decline. Already the crisis has hit the middle classes, and they too are looking around for political alternatives ... [But] the most important thing is not the simple formation of a new party – we have many of them these days – but the development of a political program on which a new party should be based, and which could attract a broad section of social interests. (Tsvangirai as interviewed in *Horizon*, September 1992)

The task as defined by the ZCTU is the development of a broad counterhegemonic force, of which one important element would be a broad political front. This is an ambitious project. The significance of this thinking within the labour movement and among other social forces lies in their awareness of the limits of political pluralism as currently constituted in Zimbabwe and of the emerging vacuum created by a deepening crisis of hegemony.

However, in spite of the organizational and ideological weakness of ZANU-PF (it now has to depend on state finances to fund its activities because membership and subscriptions have dwindled), the opposition parties are far from being a cohesive force capable of wresting power, as we observed above. This is not simple to explain in a context in which unprecedented economic and social hardships have resulted in an erosion of the popular support for the nationalist coalition assembled in ZANU- PF.

Partly the situation can be explained in terms of the similarity rather than clear differences between the ZANU-PF government economic policy and those espoused by the opposition parties. Both sides are committed to a capitalist path and elite-based politics, although differences emerge over emphasis and timing. Furthermore, the social basis of the leadership of ZANU-PF and the opposition parties is similar; the black bourgeoisie and petty bourgeoisie constitute the leadership.

Partly, the explanation has to be sought in the character of Zimbabwe's civil society. Although it is, relatively speaking, not a strongly developed civil society, its constituent elements have coalesced at critical junctures: in opposition to high-level corruption (in 1988–89), in campaigns against the one-party state (in 1990), in criticism of various manifestations of state authoritarianism *vis-à-vis* universities and trade unions (in 1991 and 1992) and in the condemnation of ESAP (particularly as from 1992 when its painful effects began to be widely felt).

Yet, as a civil society, it neither has a monolithic structure nor a common ideological outlook and agenda. Indeed, its own development is closely associated with the capitalist development process in both the private and public sectors (including the expansion of the social sector services and credit support for indigenous business interests). For instance, the emergence of pressure groups such as the black capitalist interests which are grouped in the Indigenous Business Development Centre was facilitated by access to state institutions which provided softer finance and other less stringent conditions for new businesses. However, while these interests, as well as those represented in the Indigenous Commercial Farmers' Union and the Zimbabwe Farmers' Union, may well be beneficiaries of the economic space created by ESAP, many public servants and professional associations have been alienated through ESAP-induced unemployment and the substantial drop in living standards.

Even the well-placed and influential agrarian and manufacturing bourgeoisie seems confused at the twists and turns of economic and land policies. The land owners are extremely worried about the form that land redistribution will take while the industrialists have become concerned about potential de-industrialization in certain sectors if ESAP is pursued to its logical conclusion. These contradictory aspects of the state-civil society relationship are, however, being played out in muted political struggles.

Hegemony exists when the political leadership of a group or nation is exercised with minimal dispute and resistance but constant work and struggle are required to achieve and maintain it, for no hegemony is ever complete and many attempts to establish hegemony are never realized (Gamble 1988). That is why hegemonic projects are encountered much more frequently than hegemony itself. In Zimbabwe, the hegemonic project was centred on post-colonial reconstruction biased towards social redistribution (before ESAP), and there was some popular support for this. If the project was flawed due to the inability to resolve the national question until the reintegration of ZAPU and ZANU in 1987, in the present conjuncture, contradictory aspects within the new hegemonic project of economic modernization via austerity measures and authoritarianism threaten to unravel ZANU-PF hegemony altogether.

THE 1995 ELECTIONS

The conduct of the general elections in 1995 broadly confirmed the misgivings of opposition parties and independent analysts regarding the monopoly of ZANU-PF in the present political system. This monopoly is exerted in control of and privileged access to mass media, and reinforced by the use of government funds for political purposes and patronage. Hence, the advantages conferred by incumbency provided ZANU-PF with a head start in the election campaign. The election itself was marred by instances of procedural irregularities, incompetence and unfair practices. The Electoral Supervisory Commission conceded that the voter register was riddled with errors. Up to 106 000 potential voters could not vote because of errors and omissions in the register.

The overwhelming advantages which ZANU-PF possessed and exploited, together with the defect electoral system itself, provided grounds for opposition parties to boycott the elections. The main boycott parties were the Zimbabwe Unity Movement led by Edgar Tekere, the Democratic Party led by Davison Gomo and the United Party led by Abel Muzorewa. The boycott parties argued that constitutional reforms were necessary in order to create 'a level playing field'. Critics challenged the monopoly access to government funds to finance the campaign, which ZANU-PF enjoyed, as well as the power of the president to nominate additional Members of Parliament. The nomination of governors and chiefs to the Parliament by the president was also criticized. Furthermore, ZANU-PF's unrivalled access to the mass media, including state radio and television, was viewed as decisively tipping the balance against the opposition parties.

The boycott by the opposition parties was incomplete, however, because two parties, ZANU-NDONGA and the Forum Party of Zimbabwe, decided to field candidates. Out of 120 seats, though, only 65 were contested, which in turn meant that only 2.6 million voters, out of an electorate of 4.8 million, were actually required to cast their votes. ZANU-PF won 118 seats (out of 120 which could be contested) compared to 117 seats in the 1990 election.

If the conduct, participation levels and outcome of the 1995 elections represent reliable indicators of democratization, one must conclude that the process is still immature and flawed, despite triumphant pronouncements by government spokesmen to the contrary. Constitutional reform which limits the advantage of incumbents and better registration of voters is called for. Further, the single-seat constituency system, which emulates the British method, does not work well in the circumstances. By comparison, a proportional representation system would have awarded 24 seats to the opposition, both in 1990 and 1995. The effects on the political climate of a strong representation of the opposition in Parliament are easy to imagine. A reform of the system of representation would therefore contribute significantly to the undermining of the *de facto* one-party system installed by ZANU-PF in Zimbabwe.

CONCLUSION

This chapter has attempted a critical evaluation of the content of economic reforms and political liberalization and the relationship between the two processes. The ambiguous outcomes of economic liberalization and its sustainability were assessed. It was argued that authoritarianism is still a major feature of Zimbabwean politics in spite of formal adherence to multi-partyism and other trappings of pluralism. That authoritarianism was also replicated in the top-down design and implementation of the structural reform measures as embraced in ESAP. Neither the economic nor the political liberalization processes in Zimbabwe have been characterized by democratic practice. The conditions for substantive democratization and a more equitable development strategy therefore still need to be struggled for. The present models of authoritarian multi-partyism and austere economic reforms which depend on support and conditionalities from international finance capital will continue to be challenged.

References

Democratic Party (1991), *Inaugural Statement* (Harare: Democratic Party).

First Merchant Bank (1992 and 1993), *Quarterly Guide to the Economy*, various issues (Harare: First Merchant Bank).

Forum Party of Zimbabwe (1993), *Policy Papers* (Harare: Forum Party of Zimbabwe).

IBRD (1992), *Zimbabwe: Policy Framework Paper*, 1992–95 (Washington, DC: IBRD).

Gamble, A. (1988), *The Free Economy and the Strong State* (London: Macmillan).

Leftwich, A. (1993), 'Governance, Democracy and Development in the Third World', *Third World Quarterly*, Vol. 14. No. 3 pp. 605–24.

Mandaza, I. and L. M. Sachikonye (eds) (1991), *The One-Party State and Democracy* (Harare: South African Political and Economic Series).

Mosley, P., J. Harrigan, J. F. J. Toye (eds) (1991), *Aid and Power: The World Bank and Policy-Based Lending* (London: Routledge).

Moyana, K. (1992), *Zimbabwe's Financing Needs Through 1993*, Paper presented to a Consultative Group meeting (Paris), mimeo.

Qadir, S., C. Clapham and B. Gills (1993), 'Democratization in the Third

World: an introduction', *Third World Quarterly*, Vol. 14, No. 3, pp. 415–22.

Riddell, R. (1990), *Manufacturing Africa* (London: James Currey).

Sachikonye, L. M. (1994), 'Industrial Restructuring and Labour Relations under ESAP in Zimbabwe', Paper presented to a Conference on 'Dimensions of Economic and Political Reform in Contemporary Africa', Kampala, April.

Stoneman, C. and L. Cliffe (1989), *Zimbabwe: Politics, Economics and Society* (London: Pinter).

Tsvangirai, M. (1992), Interview in *Horizon*, September.

Zimbabwe Government (1991), *Zimbabwe: A Framework for Economic Reform* (Harare: Government Printer).

Note

1. However, it should not be overlooked that, in the 1980–90 period, inflation was more stable, averaging 13% per annum. Similarly, interest rates at 28% in December 1993 were still much higher than the 17.5% rate in 1991.

Part III

State, Civil Society and Social Movements

10 Seeds of Democracy: The Chinese Students' Movement in 1989

Caixia Dong

In the spring of 1989, university students in Beijing were the first to start the protests which later developed into a mass social movement throughout China. Students took the lead in demonstrations, petitions, class boycotts, attempts at dialogue with the government and a hunger strike. They succeeded in generating massive support from wide sectors of society and in forcing the government to address the problems Chinese society faced, which posed the most severe challenge to the Party-state since 1949. With the help of the international press, student protesters became the focus of attention, receiving support from home and abroad.

At the same time, students were seriously criticized for being highly reactive rather than having a clear goal and a clear programme, for being disorganized with frequent changes of leadership, for being undemocratic and even corrupt. The students' attempts to maintain 'purity' of the movement caused anger and criticism among the worker activists (Walder and Gong 1993: 24). The movement itself ended in bloodshed. None of the students' demands was accepted. By this account, the movement was a failure.

Numerous articles and books have been written to describe and analyse the student protest movement. Discussions in the press tend to categorize the student protesters either as champions of democracy, at best, or as hot-headed youngsters, at worst. Those who hail the student protesters as champions of democracy tend to overlook the fact that the student protesters were often not clear about their own goals and programmes. Those who criticize them tend to base their arguments on the tragic end of the movement.

Academic discussions, which have covered historical, sociological and cultural aspects of the movement, are much more helpful in understanding the student protests in 1989. However, in discussions

197

about democracy as a concept as well as a concrete direction for the development of Chinese society, students are usually regarded as a part of the intellectual group rather than as having their own identity. In China, university students are not usually seen as a distinctive social group, and they are considered of secondary importance because of their youth and lack of experience. The lack of organization and reactive character of their protests also contributed to the lack of recognition of their identity.[1]

Taking a closer look at the students during their 1989 protest, one sees at least two distinctive features. First, through repeated demonstrations, petitions and finally a hunger strike, the students demanded a dialogue with the government on equal terms. Second, from very early on, the students formed independent organizations and insisted on recognition of them by the government. Other groups were not as persistent in this. Generally speaking, student radicals tend to uphold their ideals much more than other groups. However, we should also look into students' anxieties and special interests which make them different from other social groups, in order to understand what happened.

This chapter therefore focuses on the factors that distinguish the students from their closest associates, the intellectual group as a whole. The purpose is to give a more accurate picture of the movement and to contribute to further discussions on group identity and group interests in society and on social movements in general. Without a clear idea of the students' group identity, the conclusion on the students' role in the 1989 social movement can easily end up in either extreme as discussed above.

First, consideration will be given to the position of university students in the Chinese social structure in order to assess their role in Chinese society. Second, the impact of the economic reform process on university students will be discussed, and third, the analysis will focus on how the students mobilized, and will examine their concrete demands and how these were presented.

THE UNIVERSITY STUDENTS

In the 1980s, university students enjoyed significant material advantages compared to ordinary workers. Students received special treatment: the entire system of university education was free of charge, including tuition and housing. Some students even received monthly allowances from their universities. They were also promised an assigned job by the government after graduation. They did not have to deal with complicated problems like family, housing or promotion. In other words, everything was taken care of except the studies. Students were expected to devote themselves entirely to their studies and to be 'useful' to the country when they graduated.

Unlike typical state employees, university students did not belong to any work units (*danwei*). A *danwei*, or workplace, functions as an employer and also provides social services for its employees. The social services cover almost every aspect of life: as the Chinese say *sheng, lao, bing, ci* (life, retirement, sickness and death): birth, sickness, kindergarten, education, transportation, housing, medical services, pension, recreation and even family disputes. The relationship between the employer and employees can therefore become very complicated because of its multiple functions. Leaders of a 'danwei' are very powerful because they oversee not only work but also the distribution of social services to the employees. An employee has a close relationship with his 'danwei' as his work and life depend on it.

University students were usually considered as a part of the intellectual group.[2] But in terms of 'danwei', they were different. Because 'danwei' was significant for a person's work and life in China, 'danwei' members were potentially more powerful than persons who did not belong to a 'danwei', because those in 'danwei' had direct access to state property. The role and leverage of university students in society was even less because they did not have their own independent organizations. On the other hand, penalties for unacceptable behaviour were usually less severe for students than for a person who belonged to a 'danwei'. In other words, a student had much less to lose compared with a state employee from involvement in disapproved political activities.

A good example concerns the journalists during the 1989 protest. Journalists were state employees with a 'danwei': that is *People's Daily* or *Guangming Daily*. They had direct access to state-owned media equipment and other resources. Under the strict state control over the media through censorship, they could not work as independent journalists. They incurred a high risk of being punished if they did so. In May 1989 the journalists organized themselves in protest and began to report objectively on the movement. This was possible because of slacker control, which in turn resulted from the split within the top Party leadership and support from colleagues from the West. This resulted in a 'free press' during two weeks, which had been unknown to the Chinese for decades. But the media workers were also the first target of sanctions.

The university students had no independent organizations of their own that represented solely their interests and helped channel their grievances. Instead, the Communist Youth League, operating among the students, oversaw students' behaviour and made sure that the students were politically 'healthy'. Official student unions concentrated on organizing such activities as sport events, ceremonies commemorating historical events and propaganda campaigns. The official student unions were severely criticized at the beginning of the movement and the student activists started their own organizations very early.[3]

UNIVERSITY STUDENTS AND THE REFORM

The decision of developing 'key universities', with admission only by rigorous competitive examinations, marked a major institutional change in Chinese education, the first since the Cultural Revolution. At a National Science Conference in March 1978, a modernization plan gained momentum and it was later ratified at the well known Third Plenum of the Eleventh Central Committee of the Party later the same year. This was regarded as the starting point of the present university reform. In the plan, the development of key universities was incorporated in the overall plan for developing energy resources, computer, laser and space technology, high energy physics and genetics, which needed science and technology personnel most.

In the 1970s the selection of university students was based on political criteria such as class and family background. The emphasis on proletarian rule in society during the Cultural Revolution led to admission of university students only from among the 'politically correct' classes, workers, peasants and soldiers or those whose families were also from these classes. Individuals from other classes were not eligible. The new policy, in contrast, emphasized one's ability and willingness to learn. Since educational resources, including facilities, teaching staff and budgets were limited, due to the tremendous damage to the universities during the Cultural Revolution, competition for admission was fierce. Competitiveness rather than political loyalty became the basic principle of admission and the character of the student body changed, although Chinese Communist Party history and Marxist political economy remained required courses.

Years of political campaigns and class struggle became almost a way of life for the population. Many of the new students grew up in families where their grandparents might have been persecuted during the 1950s, or their parents persecuted during the 1960s and 1970s; and they had seen or heard as teenagers about their uncles or aunts, friends or neighbours who shared this same fate. Many Red Guards, active when they were 16 or 17, had missed their education during the Cultural Revolution and therefore had fewer opportunities later (Li 1990: chs 1–3). Compared with all these, the university students in the 1980s did not suffer much. Depoliticiza-tion of life, increased autonomy from direct Party control, and the opening towards the outside world created conditions for the students which previous generations could not dream of.[4]

University students closely followed the ongoing economic and political reforms because they were concerned with their own future. The economic reform programme emerged from the central planning system. This programme and decentralization of economic decision-making and power created a multitude of new power foci charged with administering investment and the allocation of resour-ces. The size of the cadre corps increased drastically, although the Party attempted to streamline the bureaucracy.[5]

Special privileges enjoyed by Party and government officials, such as spacious apartments for themselves and for their children, personal drivers, access to foreign currency for purchasing imported goods and so on were widely known among the people under the central planning system before the reform started. In the course of implementing the new programme, while keeping the old privileges intact to a large extent, a dual price system was introduced. This created new opportunities for official profiteering which became so rampant that a new term was created: *guandao*, which means 'officials engaging in trading at a profit'.

Corruption was not limited to the high ranking and middle level officials. It was widespread in 'danwei', such as factories (Walder 1991: 479–83). The legal system was unable to curb these problems and the corrupt officials could continue to ' "fish" for private (or local) gains using public "fishing equipment" without being moni-tored by the public' (Yu 1990: 35).

In 1980, Deng Xiaoping called for political reform but stressed that political reform was meant to strengthen, not weaken, the Party leadership (Deng 1984). The Four Cardinal Principles (adherence to the socialist path, upholding the leadership of the Communist Party, upholding Marxism-Leninism-Mao Zedong Thoughts, and the people's democratic dictatorship) became the golden rules. Ever since they were introduced, these principles had become instruments for restricting free debates on socialism, Marxism and the Party leadership. Initiatives towards a free press and free associations depended on the tolerance level of the central authorities. The Campaign against Spiritual Pollution (1983) and the Campaign against Bourgeois Liberalization (1987), purges against some liberal intellectuals and the forced resignation of the former Party Secretary-General Hu Yaobang indicated the narrow limits of the Party's pledge to political reform. Student activism was also carefully monitored by the school authorities.

Towards the end of the 1980s, the economic reform had come under severe strain. The inflation rate was rising fast. The serious corruption was seen by the students as a result of the reluctance to introduce political change. Further, students could not be sure of getting jobs they were interested in. This uncertainty was especially widespread among those who studied social sciences, humanities and management. They risked coming to a 'danwei' where most of the employees were more concerned about housing, bonus and personal connections rather than professional expertise. This uncertain future, together with worsening living conditions on campus and restrictions of student activities, combined to make many students apathetic.

A few students, however, decided to face reality by actively involving themselves in pushing the reform forward, believing that the solution was further reform. Intellectuals across the country were organizing unofficial discussion clubs, founding new journals, expanding contacts with Chinese outside the country and participating in international scholarly and cultural exchanges. The student activists closely followed these events and organized their own clubs and started their own journals.[6] Wang Dan, who became the most prominent student leader in the 1989 movement, organized one of the 'democracy clubs' at his university, where students gathered to discuss topics such as democratic reform and individual freedom. In Beijing University alone, there were 13 similar clubs. On 3 April 1989, together with 54 other students, Wang Dan petitioned the university leaders for open dialogue and greater democracy on campus (Han Minzhu 1990: 16–19).

STUDENT DEMANDS

The students' ideas about democracy and their understanding of China's need for reform were put to the test between April and June 1989. Mass protests were triggered by several interacting factors. One was the general international trend towards political pluralism and economic privatization. This contrasted with the centralized political power system at home. Ups and downs in the economic reform and widespread dissatisfaction about corruption and lack of freedom also contributed, as did several important anniversaries in 1989 that could be linked to the theme of democracy and the death of a popular leader, Hu Yaobang.

The students took the lead in the protests. However, the favourable conditions did not reduce the complexity of the students' task. Lack of experience in working for democracy and resistance from the authorities made the risk of failure high. To increase the probability of success, the students needed support from a broad spectrum of the population, including sympathy from within the Party.

The student movement took several forms: petitions, demonstrations, class boycotts, attempts at dialogue with the government, a hunger strike and efforts towards the legitimization of their independent organizations, all based on the principle of non-violence. Petitions, demonstrations and class boycotts were based on the students' understanding of individual rights. Direct dialogue with the government was a much more radical act, since it challenged the authorities to discuss on equal terms and was the first step towards legitimization of the independent student organizations. This could have chain effects among other social groups and could be the first step to political pluralism. The hunger strike was the direct result of the failure to develop this dialogue and brought the whole movement to a higher stage. The hunger strike succeeded in raising the consciousness of the people and won unprecedented popular support.

The independent student organizations went through turbulent periods throughout the movement. They suffered many setbacks because of lack of leadership, lack of theory and lack of coordination with other social groups as well as lack of democratic spirit. But the very existence of these independent organizations was significant for the movement.

Petition, Class Boycott and Demonstrations

The first demands the student activists tried to deliver to the government at a very early stage of their protest were as follows:

- Re-evaluate Hu Yaobang and his achievements.
- Renounce the Campaign against Bourgeois Liberalization and the Campaign against Spiritual Pollution.
- Allow citizens to publish non-official newspapers and stop censorship of the press.
- Reveal the salaries and other wealth of Party and government leaders and their families.
- Rescind the Beijing municipal government's 'Ten Provisional Articles Regulating Public Marches and Demonstrations'.
- Increase state expenditure for higher education.
- Provide objective news coverage of the students' demonstrations.

The message was to demand freedom of speech, freedom of press, fight against corruption and for more funds for education. The demands reflected students' grievances and their desire for political change. To their frustration and anger, they were directed to submit their petition to a clerk and their request for a dialogue with the government got no response. At the same time, there were beating incidents both in Beijing and Xian during the student protest. The students blamed police for the violence. A few days later, in a dramatic gesture, three of the student representatives knelt for 45 minutes in front of the People's Great Hall, the government's working and meeting building, carrying the scroll which contained their petitions. No one came out to receive them. The government's apparent indifference and the students' patience generated further support from other sectors of society (Han Minzhu 1990: ch. 1).

The students in Beijing began to establish independent student organizations in order to carry on with the protest. They declared a city-wide class boycott of indefinite duration to protest against the beating incidents, the government's failure to reply to their petition, and the distorted press coverage of their protest. This was followed by the launching of student newspapers. The government responded by cutting phone and telex lines that transmitted protesters' messages, closing down a pro-democracy newspaper based in Shanghai and firing its chief editor. On 26 April 1989, the *People's Daily* (the Party's newspaper) carried an editorial denouncing the students' actions.

If the editorial was intended to cow the students and their supporters, the effect was just the opposite. On 27 April a million people demonstrated in the capital. The students organized the demonstration under their newly established joint university organization. The students impressed the city's population by maintaining strict discipline within their ranks and avoiding violence. Their intention was clear: to press for their demands using only peaceful means. They also regarded social stability as a precondition for a smooth reform process. After the demonstration, many students went back to resume their studies and the student leaders argued over what to do next.

Dialogue and Hunger Strike

The student activists kept seeking direct dialogue with the government about their demands, while the government stalled. Dialogue with an unofficial organization could not be accepted by the government, because the top leaders were aware of the encouraging effect this would have on other social groups. However, in order to appear to accommodate the students' request, the government organized a meeting with the student's representatives, mostly from the official student unions, on April 29 and 30, but to the dismay of student activists and their supporters, this produced few meaningful results.

Outraged by the government's 'insincerity', the student activists began to pursue a 'meaningful dialogue' on condition of selecting their own representatives. On 5 May, the students submitted a new petition, but it was not until 12 May that the government replied that 'an informal meeting' (and not a dialogue) would be held on two conditions: only controlled news reporting would be permitted and the students would have to provide a list of their representatives to the government before the meeting.

The government's response divided the already highly heterogenous student leadership. The more radical student activists, always sceptical of the government's sincerity, began to prevail. A hunger strike started on 13 May to urge an immediate dialogue and recognition of the independent student organization (Han Minzhu 1990: 193).

Organization

After the memorial service for Hu Yaobang, the student activists in Beijing took a major step in establishing their own independent organizations. On 23 April the Provisional Student Federation of Capital Universities and Colleges was established, representing 40 universities and institutes. This joint organization played a crucial role in organizing the events that followed, in coordination with similar organizations in other cities. It attracted support from home and abroad and negotiated with the government for an open dialogue and recognition of the organization.

The federation was born with problems, however. First, it was a joint organization with representatives from each participating university or institute, selected without proper election procedures. Later events showed that the student participants were much more inclined to follow the leaders of their own universities than the leadership of the joint organization. If some university representatives did not agree with decisions made by the federation, all the student participants under their direct leadership withdrew from action. For example, after the 4 May demonstration, many students returned to campus to resume classes. Yet the decision to end the class boycott created controversy, which ended in another change of leadership. Beijing University and Beijing Normal University refused to end the class boycott, arguing that it was important to keep up pressure on the government.

Second, the leadership changed frequently due to differences in approach. The main controversy was between the moderate and the radical factions. When Beijing University and Beijing Normal University leaders refused to end the class boycott on 4 May, they were outnumbered by more moderate leaders who felt that further disruption of their studies was counterproductive and unnecessary. More importantly, the situation at the time favoured the moderate group. However, at receiving the government's delayed response to the students' request for a meaningful dialogue, the radical student leaders started a hunger strike that the moderate group was forced to accept. After martial law was enforced, the independent student organizations began to fall apart. The joint student organization, already overshadowed during the hunger strike, therefore held limited sway over the students from the provinces who occupied Tiananmen Square.

CONCLUDING REMARKS

University students in the 1980s were privileged because of their small number and their paid education. They were free from many problems of life and work that state employees faced. The students, therefore, had personally much less to lose by engaging themselves in social protest movements. They could also be mobilized quickly in large numbers. On the other hand, the students' leverage was relatively weak because they did not belong to any 'danwei' which had direct access to state resources. In contrast, the journalists who organized to protest in 1989 were much more effective in their actions, by making use of their access to state resources.

University students were direct beneficiaries of the new university reform. A new 'entrance examination' system gave all eligible young persons relatively equal access to higher education. The open-door policy provided them with more knowledge about advanced science and technology as well as about Western liberal ideology and value systems.

The economic and political reforms in the 1980s ran into problems that were partly attributed to rampant official corruption. Widespread dissatisfaction among the population also affected some students who did not see a future in further education and work in 'danwei'. They prepared themselves for leaving the country or killed time by idling. But other students felt that the solution to the problems lay in further reform and active personal involvement in the reform process.

The sudden death of a popular leader, combined with serious problems in the implementation of economic reform programme in the late 1980s triggered massive social protest from April to June 1989. The university students took the lead in demanding a free press and the right of free association. Two concrete steps taken by the students were significant in terms of challenging the existing social and political structure: seeking a dialogue with the government on equal terms and seeking legitimization of the students' independent organizations. The students' organizations, however, were constrained partly due to constant internal fights among the student leaders.

None of the students' demands was accepted. Their organizations fell apart after the government declared martial law. After 4 June, many student activists were arrested or went into exile. The economic reform process, however, continued. The open-door policy was not reversed. Hence, the Party-state as well as the entire population still face the same problems which the student activists addressed in 1989.

References

Deng Xiaoping (1984), 'On the Reform of the System of Party and State Leadership', in *Selected Works of Deng Xiaoping (1975–1982)* (Beijing: Beijing Foreign Languages Press), pp. 302–25.

Diamond, L., J.J. Linz and S.M. Lipset (eds) (1989), *Democracy in Developing Countries – Latin America*, Vol. IV (Boulder, Col.: Lynne Rienner).

Gold, T. B. (1991), 'Youth and the State', *The China Quarterly*, No. 127 (September), pp. 595–612.

Han Minzhu (1990), *Cries for Democracy* (Princeton, NJ: Princeton University Press).

Lee, H.Y. (1992), 'China's New Bureaucracy?', in A. L. Rosenbaum (ed.), *State and Society in China: The Consequences of Reform* (Boulder, Col.: Westview).

Li, L. (1990), *Moving the Mountain: From the Cultural Revolution to Tiananmen Square* (London: Pan).

Szabó, M. (1991), 'Changing Patterns of Mobilization in Hungary within New Social Movements: the Case of the Ecology and the Student Movements', in G. Szoboszlai (ed.), *Democracy and Political Transformation* (Budapest: Hungarian Political Science Association).

Walder, A.G. (1991), 'Workers, Managers and the State: the Reform Era and the Political Crisis of 1989', *The China Quarterly*, No. 127 (September), pp. 467–92.

Walder, A. G. and Gong Xiaoxia (1993), 'Workers in the Tainanmen Protests: the Politics of the Beijing Workers' Autonomous Federation', *The Australian Journal of Chinese Affairs*, No. 29 (January), pp. 1–29.

Yu, B. (1990), 'China in 1989: A Distorted Authoritarian State in Crisis', in J. Hao (ed.), *The Democracy Movement of 1989 and China's Future* (Washington, DC: The Washington Center for China Studies).

Notes

1. Overlooking distinctions of this kind tends to lead to misconceptions of the roles of particular groups in social movements (Diamond, Linz and Lipset 1989: pp. xii–xviii).

2. Since the overall level of education is low and few people receive higher education, the intellectuals are a very small group in China. Traditionally, Chinese intellectuals served as scholar-officials whose duty was to counsel authorities or, when need be, to remonstrate with those in power. Therefore they are inclined to view themselves as an enlightened class, an elite.

3. See 'Down with Student Bureaucrats' in Han Minzhu (1990), pp. 69–70.

4. They roughly fit 'the 1970s Reform Cohort' in Thomas Gold's cohort analysis. See Gold (1991), pp. 607–8.

5. According to Hong Yung Lee, the overall size of the cadre corps increased from 21 million in 1983 to 29 million by 1988. See Lee (1992), p. 60. A student noted in *News Herald*, No. 2/4 (May 1989) that 'during the decade from 1978 to 1987, the administrative outlays doubled, as did the number of administrative personnel' (Han Minzhu 1990: 33).

6. During the same period in Eastern Europe, students organized themselves similarly (Szabó 1991).

11 Constructing Civil Society: Election Watch Movements in the Philippines

Eva-Lotta E. Hedman[1]

'Protect the Ballot and Save the Nation'
— (National Movement for Free Elections 1953 slogan)

At three critical junctures before the recent restoration of formal democratic institutions and procedures under President Corazon Aquino (1986–92), Philippine presidential elections have seen the emergence of national campaigns for 'free and clean elections'. In each case, an ostensibly non-partisan, cross-class movement in the spirit of non-violence, citizenship and voluntarism took on the 'guns, goons and gold' long associated with Philippine electoral politics. Thousands participated in these organized efforts to check voters' registration lists, train pollwatchers, hold parallel vote counts, give voters' education seminars, host bi-partisan candidate fora, and challenge and document fraud and violence that interfered with voting and canvassing. In terms of social base, these electoral-reform campaigns counted among their ranks businessmen and women, religious and secular clergy, members of parish and civic organizations, student and professional associations, veterans' leagues and trade unions.

In their reformist orientation, citizenship-based appeal and broad social composition, Philippine election watch movements thus appear analogous to the 'resurrection of civil society' observed in transitions from authoritarian rule in Latin America and (former) Eastern Europe. Students of Latin America, for example, have emphasized the 'initiatives for change . . . from within civil society' (Stepan 1985: 316). The role of 'religious groups, intellectuals, artists, clergymen, defenders of human rights, and professional associations' in political reform and liberalization processes under

210

military bureaucratic-authoritarian regimes has also been noted (O'Donnell and Schmitter 1986: 54). In Eastern Europe, analysts have likewise interpreted the organization and eventual mobilization of workers, students, intellectuals, religious and human rights activists under state socialism as efforts towards 'the reconstitution of civil society through the rule of law and the guarantee of civil rights, a free public sphere and a plurality of independent associations' (Arato 1981: 23).

A growing body of literature has focused more explicit attention on the nature and role of 'civil society' as the concept itself has gained renewed currency in the social sciences. What appears to be the 'dominant paradigm' within this emerging field essentially assumes that a 'pluralist and self-organizing civil society independent of the state is an indispensable condition of democracy' (Keane 1988: 51). This tendency to identify democracy with a plurality of intermediary groups and networks parallels a view of democratization processes as the proliferation of such interactions and institutions within society (Cohen and Arato 1994; Gibbon, Chapter 5 in this volume).

While a welcome departure from overly deterministic structural perspectives, recent writings on civil society and its putative role for democracy tend towards both reification and voluntarism. For example, such formulations of 'civil society' and 'democratization' tend to obscure the extent to which these spheres and processes are embedded in larger social contexts, as well as defined by more narrowly construed political interests. That is, the significance of underlying socio-economic conditions and the effects of state institutions and policies upon secondary associations and networks suggests that domination and contestation, rather than 'self-organizing' citizens and 'self- limiting' solidarities, characterize what is commonly referred to as the 'sphere of civil society' (Skocpol 1985: 21). Moreover, the actual processes by which this sphere becomes politically relevant, or by which certain social groups – but not others – can successfully mobilize 'in the name of civil society' at discrete historical junctures, suggest that conflict and exclusion, rather than harmonious differentiation and all-inclusive pluralism, decisively shape the nature and direction of 'civil society' (Cohen and Arato 1994).

This chapter contributes to contemporary theorizing about civil society and its putative democratizing role by examining three cases of so-called 'national citizens movements' for free and clean elections in the post-war Philippines. Drawing on existing social movements scholarship, the analysis below identifies a set of changing political conditions which favoured a resurrection of 'civil society' and thus, much like studies debunking 'mass society' explanations for collective action, draws attention to the significance of social resources, organizations and networks for successful mobilization (McCarthy and Zald 1977). In this vein, this chapter takes as its point of departure a political process framework (Tilly 1978; Tarrow 1983) for explaining the timing and trajectory of 'civil society's' mobilization in three cases in the Philippines: the National Movement for Free Elections (NAMFREL) in 1953, the Citizens Electoral Assembly in 1969 and the National Citizens Movement for Free Elections in 1986.

THREE CRISES OF PHILIPPINE ELECTORALISM

Prior to the restoration of formally democratic institutions and procedures that followed upon the much celebrated 'People Power' revolt which ousted Marcos in February 1986, collective efforts at mobilizing support and resources for electoral reforms accompanied the 1953, 1969 and 1986 Philippine presidential elections. In each case, these self-proclaimed citizen campaigns targeted an incumbent seeking reelection, who was widely viewed as corrupt and authoritarian and, thus, as a threat to the 'future of democracy in the Philippines'. In addition, however, these campaigns also emerged against the backdrop of surfacing participatory crises and extra-electoral mobilization of previously unincorporated social groups. Significantly, each such effort originated in a crisis that threatened to undermine both the political hegemony of the dominant class and the process of capital accumulation. That is, the 1953, 1969 and 1986 presidential elections saw the organization of clean-election campaigns as a reaction to mounting political pressures from both above (in the form of a visibly anti-democratic incumbent seeking reelection) and below (in the shape of extra-electoral mobilization by previously unincorporated social groups). In combination, these political developments comprised the necessary – if not sufficient – conditions for the emergence of mobilization efforts to reform and legitimize the electoral process in the early 1950s, late 1960s, and mid-1980s.

The candidacy of a manifestly anti-democratic incumbent in the presidential elections of 1953, 1969 and 1986 led to anticipations of massive electoral fraud in these three elections. While other incumbents also used pork barrel, constabulary intervention, electoral fraud, and other dirty tricks in their bids for reelection, the aggregation of political powers and economic control under Presidents Quirino and Marcos signalled a qualitative departure from the politics of elite contestation under Philippine electoralism (Coquia 1955: 100–56; Hartendorp 1958: 281–304). Thus, Quirino's and Marcos's unprecedented efforts at expanding the powers of an already strong executive branch in the years leading up to the 1953 and 1969 elections, respectively, threatened to undermine the political hegemony of the dominant class and the process of capital accumulation (Golay 1961: 58–89, Doronila 1992: 123–49). Despite the official lifting of martial law in 1981, moreover, Marcos, backed by his military and business cronies, continued ruling by presidential decree and plundering the Philippine economy until the 1986 elections (Manapat 1991).

The ambitious reelection schemes of Quirino and Marcos – as evidenced by their unprecedented muscling of executive powers against both political opponents and the legislature as an institution – thus threatened to perpetuate the rule of a president whose authoritarian and patrimonial tendencies encroached upon the privileges of the oligarchy and undermined the process of capital accumulation in the Philippines. In this context, the electoral-reform campaigns raised the costs of engaging in 'systemic and systematic' fraud and violence (Tancangco 1992), ostensibly to all candidates but with particular relevance for the incumbent given his vast powers over political, economic and coercive resources. While the mounting patrimonial and praetorian proclivities of the presidential incumbent thus provided a conspicuous *raison d'être* for Philippine election watch movements in 1953, 1969 and 1986, these mobilization campaigns also served to mitigate long-term problems of political incorporation and to neutralize short-term extra-electoral challenges. The rumblings of latent participatory crises in the early 1950s, late 1960s and mid–1980s constituted a perhaps less obvious but equally important backdrop to the electoral-reform campaigns that appeared against Quirino's and Marcos's bids for reelection. Each of these elections saw the emergence of previously excluded social sectors – peasants, students and workers, and urban middle-class elements – acting collectively to press their political demands. Significantly, extra-electoral mobilization and election-boycott campaigns organized by an underground Left also targeted each of these three presidential contests.

The introduction of universal suffrage with independence in 1946 presaged the emergence of a serious participatory crisis in the Philippines in the early 1950s (Anderson 1993). This expansion of the political franchise took place within a social context characterized by a deepening 'disintegration of the traditional landlord-tenant relationship' due primarily to the ongoing commercialization of agriculture (Kerkvliet 1977: 249). The Second World War had also 'temporarily but severely weakened the gravitational pulls of the old Philippine institutional structure' and, as a consequence, many 'pre-war vertical ties between gentry patrons and their peasant clients had become unstuck during the occupation' (Edgerton 1975: 3 and 19).

The expansion of formal political participation and the dislodging of traditional patron-client ties thus presented the Philippine elite with a dual dilemma stemming from the need to incorporate peasants into electoral factions while preventing such institutions from serving as vehicles for popular collective mobilization. After the 1946 congressional elections, six elected candidates closely identified with peasant organizations and guerrilla networks in the rice-bowl region of Central Luzon – and enjoying the support of the Partido Komunista ng Pilipinas (PKP) and the Civil Liberties Union – were barred from ever taking their respective seats. Candidates supported by peasant organizations in Central Luzon also faced massive fraud and rampant violence in the 1947 local and 1949 national elections (Kerkvliet 1977: 173–4 and 205–11). In a related development, the extra-electoral mobilization of peasant guerrillas, known as Huks, supported by the PKP after 1948, gained in organizational strength and size between 1946 and 1948 throughout four provinces near Manila that became known as 'Huklandia' (Kerkvliet 1977: 174–202). By 1950, the Huks had expanded their areas of control to include all of Central Luzon and large parts of Southern Luzon (that is, the environs of the national capital: Kerkvliet 1977: 235). In a reversal of its legal struggle strategy, the PKP, having declared a 'revolutionary situation' in the aftermath of the 1949 presidential contest, called for a boycott of the 1951 senatorial elections to 'make the masses realize the necessity, the absolute necessity of revolution . . . [and to] complete the people's disillusionment regarding the elections' (Kerkvliet 1977: 237). According to Kerkvliet, '[m]any Huk leaders in the field

commands and Recos [regional commands] urged boycott, too'
(1977).

In the 1960s, continued economic differentiation and rapid urbanization prefigured a second major participatory crisis in the
Philippines, as the socio-demographic terrain changed to include
both an increasing segment of 'economically insecure clients' and,
in absolute terms, a growing urban middle class (Nowak and
Snyder 1974a: 1151). These developments, scholars have argued,
signalled an overall decline in the 'integrative capacity of political
machines' (Nowak and Snyder 1974a: 1165) because of the mounting costs of 'particularistic rewards' (Scott 1969: 1144) and weakening client leverage due to the 'specialization in clientelist structures'
(Nowak and Snyder 1974a: 1152).

As existing mechanisms for political incorporation appeared
increasingly inadequate, embryonic efforts at channelling social
mobilization into alternative institutions emerged in the 1960s. For
example, 1963 and 1964 saw the organization of a workers' party
supported by national labour federations, a peasant association
backed by former Huks, and a student movement endorsed by
radical nationalists, all three of which were identified with prominent Filipino socialists or communists.[2] As the 'increased vocality
of a radical intelligentsia in the 1960s helped politicize worker and
peasant discontent' (Nowak and Snyder 1974b: 154), these sectors
began mobilizing demonstrations, launching strikes and battling
court cases. The late 1960s also saw the addition of organized
political action aimed more explicitly against the forces of 'law and
order'. In this vein, the resurgence of the Huks in Central Luzon,
the founding of the Communist Party of the Philippines (CPP) and
its New People's Army (NPA: Jones 1989: 17–38), and the declaration of the Muslim Independence Movement (George 1980: 131–42;
Che Man 1990: 77–81), all signified different extra-parliamentary
approaches to the unresolved problem of wanting political integration. Finally, as the Philippines experienced rising 'violent and mass
urban activities, precisely during the period when turnout declined'
(Nowak and Snyder 1974a: 1169), calls for organized election
boycotts emanated from within the country's single most important
national institution for higher education, strategically located in the
capital city: the University of the Philippines, Diliman. Through the
Philippine Collegian, the official voice of the University of the
Philippines student body, and through reprints in national dailies
and weeklies, election boycott advocates on campus articulated

their opposition to voting in the 1967 and 1969 elections (Makabenta 1967).

This escalating participatory crisis was staved off but not resolved by Marcos's declaration of martial law, abolition of Congress and installation of so-called 'constitutional authoritarianism' in 1972 (Rosenberg 1979). In fact, continuing industrialization and increasing social inequalities in the 1970s contributed to undermining the regime's integrative capacity over time (Boyce 1993). In the 1980s, moreover, as a world recession exposed the limits to 'crony capitalism', Marcos's political coalition unravelled (Hawes 1987). While a papal visit in 1981 prompted the official lifting of martial law, Marcos's continued rule by presidential decree failed to accommodate the mounting demands for political representation voiced in the 'parliament of the streets' of the 1980s.

The most organized and sustained extra-electoral opposition to the dictatorship, the NPA, first experienced growth in the hinterlands before eventually expanding to areas surrounding towns and cities in the early 1980s. During the two final years of the Marcos regime the NPA reportedly doubled its forces and extended its influence to cover an estimated 20 per cent of all Philippine villages (Lawyers' Committee For Human Rights 1988: 3). In addition to the guerrilla war, and partly reflecting the CPP's new united front initiative (Jones 1989: 146), the Philippines also saw the resurgence of urban mass political action in the 1980s. The formation of a radical inter-university student organization, a militant labour union, and a national democratic peasant alliance, for example, reintroduced student protests, labour strikes and peasant demonstrations to the scene of Philippine politics.[3] Marcos's so-called 'demonstration elections' also met with organized boycotts successfully promoted by the CPP in the years leading up to the 1986 presidential contest. In the 1984 elections to the National Assembly, moreover, the CPP-led boycott also succeeded in mobilizing the support of more mainstream social groups and political organizations. Finally, as the CPP's Executive Committee ordered an election boycott of the 1986 snap elections, its affiliate labour and student organizations, as well as the united front's national council, 'formally approved an active boycott position' (Jones 1989: 158).

Although the participatory crises discussed above manifested important differences in terms of their respective historical origins and political magnitude, they presented challenges of a similar kind in the 1953, 1969 and 1986 elections. In all these cases, election watch movements emerged when the policies of an authoritarian incumbent and the extra-electoral mobilization of previously unincorporated social groups threatened both the political hegemony of the ruling class and the process of capital accumulation itself. These movements thus mobilized not merely in support of democracy but also in opposition to extra-electoral challenges directed against both the incumbent regime and the ruling class. While mobilizing in the name of 'civil society', Philippine election watch campaigns thus emerged in a process of political contestation and conflict and at the expense of more radical demands for social change and democratization.[4]

THE CITIZEN

Against the backdrop of these deepening participatory crises and attempts to prolong presidential rule by unconstitutional means, a proliferation of civic and lay organizations marshalled their respective networks to champion collective campaigns for reform in the electoral process. In 1953, for example, NAMFREL drew support for its high-profile campaign from Second World War veteran and anti-communist leagues, civil liberties and Catholic action groups, as well as professional and student associations (Coquia 1955: 282–311). Volunteers with such affiliations provided critical backing for NAMFREL by organizing and participating in activities ranging from civic-consciousness caucuses and clean-election rallies to voter-registration drives and election-watch vigils during the 1953 presidential contest.[5]

The 1969 presidential elections, moreover, saw Catholic (and, to a lesser extent, Protestant) lay organizations, professional and student associations supply the Citizen National Electoral Assembly (CNEA) with resources and networks linking them up with cities and towns beyond Manila's orbit (Tutay 1969a: 10–11). While rural – and mostly poor – people still made up more than two-thirds of the total population, socio-economic development and demographic change nevertheless saw the emergence of a nascent middle-class sector and a concomitant increase in voluntary association membership, reflected in part in CNEA's national network. In the case of the actual ballot-watching, for example, college students from private – and especially sectarian – schools served as volunteer poll-watchers in the national capital region, as well as in some provincial cities and towns. As regards the vote-count effort, moreover, Philippine media associations provided the infrastructure for speedy transmission of vote returns under the framework of 'Operation Quick Count '69' (Tutay 1969b: 10–19).

The 1986 presidential elections, finally, occasioned the mobilization of more than half a million NAMFREL volunteers who collectively guarded the ballot in the name of the *Bantay ng Bayan* – 'Watchdog of the Nation' – at precincts throughout the Philippines (NAMFREL 1987; Byington 1988). These volunteers participated in nationwide efforts to check the voters' registration lists, train pollwatchers, organize NAMFREL vote counts, hold voters' education seminars, host bi-partisan candidate fora, and challenge and document fraud and violence which interfered with voting and/or canvassing. With two-thirds of the country's urban population (42 per cent) living outside the national capital region, which covered some 7 million inhabitants, NAMFREL's 1986 mobilizing effort benefited from the expansion of tertiary educational institutions and a multitude of professional, civic and religious associations with links throughout the Philippines. For example, students at colleges and universities run by Jesuits and other religious orders and members of amateur radio clubs, certified public accountant and lawyers associations, and Catholic lay organizations (such as the Legion of Mary, Catholic Women's League, Knights of Columbus, and Charismatic Cursillistas) manned precincts and served as volunteers on special task force teams in 'hot spot' areas in various parts of the country.

THE 'COMPANY', THE CHURCH, AND THE CHAMBER

While the much publicized role of these so-called 'intermediary associations' in the 1953, 1969 and 1986 electoral-reform campaigns seemingly validated the universal, apolitical and non-hierarchical official identity of the two NAMFRELs and of CNEA – aptly reflected in their emphasis on both the 'national' and the 'citizen' – the nature of their involvement underscored the importance of powerful institutional and class interests in these movements. In fact, a high degree of social embeddedness – rather than 'intermediate autonomy' – characterized these civic and lay associations and, significantly, conditioned their support for Philippine election watch campaigns. For example, the prominent backing of Philippine Second World War veterans associations for NAMFREL in 1953 resulted largely from the close ties such organizations maintained with the US government, the main source of all veterans' benefits. The enthusiastic support by many Catholic school students and seminarians for CNEA, moreover, reflected in large part the official position of both the secular and religious clergy, who publicly endorsed and actively advanced the 1969 electoral-reform campaign. Finally, the decisive intervention by professional associations of lawyers, accountants and communications experts, and by civic organizations like the Jaycees, Lions and Rotary in NAMFREL's 1986 campaign, followed the lead of national 'captains of industry' and major provincial business interests.

Overall, the composition, resource-flow and diffusion of the two NAMFRELs and CNEA further indicated the extent to which involvement by 'civic volunteers' was conditioned by these 'professional political and ideological intermediaries' (Gramsci 1971: 286). First of all, these campaigns typically manifested an organizational hierarchy which placed executives, clergymen and other prominent figures in leadership positions while their respective employee, student and plain-folk 'clients' filled the ranks of these movements. Moreover, the transportation costs, food expenses and insurance policies provided to many participants in these mobilizing efforts rested on an essentially top-down resource flow of American, Church and big business benefactions. Finally, the overall diffusion pattern of these organizational efforts – originating in the national capital and radiating out from major cities to provincial towns – closely paralleled pre-existing socially embedded institutional networks.

Overall, the involvement of dominant institutional and class interests determined the mobilizing scope and intensity of these three election watch campaigns. The support of the same key institutional and class interests – the US government, the Catholic Church and the business elite – for a charismatic reform-oriented opposition candidate to replace the discredited authoritarian incumbent and, thus, to restore political stability, further shaped the 1953 and 1986 electoral-reform campaigns. Circumventing traditional party machines by means of mass mobilizations and reformist appeals, the 1953 Magsaysay for President Movement and the 1986 Cory Aquino for President Movement drummed up widespread popular support for famed Huk fighter Ramon Magsaysay and martyr's widow Corazon Aquino, respectively (Thompson

1988). Prevailing anticipations of massive electoral fraud and violence by presidents Quirino and Marcos, however, underlined the need for mechanisms to counter the incumbent administrations' vote-producing machinery. In the 1969 election, by contrast, it was (the then quite respected) Marcos who most successfully bypassed elected officials at the municipal and provincial levels in order to mobilize direct support at the *barangay* level, while his sole opponent, a long-time machine politician, hardly captured the imagination of those clamouring for change (Mojares 1985, Rafael 1990: 282–384). Under these circumstances, the 1969 presidential election presented the hegemonic bloc with less of an opportunity for political re-equilibration by means of electoral reformism than the contests of 1953 and 1986.

US GOVERNMENT INTERVENTION

Activities that effectively amounted to foreign intervention aided the mobilization of the two NAMFRELs in significant (albeit different) ways in the 1953 and 1986 presidential elections. The critical role of the US Central Intelligence Agency (CIA) in promoting the first NAMFREL is widely recognized (for example, Abueva 1959: 100–8; Currey 1988: 126–30). Moreover, the second NAMFREL – contrary to repeated refutations by its leadership – also received substantial support from foreign sources (Bonner 1987: 408–9).

The US government, in fact, played a pivotal part in introducing electoral-reform campaigns on to the scene of Philippine electoral politics in the early 1950s. As the 'loss' of China and the outbreak of the Korean War signalled the coming of the Cold War to the region, the USA was anxious to safeguard Asia's 'showcase of democracy' against challenges from both the local peasant-based insurgency and the incumbent presidency in the years leading up to the 1953 Philippine presidential elections (Berry 1967; Gaddis 1982). US foreign policy toward its former colony in the early 1950s thus involved extensive counterinsurgency measures, economic development assistance programmes, and pressures for reformist legislation (Golay 1966), as well as blueprints for building a nationwide election watch movement for the 1951, and, more importantly, the 1953 presidential elections.

While the CIA assisted in organizing support and procuring

resources for the first incarnation of NAMFREL, the US government publicly signalled its approval for this effort. The US Embassy and the Joint US Military Assistance Group (JUSMAG) in Manila, as well as high government officials back in Washington, DC, openly declared their support for 'clean and free elections'. US Embassy personnel commented favourably upon NAMFREL and even appeared at rallies organized by the movement (Westerfield 1963: 417–19). Due to its close identification with American objectives in the 1953 Philippine elections, NAMFREL also gained a great deal of mileage from foreign – especially American – media publicity.

In the 1980s, moreover, wary of losing yet another ally to an anti-American social revolution, the USA, under the zealously anti-communist administration of Ronald Reagan, again assumed an important – if less conspicuous – role in supporting the mobilization of the (second) NAMFREL in the 1986 presidential elections (Bonner 1987: 408–9). Publicly expressing concern that 'Marcos has failed so far to take political, military and economic steps necessary to defeat the Communists, who seem to have seized the battlefield initiative',[6] the US government applied increasing pressures on the Philippine president to implement economic, political and military reforms. While the US Embassy in Manila maintained close contacts with NAMFREL up until the elections, US government and quasi-government agencies helped finance NAMFREL's mobilizing campaign by, for example, channelling funding to participant organizations such as the Bishops-Businessmen Conference and the Trade Union Congress of the Philippines.[7]

In the 1967 senatorial and the 1969 presidential elections, by contrast, no analogous international intercession advanced the cause of the CNEA.[8] In fact, against the backdrop of resurging nationalism and mounting anti-American sentiment, triggered in part by the Vietnam War, the US government, which 'relied increasingly on the US bases and facilities in the Philippines' as the war progressed (Shalom 1986: 99), showed scanty interest in pressuring for political reforms in ways that might have been construed as criticism of the incumbent Philippine president in the late 1960s (Bonner 1987: 73–6).

CATHOLIC CHURCH BENEDICTION

The Catholic Church, another important internationally-linked institution with a powerful presence in the Philippines, also contributed both ecclesiastical blessings and more substantive support to the clean-election crusades. In 1953, expressing distress over the continued 'communist' challenge and concern about the growth of 'immoral' graft and corruption linked to the Presidential Palace, the Catholic Church stressed the import of voting as a 'means of political reform', and admonished its flock from pulpits across the country to protect the 'sacred freedom of the poll'.[9] In addition, several Church-owned and -operated radio stations disseminated NAMFREL's calls for vigilance and volunteers in many parts of the Philippines. Finally, the Catholic Action of the Philippines, the federated umbrella for all Catholic lay organizations, publicly endorsed NAMFREL and printed its appeals for support in the organization's official weekly publication.

Against the backdrop of the Second Vatican Council in 1965, mounting student activism in sectarian schools and among Catholic youth organizations in Manila (Diel 1974: 158), and calls by Filipino Catholics for a more politically relevant church (Youngblood 1990: 65–83), the Catholic Church hierarchy threw its official support behind CNEA's campaign for 'clean and peaceful elections' in 1969. In an effort to provide morally salient leadership in a politically volatile situation, Bishop Gaviola, then Secretary-General of the Bishop's Conference of the Philippines and CNEA national chairman, 'appealed to all parish priests, nuns, and other religious elements . . . all over the country to participate in the campaign for free, honest and peaceful elections' (Tutay 1969b: 18; *Manila Times*, 23 October, 1969: 6). In response to such appeals, Catholic priests organized and addressed CNEA rallies in many parts of the country, and Philippine clergymen, including one archbishop and four bishops, served as CNEA chairmen in at least 25 per cent of all provinces. In addition, priests and seminarians at private, sectarian schools encouraged the organization of students, many of whom were affiliated with Student Catholic Action, into CNEA poll-watch teams in many parts of the Philippines.[10]

In 1986, moreover, afflicted by the deteriorating dictatorship and the growing guerrilla movement and besieged by deep internal rifts between conservative, reformist and revolutionary clergy, the Church and many religious orders lent critical support to NAMFREL's campaign for clean elections. As government '[r]aids on church institutions and the arrest of priests, nuns, and lay persons suspected of leftist tendencies' increased sharply in 1982, Philippine bishops adopted a markedly confrontational position reflected in its

February 1983 'blistering pastoral letter accusing the regime of repression, corruption and economic mismanagement' (Young-blood 1990: 196–7; Lawyers' Committee for Human Rights 1985: 70–4). In this situation, the Catholic Hierarchy seized upon NAM-FREL's clean-election campaign as a means of advancing the 'middle road' of electoral democracy.

The Catholic Bishops' Conference of the Philippines, whose national president Cardinal Vidal served as a regional coordinator of NAMFREL, thus expressed its 'wholehearted support for NAM-FREL' in a joint pastoral exhortation released before the election (*Pulso* 1986). Some 20 bishops served as official NAMFREL coordinators, including the national co-chairman, while the Philip-pine Church's most politically prominent prelate, the Manila Cardi-nal, played a critical behind-the-scenes role (Johnson 1987: 47). With the official endorsement of the secular hierarchy, moreover, local parish networks and Catholic lay organizations as well as the Council of the Laity of the Philippines (the lay counterpart to the Church hierarchy), provided generous logistical assistance, man-power and moral support to NAMFREL.

Similarly, colleges and universities run by Jesuit and other relig-ious orders and incorporated into the nationwide Catholic Educa-tion Association of the Philippines offered venues for volunteer meetings, headquarters for both poll-watch and vote-count efforts, and critical logistical support for NAMFREL in many parts of the Philippines.[11]

BUSINESS ELITE BACKING

In contrast with the long-standing institutional presence of the US government and the Catholic Church, a Philippine business sector only gradually emerged as a unified and self-organized social actor in the post-war period, a development which, in turn, was reflected in the increasing involvement of businesses in the three electoral reform campaigns. In the early 1950s, for example, NAMFREL benefited not so much from initiatives from the business community *per se*, as from benefactions from prominent economic interests identified with the 'outs' and channelled primarily via political machines. The Quirino administration's unprecedented record of corruption in government-run corporations (Golay 1965: 291) and its highly 'selective' implementation of fiscal and trade regulatory policies (Philippine Chamber of Industries 1977: 59–60) became a major campaign issue for the political opposition in the 1953 election (Coquia 1955: 100–10). Meanwhile, 'a fight for supremacy between the two biggest rival sugar blocs' (Coquia 1955: 195) in the Philippines' premier industry erupted during the 1953 elections, as sugar planters and owners of sugar centrals provided massive financial backing for the opposition and the incumbent presidential candidates, respectively. In this context, prominent economic interests closely affiliated with the opposition Nacionalista Party and/or the Magsaysay for President Movement also helped advance NAMFREL's campaign. While ostensibly independent efforts, these three organizations were, in fact, closely intertwined (Coquia 1955: 291). In addition to indirect financial and logistical support, NAMFREL benefited from publicity in opposition-controlled newspapers[12] and from the well-oiled Magsaysay for President Movement and Nacionalista Party machineries at the precinct level.

In the late 1960s, by contrast, CNEA banked on the direct support of an emerging domestic financial capitalist class for the organization and execution of the parallel vote-count effort (Hutchcroft 1993). As fiscal, monetary and trade policies in the late 1960s signalled growing government regulation of the economy, the Marcos administration's public borrowing bonanza and spending spree increasingly dwarfed private sector investments. As of 1967, the government, while exempting its own development programmes from the Central Bank's credit squeeze, began implementing several 'steps to limit credit and reduce the drain on foreign exchange' (Baldwin 1975: 69). Similarly, trade policy under the Marcos administration, with its newly established Board of Investment, offered incentives for particular industries and economic activities while discriminating against others deemed neither 'preferred' nor 'pioneer'. In the election year of 1969, as the private sector experienced a dramatic downturn due to the cumulative effects of Marcos destabilizing economic policies, Congress, in a feeble attempt 'to regain the initiative in setting policy', passed the so-called Magna Carta of Social and Economic Freedom (Doronila 1992: 129). Against this backdrop, business leaders in banking, finance, insurance and media lent their resources and networks to the 1969 electoral-reform campaign. For example, the Friends of CNEA-OQC'69, a group of mostly bank managers and finance executives, charitably offered to provide insurance to 'cover hospitalization expenses, accident and disability benefits, death and all other risks the CNEA and OQC [Operation Quick Count] volunteers may suffer during the full 72 hours' of the elections (*Manila Times*, 1 November, 1969: 1 and 8). Moreover, the Philippine Bankers Association and two of the largest insurance companies in the country donated thousands of pesos to OQC. In addition, the Advertising Council of the Philippines publicly endorsed the 1969 clean-election campaign (*Manila Times*, 6 November, 1969: 1 and 6) while media moguls provided critical logistics and organizational infrastructure to facilitate the speedy transmission of vote returns over '137 radio and nine TV stations throughout the country and at least 12 major Manila dailies' (*Manila Times*, 20 October, 1969: 1; Tutay 1969b: 10 and 18–19).

Finally, in the mid–1980s, NAMFREL appeared, largely because of the machinations of a vastly expanded business community, now clearly an actor in its own right. In 1986, as the NPA collected 'revolutionary taxes' from business ventures in many parts of the Philippines and as 'patrimonial plunder' continued to undermine the prospects for economic recovery (Aquino 1987; Manapat 1991), the (non-crony) business elite threw its support and resources behind NAMFREL's campaign for free and clean elections.

Further, as Marcos's most notorious crony Eduardo 'Danding' Cojuangco, whose seemingly insatiable appetite for devouring others' business ventures earned him the alias 'Pacman', moved to establish control over both the marketing of sugar and the flour industry in the mid-1980s, sugar planters helped underwrite NAM-FREL, and a major food tycoon and flour magnate, serving as the movement's chairman, channelled massive corporate resources into the 1986 clean-election campaign (see Manapat 1991: 240–1). More generally, critical backing from the Makati Business Club and widespread support among corporations located in Makati's financial district significantly advanced NAMFREL's mobilizing efforts.[13] Similarly, large companies lent their managers, employees, and logistics to advance NAMFREL's organizational tasks, volunteer teams and communication/transportation systems in provincial cities throughout the Philippines.[14]

In short, the involvement of 'civic associations' and the participation of 'citizen volunteers' in these clean-election movements occurred largely at the bidding of well-entrenched institutional and class interests. Overall, the organizational resources and networks supplied in varying degrees by the US government, the Catholic Church and Philippine business elites accounted for variations in mobilizing process and outcome across the three election-watch campaigns. In 1953, with critical backing from the CIA and the JUSMAG, NAMFREL's highly publicized campaign for free and fair elections contributed to thwart Quirino's ambitions to remain in office, and to tallying up the votes for victorious reformist presidential candidate Magsaysay. Similarly, in 1986, with significant – if less conspicuous – US support and decisive Bishops-Businessmen promotion, NAMFREL's internationally televised campaign to 'protect the ballot' successfully undermined Marcos's designs for renewing his mandate by means of a so-called 'demonstration election' and produced a winning margin for the popular presidential candidate, Aquino. In 1969, by contrast, in the absence of US endorsements, CNEA's clean-election campaign failed both to counter and to document the widespread electoral fraud and violence that accompanied Marcos's (unprecedented) reelection to another full presidential term. More generally, CNEA's failure to 'stimulate and insure a massive citizens' participation in the 1969 elections' (Commission on Elections 1971: 4) presaged the deterioration of Philippine electoralism in the face of mounting executive authoritarianism and escalating participatory pressures, a contradiction which eventually culminated in the declaration of martial law in 1972.

CONCLUSION

This chapter has examined the conditions and processes favouring the emergence and mobilization of collective campaigns for free and clean elections at three distinct conjunctures in the post-war Philippines. Mobilizing as 'national citizens movements' to safeguard the electoral process, these efforts suggest themselves as instances of a 'resurrected civil society' fighting the good fight on behalf of democracy. Upon closer examination, however, the trajectory of Philippine clean-election campaigns draws attention to patterns of political conflict and ideological contestation over the sphere of civil society.

Whereas their broad social composition, citizenship-based appeal and reformist orientation appear to authenticate the universal objectives endorsed by Philippine election watch movements, the timing of these mobilizing efforts suggests that contestation and exclusion, rather than harmony and inclusion, have characterized such collective campaigns. To a considerable extent, these move-ments emerged in response to the unprecedented usurpation of political power by the presidents, whose ambitions to continue in office threatened the stability of Philippine electoralism. However, these election watch campaigns also arose as reactions to surfacing participatory crises and extra-electoral mobilization by previously unincorporated social groups, whose demands threatened to under-mine the political hegemony of the ruling class and the process of capital accumulation in the Philippines.

While the participation and support offered by thousands of 'plain folks' apparently confirmed the self-organizing, non-hierar-chical and volunteer-based nature of these clean-election move-ments, powerful institutional and class interests conditioned the actual mobilization processes in each of the three campaigns. That is, the backing of US government agencies, Catholic Church institu-tions and Philippine business elites structured the composition, resource-flow and diffusion of these collective efforts in an essen-tially top-down, centre-periphery pattern. Without trivializing the sacrifices made by many NAMFREL and CNEA participants, or diminishing the political significance of these collective manifesta-tions of democratic citizenship, this chapter underscores how 'the actions and organizations of "volunteers" must be distinguished from the actions and organizations of homogenous social blocs, and judged by different criteria' (Gramsci 1971: 202–3).

In conclusion, this analysis of three collective campaigns for 'free, clean and honest elections' in the post-war Philippines draws atten-tion to the complex processes by which a given 'civil society' emerges as an actor on the stage of national politics. Moreover, it emphasizes the significance of changing political conditions for the timing of mobilizations in the name of civil society. Finally, it underlines the salience of powerful institutional and class interests for structuring the nature and direction of such national citizens' movements.

References

Abueva, J. V. (1959), *Focus on the Barrio* (Manila: Institute of Public Administration, University of the Philippines).

Anderson, B. R. (1996), 'Elections and Participation in Three Southeast Asian Countries', in R.H. Taylor (ed.), *The Politics of Elections in Southeast Asia* (Cambridge: Cambridge University Press).

Aquino, B.A. (1987), *Politics of Plunder: The Philippines under Marcos* (Quezon City: Great Books Trading).

Arato, A. (1981), 'Civil Society against the State: Poland 1980–81', *Telos*, No. 47, pp. 23–48.

Baldwin, R.E. (1975), *Foreign Trade Regimes and Economic Development: The Philippines* (New York: Columbia University Press).

Berry, N.O. (1967), 'Representation and Decision-Making: A Case Study of Philippine-American War Claims', PhD dissertation, University of Pittsburgh.

Bonner, R. (1987), *Waltzing With a Dictator: The Marcoses and the Making of American Policy* (New York: Times Books).

Boyce, J.K. (1993), *The Philippines: The Political Economy of Growth and Impoverishment in the Marcos Era* (Honolulu: University of Hawaii Press).

Byington, K. (1988), *Bantay ng Bayan: Stories from the NAMFREL Crusade 1984–86* (Manila: Bookmark).

Che Man, W.K. (1990), *Muslim Separatism: The Moros of Southern Philippines and the Malays of Southern Thailand* (Singapore: Oxford University Press).

Cohen, J.L. and A. Arato (1994), *Civil Society and Political Theory* (Cambridge, Mass.: MIT Press).

Commission on Elections (1971), *Report of the Commission on Elections to the President of the Philippines and the Congress on the Manner the Elections were Held on November 11, 1969* (Manila: Bureau of Printing).

Coquia, J.R. (1955), *The 1953 Philippine Presidential Election* (Manila: University Publishing Co.).

Cruz, A.C. (1966), 'A Natural History of Our Nationalist Demonstrations', *Graphic*, 9 February.

Currey, C.B. (1988), *Edward Lansdale: The Unquiet American* (Boston, Mass.: Houghton Mifflin).

Diel, D. (1974), 'The Confrontation of the Roman Catholic Church with the Economic and Social Development in the Philippines in Relation to the Influence of the Socio-Theological Position of the II Vatican Council', PhD dissertation, University of Hamburg.

Doronila, A. (1992), *The State, Economic Transformation, and Political Change in the Philippines 1946–1972* (Singapore: Oxford University Press).

Edgerton, R.K. (1975), 'The Politics of Reconstruction in the Philippines: 1945–48', PhD Dissertation, University of Michigan.

Free Philippines (1953), 'Observers from Foreign Nations to View Philippine Democracy at Work', 19 October.

Gaddis, J.L. (1982), *Strategies of Containment: A Critical Appraisal of Postwar American National Security Policy* (New York: Oxford University Press).

Gates, R.M. (1987/88), 'The C.I.A. and American Foreign Policy', *Foreign Affairs*, Vol. 66, No 2, pp. 215–30.

George, T.J.S. (1980), *Revolt in Mindanao: The Rise of Islam in Philippine Politics* (Kuala Lumpur: Oxford University Press).

Golay, F.H. (1961), *The Philippines: Public Policy and National Economic Development* (Ithaca, NY: Cornell University Press).

Golay, F.H. (1965), 'The Environment of Philippine Economic Planning', *Philippine Economic Journal*, Vol. 4, No. 2, pp. 284–309.

Golay, F.H. (ed.) (1966), *Philippine-American Relations* (Manila: Solidaridad).

Gramsci, A. (1971), *Selections from the Prison Notebooks* (New York: International Publishers).

Guevarra, D.G. (1992), *Unyonismo sa Pilipinas* (Manila: May Akda).

Hartendorp, A.V.H. (1958), *History of Industry and Trade of the Philippines* (Manila: American Chamber of Commerce).

Hawes, G. (1987), *The Philippine State and the Marcos Regime: The Politics of Export* (Ithaca, NY: Cornell University Press).

Hutchcroft, P.D. (1993), 'Predatory Oligarchy, Patrimonial State: The Politics of Private Commercial Banking in the Philippines', PhD dissertation, Yale University, New Haven, Conn.

Johnson, B. (1987), *The Four Days of Courage* (New York: Free Press).

Jones, G.R. (1989), *Red Revolution: Inside the Philippine Guerilla Movement* (Boulder, Col.: Westview).

Keane, J. (1988), 'Democracy and Civil Society', in John Keane (ed.), *Civil Society and the State* (New York: Verso).

Kerkvliet, B.J. (1977), *The Huk Rebellion: A Study of Peasant Revolt in the Philippines* (Berkeley: University of California Press).

Lawyers' Committee for Human Rights (1985), *Salvaging Democracy: Human Rights in the Philippines* (New York: Lawyers' Committee for Human Rights).

Lawyers' Committee for Human Rights (1988), *Vigilantes in the Philippines: A Threat to Democratic Rule* (New York: Lawyers' Committee for Human Rights).

Makabenta, Y. (1967), 'We Will Not Vote', *Graphic,* 15 November, p. 29.

Manapat, R. (1991), *Some Are Smarter Than Others: The History of Marcos' Crony Capitalism* (New York: Aletheia).

McCarthy, J.D. and M.N. Zald (1977), 'Resource-Mobilization and Social Movements: A Partial Theory', *American Journal of Sociology*, Vol. 82, pp. 212–41.

Mojares, R.B. (1985), *The Man Who Would Be President: Serging Osmena and Philippine Politics* (Cebu City: Maria Cacao).

NAMFREL (1987), *The NAMFREL Report on the February 7, 1986 Philippine Presidential Elections* (Manila: National Citizens Movement for Free Elections).

Nemenzo, F. (1988), 'The Philippine Labour Movement and the Continuing Struggle for Democracy', paper presented at 'Conference on Labor Movements in Transitions to Democracy', Kellogg Institute for International Studies, University of Notre Dame.

Nowak, T.C. and K.A. Snyder (1974), 'Clientelist Politics in the Philippines: Integration or Instability?', *American Political Science Review*, Vol. 68, No. 3, pp.1147–70.

Nowak, T.C. and K.A. Snyder (1974b), 'Economic Concentration and Political Change in the Philippines', in B.J. Kerkvliet (ed.), *Political Change in the Philippines: Studies of Local Politics Preceding Martial Law*, Asian Studies monograph, No.14 (Honolulu: University of Hawaii Press).

O'Donnell, G. and P.C. Schmitter (1986), 'Resurrecting Civil Society, and Restructuring Public Space', in G. O'Donnell and P.C. Schmitter (eds), *Transitions from Authoritarian Rule: Tentative Conclusions about Uncertain Democracies* (Baltimore, MD: Johns Hopkins University Press).

Philippine Chamber of Industries (1977), *A White Paper on Philippine Industry* (Manila: Philippine Chamber of Industries).

Pulso (1986), 'We Must Obey God Rather Than Men', Joint Pastoral Exhortation of the Catholic Bishops' Conference of the Philippines on the Snap Election, reprinted in *Pulso*, Vol. 1, No. 4, pp. 327–31.

Putzel, J. (1992), *A Captive Land: The Politics of Agrarian Reform in the Philippines* (Quezon City: Ateneo de Manila University Press).

Rafael, V.L. (1990), 'Patronage and Pornography: Ideology and Spectatorship in the Early Marcos Years', *Comparative Studies in Society and History*, Vol.32, No.2, pp. 282–97.

Ramos, E.T. (1976), *Philippine Labor Movement in Transition* (Quezon City: New Day).

Rosenberg, D.A. (ed.) (1979), *Marcos and Martial Law in the Philippines* (Ithaca, NY: Cornell University Press).

Scott, J.C. (1969), 'Corruption, Machine Politics, and Political Change', *American Political Science Review*, Vol. 63, No. 4, pp. 1142–58.

Shalom, S.R.A. (1986), *The United States and the Philippines: A Study of Neocolonialism* (Quezon City: New Day).

Skocpol, T. (1985), 'Bringing the State Back In: Strategies of Analysis in Current Research', in P.B. Evans, D. Rueschemeyer and T. Skocpol (eds), *Bringing the State Back In* (Cambridge: Cambridge University Press).

Stepan, A. (1985), 'State Power and the Strength of Civil Society in the Southern Cone of Latin America', in P.B. Evans, D. Rueschemeyer and T. Skocpol (eds), *Bringing the State Back In* (Cambridge: Cambridge University Press).

Tancangco, L.G. (1992), *The Anatomy of Electoral Fraud: Concrete Bases for Electoral Reforms* (Manila: MJAGM).

Tarrow, S.G. (1983), *Struggling to Reform: Social Movements and Policy Change During Cycles of Protest*, Western Societies Paper No. 15 (Ithaca, NY: Cornell University).

Tarrow, S.G. (1994), *Power in Movement: Social Movements, Collective Action and Politics* (Cambridge: Cambridge University Press).

Thompson, M.R. (1988), *Cory and the Guy: Reformist Politics in the Philippines*, UFSI Reprint, No.16, (Indianapolis: Universities Field Staff Internationals).

Tilly, C. (1978), *From Mobilization to Revolution* (New York: Random House).

Tutay, F.V. (1969a), 'Policing the Polls: CNEA and OQC 1969 Join Hands with PC to Ensure Clean, Free and Orderly Elections on November 11', *Philippines Free Press*, 1 November.

Tutay, F.V. (1969b), 'Operation Quick Count 69', *Philippine Free Press*, 8 November.

Westerfield, H.B. (1963), *The Instruments of America's Foreign Policy* (New York: Thomas Y. Cromwell).

Youngblood, R.L. (1990), *Marcos Against the Church: Economic Development and Political Repression in the Philippines* (Ithaca, NY: Cornell University Press).

Notes

1. The author would like to thank Benedict Anderson, Peter Katzenstein, Jonas Pontusson and Sidney Tarrow for encouragement and guidance, and John Sidel for everything from thoughtful criticism to welcome distraction. Research for this chapter was assisted by grants from the Albert Einstein Institute, the Andrew W. Mellon Founda-

tion and travel grants from Cornell University. Of course, responsibility for the ideas and opinions expressed below fall solely on the author.

2. The Lapiang Manggagawa [Labour Party] briefly united the National Association of Trade Unions (NATU) with the Philippine Association of Free Labor Unions (PAFLU) (Ramos 1976). The Malayang Samahang Magsasaka (MASAKA, or Free Peasants' Union) became one of two major peasant organizations in Central Luzon in the 1960s (Guevarra 1992: 115–16). In 1967, moreover, NATU and MASAKA, under the radical leadership of Ignacio Lacsina and Felixberto Olalia, Sr, respectively, formed the core of the Socialist Party of the Philippines (Ramos 1976: 56). The Kabataang Makabayan [Nationalist Youth] was founded by Jose Ma. Sison in 1964 (Cruz 1966: 20–1).

3. Leading student demonstrations for the restoration of autonomous student councils, the League of Filipino Students, emerged in the autumn of 1979 and led more student protests in March, July and August 1980. In 1981, on the first anniversary of a successful boycott of government-sponsored Labour Day activities and demonstrations against the Marcos regime's anti-labour policies, the militant Kilusang Mayo Uno (First May Movement) held its founding congress and resolved to launch a 'strike movement' (Nemenzo 1988: 34). Formally organized in 1985, the Kilusang Magbubukid ng Pilipinas [Philippine Peasant Movement] 'was an alliance of local peasant organizations that had adopted an unambiguous national democratic platform . . . clearly the largest organized bloc among the peasantry' (Putzel 1992: 218).

4. In this regard, while clean-election campaigns were 'not quite electoral', their obvious affinity with electoral associations and assemblies, especially when compared to their more radical contemporaries, surely afforded a certain 'grant of legality' which lowered their 'costs of mobilization and collective action' (Tilly 1978: 167). On the significance of movements' 'capacity to embody politically advantageous and culturally appropriate frames of meaning', see Tarrow (1994: 117). For a thoughtful discussion of the 'framing of collective action', see Tarrow (1994: 118–34).

5. For a contemporary overview of NAMFREL's activities, see *Free Philippines*, issues from September to November 1953.

6. Statement by Assistant Secretary of State Paul D. Wolfowitz, reprinted in, for example, *Malaya*, 29 October, 1985, p. 1.

7. Bonner (1987: 408–9) argues that the US Agency for International Development 'gave at least $300,000 to NAMFREL through these organizations', and also discusses the financial support provided to NAMFREL by the National Endowment for Democracy. He also claims that NAMFREL 'received money, surreptitiously, from the Japanese government and Japanese businessmen' (Bonner 1987).

8. However, the American Chamber of Commerce in the Philippines provided donations to the clean election effort in 1969. See, for example, 'L'Affaire Ferrer', *Philippine Free Press*, 3 October, 1970, pp. 1,12 and 51.

9. Statements by Iloilo Archbishop Jose Ma. Cuenco and Archbishop Santos, cited in Coquia (1955: 208).

10. Interviews, former seminarian and CNEA coordinator at University of San Augustin, Iloilo City, William Felix Martirez, Iloilo City, 2 October, 1992; former Ateneo High School principal and CNEA coordinator at Ateneo de Zamboanga, Zamboanga City, Fr Katigbak, Quezon City, 19 October, 1992; and former CNEA vice-chair Jose Concepcion, Makati, 29 October, 1992.

11. Interview, then NAMFREL national coordinator and La Salle University and CEAP president Bro. Roland R. Dizon, 29 September, 1992, Bacolod City. Interviews, local NAMFREL organizers Dra. Villanueva, 2 October, 1992, Iloilo City; Adrelina Hitalia, Zamboanga City, 21 September, 1992; and Mrs Lualhati Hilario, Davao NAMFREL treasurer, Davao City, 17 September, 1992.

12. See, especially the Lopez-controlled *Manila Chronicle* and the Roces-owned *Manila Times*. The Philippine News Service, which included both Joaquin Roces and Magsaysay look-alike and supporter Manuel Manahan on its board, also assisted NAMFREL greatly in this regard. The *Manila Times* even printed NAMFREL press releases, which were subsequently distributed to other papers. Interview, Armando Malay, Sr, Quezon City, 13 August, 1992.

13. Interviews, Jose Concepcion; company president and NAMFREL-Makati chair Isobel Wilson, Makati, 15 October, 1992; and NAMFREL Treasurer Teresa F. Nieva, Manila, 5 November, 1992.

14. Interviews, Aboitiz-company executive and NAMFREL-Cebu chair Jake N. Marquez, Cebu City, 6 October, 1992; Aboitiz-company executive and NAMFREL-Davao chair Alfonso S. Ybañez, September 1991; and NAMFREL-Davao Treasurer Lualhati Hilario, Davao City, 17 September, 1992.

12 Conservation for Whom? Van Gujjars and the Rajaji National Park

Pernille Gooch[1]

This chapter discusses the growing conflict between people and national park administrations using the example of the Van Gujjars, a people of transhumant buffalo herders. In 1992, after returning from their summer pastures in the higher ranges of the Himalayas, the Van Gujjars were denied entrance to parts of their winter quarters in the Shivalik forest in the state of Uttar Pradesh, which had been proclaimed a national park in 1983. This was the beginning of an open conflict, which has given the 'victims of conservation' a human face among the Indian public.

The following account is based on observation, interviews with actors in the struggle and documentary evidence. It narrates the story of how the Van Gujjars defended their right to live in the Shivalik forest. It explains why they did what they did, how their resistance grew into a movement, and how this movement has reverberated nationally through the effort of intellectuals within and allied to the movement. At the same time, it critically addresses an intrinsic problem of environmentalism, which the Van Gujjar movement put in focus. This is the conflict between the interests of local populations and the policy of creating small oases of pristine nature in an otherwise abused environment.

Usually, resistance to conservation has started as local struggles by communities losing their livelihood, leading to ideological debates as middle-class actors joined the movement. This pattern is repeated in environmental movements all over India. Further, as Sethi (1993: 140) points out, conflicts around questions of survival raise two sets of issues: those that concern the specific struggle in question, and those related to the nature of the discourse they give rise to. In this chapter, I will address both.

VAN GUJJARS AND THE SHIVALIK FOREST

India's first national park was set up in the early 1930s. In 1991 there were 75 national parks and 421 sanctuaries and proposals for a further 72 parks and 212 sanctuaries. This means that at present 3.5 per cent of India's total area and almost 20 per cent of the forests are protected by law as nature reserves, and there are plans to increase this area to 5 per cent of the country. All these figures show that preservation of flora and fauna has been given high priority in national policies during the last decades and indicate the present strength of the conservation lobby in the country. But behind this conservation strategy lies another reality, the displacement of hundreds of thousands of forest dwellers, and the threatened livelihood of villagers living on the fringe of the protected areas.

In 1983 the Uttar Pradesh Government notified its intention to amalgamate three former sanctuaries into the Rajaji National Park because of 'increasing pressure on forest and wildlife in this delicate ecosystem'. The area is only about 250 km from Delhi, and was earlier a favourite hunting ground for the Mughals as well as the British. The proposed park covers an area of 831 sq.km and it will be the largest national park in the state. It has about 400 elephants, a number of tigers and leopards, and also a wide variety of deer and birds. Like other national parks in India, Rajaji has a large human population both within the park area and in towns and villages on the periphery.

Modern development has also made major encroachments on the park. Among the more significant are: a large army ammunition dump, an electricity plant with an adjoining township, a chemical factory, a railway line, a railway station and several major roads. The area has been part of forest development schemes where indigenous species, providing food for the wild animals, have been cut down and replaced with plantations of commercially valuable trees. The population pressure (from others, not the Van Gujjars) in and around the park is immense. Within the park there are 12 revenue villages and a number of settlements, and just outside its boundaries about 80 villages are dependent on the resources of the park for gathering of firewood and fodder. Close by are also a number of towns, including Dehra Dun with a population approaching one million.

The Van Gujjars have been using the forest for ages as pasture and as a home during the winter season. They practise a forest-based form of animal husbandry and produce good quality milk and dairy products, which are widely sold. While most of the other transhumant Gujjars communities in the Himalayan region have a village base where they practise agriculture for a part of the year, this is not the case for the Van Gujjars, who live scattered in temporarily erected camps in the forest both during summer and winter. This means that they are completely dependent on access to state forests. The forest is the world of Van Gujjars and they know it intimately. Their whole existence is dependent on it, and the name they have given themselves indicates the strong ties between the Van Gujjars and their forest environment. *Van* is the word for forest.

Controversies between the Van Gujjars and officials of the Forest Department have been going on for at least a hundred years. During the last decade of the nineteenth century the British colonial power set up checkpoints along the traditional migration routes of the Gujjars in order to control the number of buffaloes which the nomads brought into the hills. The Gujjars were given permits to bring a stipulated number of cattle into the mountains and a police guard was stationed at the entrance to the hills to prevent entry without a permit.[2] In this way mobility, one of the most important factors in ecologically sound herd management, was severely restrained. As permits were not revised although herds multiplied, this policy gave ample opportunity for the forest officials to exploit the Gujjars by letting more animals slip through after receiving a bribe in kind or in cash. This practice continued after independence and it was not until the summer of 1993 that the Gujjars were allowed to migrate without a permit.[3]

The Gujjars also need permits to use the forests as their winter-quarters. During the colonial period, the forests were taken over by the State as an important national asset and their use by local people was regulated by a state monopoly. For the Gujjars this meant that *customary rights* to the forest and its product became *concessions* in the form of lopping and grazing permits given to the heads of households. The permits stated the number of cattle a family was allowed to keep. Most permits are now old and have not been updated. Hence bribes are necessary, and the Gujjars have to give a large share of their income in the form of milk, butter and cash to forest officials in order to avoid the perpetual threat of eviction.

The Van Gujjars have been constructed by the forest authorities as one of the main threats to the ecosystem of the national park, in spite of the presence of many other threats, as enumerated above. The Van Gujjars question the rationale behind this. Says Mustooq, one of their leaders: 'Why start with us? Shifting out the Gujjars is the easiest part of all but what use is it that we have been removed when the ammunition dump and the industrial plants are still there. Move them first and then you can think about the Gujjars.' Representatives from the Forest Department and the Indian Wildlife Institute in Dehra Dun have claimed that the Van Gujjars' lifestyle in the forest is no longer sustainable. According to this view the Gujjar pastoralists earlier managed to live in a sustainable way in harmony with nature. This has now changed with increased population pressure both in the hills, where the Gujjars stay in summer, and in the villages surrounding the forests of the foothills, resulting in a disastrous destruction of the vulnerable ecosystem, the very foundation of Gujjar survival. One of the main reasons given for this is that a large part of the Gujjars have stopped migrating to the mountains in the summer. This increases pressure on the lowlands. It is also maintained that the removal of the forest canopy through lopping by the Gujjars increases erosion as the monsoon rains wash away the top soil (Khati 1993: 18). The Gujjars are also accused of poaching.

These views are not supported by a report of *Habitat Utilization by Gujjar Pastoralists in Rajaji Wildlife Sanctuary* by Clark Seuril and Watts (1986). They found that the crown cover was 'relatively unaffected by lopping' and that there was: 'an increase in ground vegetation in areas with lopped trees which actually decreased the possibility of erosion'. Further, the study team 'saw no evidence of dead or dying trees other than those knocked over by elephants'.

The Van Gujjars are vegetarians and do not hunt. The larger carnivores kill a calf from time to time but the Gujjars are quite 'philosophical about their losses', and the wildlife is usually not disturbed by the Gujjars. Further, 'land is appointed to each family and boundaries respected. Families practicing transhumance always return to the same area year after year' (Clark *et al.* 1986: 51).

My field work points in the same direction. The Gujjars manage their allocated areas in a sustainable way to ensure continued survival. In winter the Gujjars feed their buffaloes with leaves lopped (harvested) from certain species of trees. As they use the yield of the same trees for fodder year after year it is of vital interest to them that the forest is regenerated. The trees are lopped in a sequence starting with the ones that shed their leaves first and finishing with the ones that keep their foliage until late spring. Each tree is lopped only once during a season, which gives it time to recuperate. I also found that most families still practise transhumance. Here there is a discrepancy between what people say and what they actually do. If the Gujjars from the park are asked if they migrate or stay, they will answer that they stay in the Shivaliks for all twelve months, because the transhumant households are the first to be relocated. Like one Gujjar said, 'if you are settled, you are like a stone and not so easily removed'. However, only a few families can stay in the foothills in summer as the area dries up and there is neither enough water nor fodder to sustain the herds.

The Forest Department, just like any other state agency dealing with nomadic peoples, sees sedentarization as the only solution to 'the nomadic problem' and the only possible way of development. The department has tried to resettle the Gujjars from the park at Pathri block in Haridwar District. Pathri was chosen in order to resettle the Gujjars as far away from the forest as possible and make it impossible for them to return unseen to their former homes in the forest (K. N. Singh 1987).

According to this scheme the Gujjars are supposed to sell all their own cattle and replace it with buffaloes of high quality breeds, and they will have to replace traditional pastoral management with stall feeding. It is estimated that each family should earn a living by keeping three milking animals and buying all the fodder for them. To quote D.S. Khati who was Director of Rajaji National Park at the time: 'They (the Gujjars) should be rehabilitated in a just and sustainable manner, thus returning health to the forest and dignity and survival to the Gujjars themselves. It was such a reasoning that prompted us to move the Gujjars out from the proposed park area' (Khati 1993: 20). The only problem was that, for the Van Gujjars, Pathri did not represent 'a just and sustainable manner'.

First of all, the Van Gujjars do not want to be cut off from the forest. Second, pastoralists form affectionate relationships with their cattle. All buffaloes have histories and individual names, and they are even seen as 'personalities'. As with all other nomadic pastoralists, livestock plays a very important role in the cultural and social life of their community. The idea of parting with the buffaloes is unacceptable.

The Gujjars want a way of development that takes their special mode of production as nomadic pastoralists into consideration. What the planners have not realized is that for pastoralists everywhere the life is 'more than just means of making a living, pastoral systems are ways of life', and it gives pastoralists (or nomads) a perspective on life which is different from that of settled populations (Galaty and Johnson 1990).

Further, space in Pathri has been allocated on the basis of grazing permit ownership. However, most permits were issued in 1937 and by now a permit might cover as many as 70–80 people and 100–50 buffaloes. As one young Gujjar said, looking at his large family, 'We won't even get enough space to stand there.' The Pathri colony was constructed during 1987–90, but by 1992 it was still empty, derelict and overgrown with weeds.

THE GUJJAR MOVEMENT

In autumn 1992, upon reaching Jamuna Bridge, the last halt on the journey and a meeting place for all the Gujjars descending from the hills, they found that all roads and paths leading into the park area were closed for them and their herds. The strategy of the Forest Department was clear: to force the Van Gujjars of the park to move to Pathri by closing every alternative. However, the Gujjars camped at transitory campsites at the edge of the park or went into hiding in the dense forests outside the park area. Resistance transcended individual, survival-oriented, acts evading the alien codes of the Forest Department, and became outspoken collective defiance.

At this point it would have been very difficult for the Gujjars to continue their struggle alone. Being illiterate, marginalized and having spent most of their lives in the interior of the forest they did not have the necessary means to take the conflict from the local to the state level where it would ultimately have to be fought. Help came in the form of a local NGO, RLEK. RLEK was preparing an adult literacy campaign among the Gujjars at the time, which had been approved by the National Literacy Mission. The situation now developed according to a classical pattern for similar movements in India. The chairperson of RLEK is Avdesh Kaushal, a well-known environmental and social activist.[4] He had the necessary connections with key persons within media, research, administration, NGOs and policy-making. This started a process in which a 'whole chain of actors at different levels' got involved in the struggle (Sethi 1993).

At the first meeting it was decided to give the Forest Department an ultimatum. If the Gujjars were not allowed to enter the park by their next meeting on 10 October they would resort to road blockage, coming with all their families, cattle, tents and luggage to camp on the very busy Delhi–Dehra Dun highway which passes through Mohand. This idea came originally from the RLEK and many expected it to be too radical for the Gujjars, who had avoided confrontation before. But at the meeting the suggestion was received with enthusiasm by all the Gujjars present, among other things because buffaloes were dying from hunger in the transitory camps outside the park. However, on 7 October permission was granted to the Van Gujjars by the Uttar Pradesh government to re-enter the forest for one more winter season. Avdesh Kaushal described the events as follows:

> On the 3rd of October, there was a Gujjar meeting. It was decided that we will block the highway on the 10th. As soon as they heard this they, (the forest officials) who were pretending to be tigers, lost their nerve. They suddenly became frightened. A day before that, on TV, all over India a film was shown about the Wildlife Institute. A Gujjar woman was also shown in the programme. That woman said a number of things, good things. For example, that 'when we lop leaves from the trees for our buffaloes, the wild deer also join our animals and feed on the leaves with them.' Secondly she said: 'whenever we go to lop leaves we leave our women and young daughters in the forest. We are not afraid of anything in the forest. But in the cities where will we leave them? In the cities they have lots of fear. They cannot live in the cities at all.'

As the experiences of this particular struggle became an issue through the media, the Van Gujjar movement became part of a general debate between, on the one hand, those who see the Van Gujjars as examples of how tribals and other forest dwellers destroy their habitat, and, on the other hand, those who maintain that local forest dwellers, such as the Van Gujjars, live in harmony with the forest and are the true guardians of their habitat. From being a local conflict the Van Gujjar struggle was from then on fought with strategic use of the media. They told everyone that 'We, the Van Gujjars are not the ones who destroy the forests; how can we destroy the trees when our whole livelihood is dependent upon them.'

Sethi (1993: 137) writes that 'unlike earlier and other struggles where the burden of mobilization and agitation is primarily borne by those directly affected ... ecological struggles by their very nature tend to draw in widely disparate and sometimes conflicting actors'. Sethi defines a whole chain of actors at different levels that tend to get involved in this particular kind of struggle. At the first level are voluntary (or political) organizations that already happen to be working with the affected community or in the area in question. Another set of actors are media people, like journalists, film-makers, and so on who have to be involved in order to communicate the protesters' message to the world outside. Apart from those it will be necessary to get the support of middle-class professionals such as lawyers, scientists, researchers and so forth; that is, a whole group who can help with tasks that demand professional knowledge such as providing background material, producing research material or helping to argue the cases in court. Their open support for the case in question in the media, especially if they are already well known, will also be important for the outcome of the conflict. Even though the main adversary will be the bureaucracy, at either local or central state levels, it will often be possible to find bureaucrats and policy-makers who are sympathetic to the cause. In this way 'we can in each struggle, trace a chain of actors, each with their own functional role and removed from the actual struggle to different degrees' (Sethi 1993: 137).

In the Van Gujjar struggle all these different levels of actors can be traced. At the core of the agitation are the pastoralists themselves struggling to keep their resource base in the forest. As their main allies, who first entered the struggle at their side, we find Kaushal and his organization RLEK, which in turn mobilized their intellectual and political peers.

ENVIRONMENTAL MOVEMENTS IN INDIA

After independence India chose a path of economic development based on modernization of industry and agriculture as advocated by Nehru, rather than the Gandhian way, which favours decentralization and small-scale rural development. Because of this the degradation of India's natural resources and the disruption of the relationship between nature and local communities accelerated in the decades after independence. It was even argued that 'environmentalists were anti-national and anti-people, agents of Western imperialism, wedded to blocking the necessary development of industry in India' (Sethi 1993: 126).

The result of these early discussions on ecology was, according to Sethi, an 'uneasy consensus' between the conservation lobby and those who advocated economic development based on modern technology. Both have had direct implications for the Van Gujjars. Conservation policies evict them from their forest, and development policies imply that they should be settled and pulled into the mainstream of economic development.

However, other points of view were not completely absent from the Indian debate. Marxists advocated a shift in the distribution of benefits from the use of natural resources from a global to a national level. At the same time, alternative development models based on a Gandhian ideology were still present in India and much of the criticism against Western modernity, inherent in the new Indian environmental movement, takes inspiration from Gandhian thoughts (Nandy 1987: 127–62).

The conflict between the Van Gujjars, the Forest Department and the conservation lobby is therefore a part of a larger conflict over 'conservation' and 'sustainable development'. The use of these expressions in India was inspired by the World Conservation Strategy adopted in India in 1980 (Indira 1992: 1650). The measures suggested for conservation and sustainable development were ambivalent. Anti-people measures such as population control and preventing people using natural resources through the creation of protected areas was mixed with ambitions to prevent dispossession of rural people, recognize traditional rights, and guarantee secure access to land, water and forests for the tribal groups. However, it is mainly the first part of the equation which is implemented and it is mainly the poorest and most backward sections of the people who bear the burden of the 'preservation of the local and global commons'. A destructive type of development benefiting only a small section of the population is allowed to continue (Indira 1992: 1650).

The criticism of 'the dominant Western world view' has created a space in the ideological discussions that has been occupied by voices from the weaker sections of society, tribals, poor peasants and women, in search of an 'Indigenous Vision' (Sen 1992), simultaneously genuinely Indian and genuinely human:

Learning from indigenous cultures assumes special relevance at a
time when alternative modes of development are being looked at
... In these indigenous cultures, people interacted with their
resource base ... People had intimate knowledge of their environment, and according to their technological level, world view
and priorities, used their resources optimally. (Chatterji 1992:
234)

It was the Chipko movement (1973–85, originating in the region
where Van Gujjars have their summer pastures) that focused the
national interest on issues of humans and their environment and
gave them an 'Indian face'. The Chipko movement has become a
legend: the powerful image of local women embracing trees penetrated the media as well as the public consciousness.

There are few movements that have been as misunderstood as the
Chipko. It was mainly active in outlying parts of the hills and few
reporters or researchers went there and talked to the grassroots
participants. Instead, the movement was interpreted by intellectuals
in more accessible places.

According to Mitra, Chipko was not a conservation movement
from the beginning. It was a movement for local control of local
resources:

Chipko was primarily an economic struggle. Environment and
ecology were attributed to it later ... the local people wanted
their economic survival first ... The transformation of Chipko
from a struggle to control local resource use to a national
movement was influenced heavily by a growing global environmental concern: Chipko began independently of global environmental consciousness, but in interacting with the rest of the
world, it assumed a deep conservationist bearing. In the process,
its utilitarian and developmental stance was steadily eroded.
(Mitra 1993: 30)

Two very important new insights emerged from the Chipko movement. One was that 'Chipko dismissed the notion that it is the poor
who wantonly destroy their environment and do not want to
protect it' (Mitra 1993: 31). The other was that 'Chipko fostered the
realization that people are an integral part of environment' (Mitra
1993: 27). Unfortunately it was mainly on the ideological level that
local people and their use of local resources were seen as integrated

in nature, while in practice their needs for means of survival were subordinated to the need for preserving trees.

As the Chipko movement shows, environmental movements are contradictory. Chipko advanced an alternative small-scale village development strategy while simultaneously fighting for the conservation of nature. However, in the course of the struggle, the former was sacrificed for the latter. As a result of the conservation struggle *all* tree felling was prohibited. This left the small village saws idle, but they had been part of the local survival economy. (Mitra 1993: 27). The villagers were disappointed and left with a feeling that they got nothing out of the struggle. Indeed, they were worse off than before. The frustration among the people of Uttarkand was expressed by a woman from the village of Reni, the place that is hailed as the birth place of Chipko. When asked why Chipko cannot be revived, she replied: 'What did we get out of the first one? Now they have made this area the Nanda Devi Biosphere Reserve and I can't even pick herbs to treat a stomach-ache' (Mitra 1993: 32).

The idea of local control of local resources and the rights of people to manage their environment was an inherent part of the Chipko movement, but it never materialized in the form of action programmes. In this respect the current Van Gujjar movement is going one step further by defending the pastoralists' right to stay in the forest and their right to use its resources. One of the main aims of the Van Gujjar movement is to show that forest dwellers are an integrated part of their environment, that they are the best guardians of the forests and that they can protect and regenerate their habitat while using it.

CONFLICT OVER CONSERVATION

According to Guha 'in India a select group of ex-hunters and naturalists has been in the forefront of wilderness conservation' (Guha 1994: 2192). Their main interest has been in the protection of the large mammals such as elephants and tigers. He further defines them as an 'interest group with an influence on state policy wholly out of proportion to their numbers'. They also share their cultural and educational background with senior bureaucrats (Guha 1994). This picture fits very well with what happened on the local scene in Dehra Dun. Here the 'wilderness conservationists' are mainly represented by the organization Friends of Doon, which is a pressure group of influential citizens of Dehra Dun. The organization had been cooperating with Kaushal in the 'limestone quarrying case' (Madsen, Chapter 13 below), but in the Van Gujjar case they have been on opposite sides of the controversy. In the latter case there has been cooperation between the wildlife conservationists and senior forest officials, and members of Friends of Doon have been actively lobbying to get the Gujjars ousted from the National Park (see Gosh 1993; and Mazumdar 1993).

The Van Gujjar conflict over the Rajaji National Park emerged as a rallying point for an already existing debate over what has been termed 'conflict conservation'. The general awareness of this problem is recent:

> It is only over the last one or two years that NGOs have begun to advocate the case of those deprived people (who lose access to natural resources because of Protected areas) and build awareness about laws and issues. But they soon found themselves in conflict with both the government and *vested interests*. (Cherail 1993, my emphasis)

While the Van Gujjar movement in Rajaji, like all the other local conflicts around Protected Areas, was rooted in local survival practices, it was the 'movement intellectuals' who broadened the movement and created a 'collective identity' for all afflicted communities. This discourse obtained its material from struggles going on all over India.

Eyerman and Jamison point out that 'All activists in social movements are in some sense "movement intellectuals", because through their activism they contribute to the formation of the movements collective identity, to making the movement what it is' (1991: 94). The Van Gujjar movement also had its own 'intellectuals' who emerged in the struggle. Important here were representatives of the Van Gujjars who contributed with their particular experience to the development of the collective identity of the movement. One of these is Mustooq Lambardar. It is worthwhile quoting him at length to communicate the force of the Gujjars' arguments:

> The forest belongs to us just as well as it belongs to the wild animals. The forest is our mother. We were all born here, my wife, my children and I. The Van Gujjars have been in these

forests for hundreds of years. Now we are treated as criminals and we will all perish if we are forced to leave the forest . . . The Government wants the wild animals like tiger, elephant and wild boars to come here and multiply but this should not be at our expense. We consider the growth of the wild animals as a very good thing but we should also be given shelter . . . The Director of the park threatened to have me arrested. I answered that you may arrest me even put me into jail but I am not prepared to leave this land [the forest] and go out from here . . . I have come here to plead the case of my fellow Gujjar brothers. We do not want to go to Pathri, instead we want to tell all our problems to the people who have come from Delhi. All that we want is that we should not be disturbed in this place. We want to remain here and earn our livelihood, we do not want to go to Pathri and live in the rooms allotted to us there . . . The Government wants to send all of us to that place, but we know that our animals will die there and we know that once we leave this place [the forest] we will never be able to return.

Although illiterate, Mustooq Lambardar played a major role in giving the Van Gujjars a collective identity through speeches at local rallies and by representing his people at national seminars and meetings.

One of the first people from the national environmental movement to openly support the Van Gujjars was Anil Agarwal, chairman of the Delhi-based Centre for Science and Environment and editor of the magazine *Down to Earth*. Agarwal's role in India is what Eyerman and Jamison (1991: 103) call an 'established intellectual'. Agarwal had already achieved legitimacy as well as national and international fame, and he could challenge dominant conceptions and thus open up a space for the redefinition of existing concepts of the relationship between man and nature. In January 1993 (that is, three months after the Van Gujjars and their conflict with the conservation lobby started to appear in the press) Agarwal wrote:

Because it is near Delhi, the conflict between foresters managing the proposed Rajaji National Park and the Gujjars who have been using these forests for a long time has been reported extensively in the national media . . . This conflict can become a blessing in disguise as it offers the Union Ministry of Environment and Forests its first opportunity to set up the country's first people's national park ... All those who talk of the need to conserve the world's biological diversity must understand the importance of protecting the world's cultural diversity.[5]

Another key actor on the national arena who supported the Van Gujjars was Roy Burman, anthropologist and, as stated in one newspaper article, 'the last word on tribals in the country'. He also challenged earlier statements made by forest officials and conservation lobbyists that it was the Van Gujjars who destroyed the forests. He argued that national parks had been set up in sparsely populated areas like the USA and Canada, but that this could not be considered correct in India. In India people should be included in conservation planning. Burman maintains that there is a 'symbiotic relationship of Gujjars and forests which should not be disturbed'.[6]

Eyerman and Jamison argue that a central theme in 'facilitating the constitution of a movement's collective identity' is the *Other* (1991: 101) against which the main part of criticism will be directed but also an *Other* with whom the movement will have to interact in order to proceed. In the Gujjars' case, as we have already seen, this principal Other was the Forest Department and its representatives. But among the movement's intellectuals, the conservation lobby has been constituted as the principal Other:

Over the last few years, the conservationist lobby has been gaining strength world-wide and in India. This lobby conceives local forest dependent communities as a major threat to forest and wildlife. Under pressure from them the government has been enacting laws that pay little attention to the local people and their needs. (Cherail 1993: 9)

By many, the 'conservation lobby' is usually seen as a 'Westernized' elite 'alienated from the vast majority of Indians, and especially ignorant if not disdainful of tribal society' (Kothari 1993). However:

The only way national parks can be a success *in India* is if people are made to feel that they are part of their heritage. But the government's *imported* nature conservation strategy begins by treating people as outcasts. In park after park therefore resentment is building up. Unless the villagers have a stake in the forests and their wildlife, the existing tension will continue. The easy money now available from *West-sponsored funds* such as the

Global Environment Facility may give a new lease of life to the law and order approach now in vogue, but in the long run it will backfire. (my emphasis)[7]

An important milestone was the 'National Workshop on declining access to and control over National Resources in National Parks and Sanctuaries' held in Dehra Dun in October 1993. The seminar was attended by grassroots groups, NGO activists, forest administrators and researchers from all over India, and it was well covered in the media. At the workshop, D. N. Tiwari, Director General of Indian Council of Forest Research and Education, saw tribals as a part of the environment and was in favour of models involving people: 'Without people's involvement, conservation cannot succeed. Tribals are also part of the biosphere, and their existence is as much endangered as that of any animal species we may try to conserve' (Society for Participatory Research 1993). Similar thoughts were expressed by S. Raju, a university lecturer, who saw the conflict as a clash between the 'park model' and the 'habitat model'. That is, both models want to conserve forests, but the park model excludes forest dwellers, while the habitat model sees them as part of the environment (D. Singh 1993).

The workshop concluded with the passing of a resolution called the 'Doon Declaration on People and Parks'. The Doon Declaration is important because it is the first attempt to transcend the particular struggles at grassroots level in order to create a general blueprint for a national movement. Its central message was as follows:

Local forest dwellers and tribals have been the major agents of protection and conservation of our forest and wildlife. They have developed insights and valuable knowledge about ecological preservation and sustainable use of such resources. They have created institutional mechanisms and norms to ensure that people live in balance and harmony with nature . . . The protection of our forest flora, fauna and wildlife is critical for conservation of biological diversity in the country. This is a common purpose among tribals and forest dwellers, environmentalists, voluntary organizations and social activists, Ministry of Environment and Forests and the management of National Parks and Sanctuaries. (Society for Participatory Research 1993)

The specific recommendations adopted include:

a campaign for recognition of customary rights of local people (including nomads), living inside and around protected areas, to the use of natural resources, and for making local people responsible for management of local parks and sanctuaries. The management proposal put forward by RLEK and CSE [Centre for Science and Environment], which was worked out with the Van Gujjars, was considered an appropriate model to be followed in sanctuaries where wildlife conservation and people's needs are in conflict. (Society for Participatory Research 1993)

One of the conclusions reached was that NGOs should form a network which could raise such issues in public fora and put pressure on the government to modify laws or reform the implementation process.

CONCLUSION: A PARADIGM FOR ALTERNATIVE DEVELOPMENT

Above, I have discussed how the interests of the Van Gujjars (staying in the forest) and the aim of the movement intellectuals (to create a development alternative) have converged in a strategy for people-oriented conservation. This strategy works for the Gujjars and is also a model for alternative development. The Gujjars have become a showpiece of survival as well as pioneers in an ideological debate. Instead of the creation of a 'traditional' national park, which means that they would be cut off completely from their natural resources, the Van Gujjars have suggested that they should be entrusted with the management of the Rajaji Park, making it into India's first 'People's National Park'. This would set an important example for others living in and around national parks. This idea was first expressed by Mustooq Lambardar and the Gujjars have declared: 'give *us* the management and we will turn this forest into a diamond'.

Handing over the management of the National Park to the Van Gujjars is, of course, not without problems. The complex context of social and economic structures of which the Van Gujjars and their utilization of the forest is only one part will have to be considered. This is something that both Van Gujjars and the involved NGOs realize. However, in the words of C. R. Bijoy, a social activist from Coimbatore: 'While each of the sanctuaries and regions have unique characteristics, a beginning has to be made in suggesting a clear alternative model for conservation. The Gujjars have indeed set a unique example' (Cherail 1993).

References

Chatterji, S. (1992), 'The Indigenous Culture of Sanskar', in S. Geeti (ed.), *Indigenous Vision: Peoples of India, Attitudes to the Environment* (New Delhi: Sage).

Cherail, K. (1993), 'Time to Change, Wildlife Conservation Strategy', *Down to Earth*, 30 November.

Clark, A., H. Seuril and R. Watts (1986), *Habitat Utilization by Gujar Pastoralists in Rajaji Wildlife Sanctuary*, Dehra Dun, mimeo.

Down to Earth (1993), 'Unique Opportunity for Kamal Nath', Editorial, 31 January.

Eyerman, R. and A. Jamison (1991), *Social Movements: A Cognitive Approach* (Cambridge: Polity Press).

Galaty, J. G. and D. Johnson (1990), *The World of Pastoralism: Herding Systems in Comparative Perspective* (London: Guilford Press).

Gosh, M. (1993), 'Why Pick on the Gujjars?', *The Himachal Times*, September 1993.

Guha, R. (1994), 'Forestry Debate and Draft Forest Act: Who Wins, Who Loses?', *Economic and Political Weekly*, 20 August.

Himachal Times, The, (1993), 'Symbiotic relations of Gujjars, forests should not be disturbed', 27 August.

Indira, (1992), 'Conservation at Human Cost. Case of Rajaji National Park', *Economic and Political Weekly*, 1–8 August.

Khati, D. S. (1993), 'Problems in Paradise', *Sanctuary Asia*, Vol. XIII, No. 4, pp. 15–21.

Kothari, A. (1993), 'Wildlife and Tribal Rights: Is a Resolution Possible?', Paper presented at the National Workshop on *Human Rights, Environment and the Law*, Bangalore.

Mazumdar, D.N. (1993), 'Van Gujjars Problems', *The Himachal Times*, 4 June.

Mitra, A. (1993), 'Chipko, an Unfinished Mission', *Down to Earth*, 30 April.

Nandy, A. (1987), *Traditions, Tyranny and Utopias: Essays in the Politics of Awareness* (New Delhi: Oxford University Press).

Sen, G. (ed.) (1992), *Indigenous Vision, Peoples of India: Attitudes to the Environment* (New Delhi: Sage).

Sethi, Harsh (1993), 'Survival and Democracy: Ecological Struggles in India', in P. Wignaraja (ed.), *New Social Struggles in the South: Empowering the People* (New Delhi: Vistaar).

Singh, D. (1993), 'In search of the guardians of nature', *Business Standard*, 9 Nov.

Singh, K. N. (1987), *Working Plan for the East Dehra Dun Forest Division, 1977–1988–89*, Dehra Dun, Forest Department.

Society for Participatory Research in Asia and Rural Litigation and Entitlement Kendra (1993), *Report on National Workshop on Declining Access to and Control over National Resources in National Parks and Sanctuaries*, Dehra Dun, 28–30 October.

Notes

1. The author is grateful to Avdesh Kaushal and his family in Dehra Dun for their hospitality and friendship during fieldwork. I also want to thank Praveen Kaushal for assistance and for all the discussions we have had about the Van Gujjars and their situation in the forest. The research reported were was financed by SAREC.

2. Letter from Forest Conservation officer, Jaunsar Division, to the Superintendent of Police, 26 May 1892.

3. In 1993 the State Government of Uttar Pradesh, through a Forest Secretary benevolent to the Van Gujjar case, accepted transhumance as their 'traditional right'. This was one of the first visible results of the present Van Gujjar movement and the result of pressure and appeals from the Gujjars with the help of RLEK, the local NGO working for their rights (see below).

4. The most spectacular of his cases, and the one which put him at the front of the environmental battle in India, was the case against limestone quarrying in the Garhwali hills (for details, see Madsen Chapter 13 below).

5. 'Unique Opportunity for Kamal Nath', editorial in *Down to Earth*, 31 January 1993.

6. *The Himachal Times*, 27 August 1993.

7. 'A lesson in bad environmental management', editorial in *Down to Earth*, 31 May 1993.

13 Between People and the State: NGOs as Troubleshooters and Innovators

Stig Toft Madsen[1]

This chapter deals with NGOs as agents of change. It presents two Indian NGOs which operate in the field where economic development, human rights, and conservation intersect. It aims to identify what has made these NGOs capable of exerting influence on policy change and judicial reform to secure livelihood rights and environmental rights for their beneficiaries.

The number of NGOs registered under the Foreign Contributions Regulation Act in India is estimated at 12–15 000 (Dhanagare 1993; Webster 1993). In 1987, the Government of India disbursed about Rs 3,000 m^2 through the Council for Advancement of People's Action for Rural Technology to more than 900 NGOs in India (Dhanagare 1993: 137). According to Robinson, Farrington and Satish (1990: 93), annual NGO revenue may have reached Rs 10 000 m. in the early 1990s, of which about 90 per cent was from abroad.

I make no claim that the two NGOs I have studied are representative of all NGOs. The NGOs analysed in this article may be termed troubleshooters and innovators; others might call them advocacy NGOs (Farrington and Lewis 1993: 311). I would like to argue that these NGOs involve themselves in complex processes of interaction with the state in order to influence policy and legal structures. Such NGOs are not spontaneous grassroots organizations, but elite brokers and innovators with links to power centres as well as to the grassroots. To a considerable extent, their 'NGO-ing' consists of penetrating a number of villages (or towns and cities) and building up support there in order to demonstrate to significant others in positions of power and influence that justice in a particular case would be better served if those significant others used their power and influence to support the case as defined by the

NGO. The pressure applied by the NGOs is persistent, but not too strong as very heavy pressure would de-activate their links to the centres of power. Reform and success ensue when a critical mass of influential, knowledgeable and respectable persons, officials as well as non-officials, find themselves in agreement on a course of action. This informal or quasi-formal consensus is shaped into appropriate directives which may be of relevance not only to the beneficiaries as originally defined by the NGO but to others as well.

The first case to be discussed concerns limestone mining in Dehra Dun. The case provided one of the first occasions where an NGO, the RLEK, successfully elicited the intervention of the Supreme Court. It is shown that the success of the RLEK was predicated on a number of factors, one of which was an enabling social network. The role of the RLEK in the limestone mining case is then juxtaposed to its role in its current campaign on behalf of a tribe, the pastoralist Gujjars, threatened with eviction from the forests near Dehra Dun.

The second case is the AKRSP in Gujarat. It has been active in influencing policy, and is known for its contribution to the creation of FM in India. Unlike the RLEK, which is exclusively Indian, the AKRSP is affiliated to a metropolitan umbrella NGO, the Aga Khan Foundation (AKF). It is argued that the high national and international profile of the AKRSP, as well as the commitment and quality of its staff, have contributed to its efficiency.

THE RURAL LITIGATION AND ENTITLEMENT KENDRA

Quarrying high-grade limestone in the Doon valley and Mussoorie Hills began in the late 1940s when Punjabi refugees brought the technology from West Pakistan. By 1981 fourteen Punjabi families operated 61 mines spread over an area of 1185 ha.[3] The method was open-cast mining, mainly on the slopes, which according to the 1952 Forest Policy were to be 60 per cent forested to protect them against landslides and other hazards (in places they were less than 50 metres from the Dehra Dun-Mussoorie main road). Safety standards were poor, and in the event of fatal accidents, survivors were paid off with as little as Rs 25, and warned to keep quiet. The mining seriously affected the water regime on the slopes and in the valley. In short, it was entrepreneurship at its worst, but it was not

illegal as the mine-owners held leases under Central and Uttar
Pradesh laws.[4]

Opposition to the mines increased around 1970 when local organizations such as Save the Village Committees (*Gram Bachao
Samitis*) petitioned the authorities. Residents of Dehra Dun city
also protested against the lime kilns operating in the city itself (for
example, Sethi 1976). Such action proved far from sufficient. A
breakthrough required a much broader and more long-term effort
in which NGOs, courts and a plethora of consultative and depart-
mental bodies interacted. The main group favouring continued
limestone mining was the lease-holders. They were usually supported, more or less actively, by the local authorities and the Uttar
Pradesh government. The State Government itself owned one of the
mines. In other words, the conflict aligned commercial interests
with the State Government, while the NGO sought support from
central government and other central institutions.

The Role of Public Interest Litigation

The catalyst which brought the above actors into play was writ
petition no. 8209 dated 2 July 1983, filed by Avdesh Kaushal with
accompanying affidavits, and brought before the Chief Justice on
14 July 1983. The writ petition turned the campaign against mining
into a public interest litigation (PIL) case. PIL is a form of litigating
in which an organization or an individual is granted *locus standi* to
bring a case to the higher courts on behalf of a deprived body of
people whose rights are being violated and who are claimed to be
unable to obtain justice otherwise. Through a process of judicial
innovation, individual judges of the Supreme Court, led by Chief
Justice P.N. Bhagwati, began admitting PIL cases in the 1970s, thus
short-cutting the judicial process which normally involves a series
of extremely time-consuming appeals (Bhagwati 1985; Baar 1990).
PIL has been used in all types of cases, not only on behalf of the
poor and powerless, as was originally envisaged, but on behalf of
people in general, and also on behalf of the rich and powerful
(Menski 1990). The petition filed by the RLEK was not of the
'postcard' size, but a detailed report.

On 12 March 1985, a three-judge bench of the Supreme Court
banned the operation of all but six of the 52 mines named in the
writ petition. Further, it directed the Government of India and
the state of Uttar Pradesh to seek alternative employment for the

lessees, and to reclaim the degraded lands with the help of an Eco-Task Force consisting of officers and ex-servicemen of the Indian army and the workers who were going to lose their jobs when the mines were closed. Under the National Rural Employment Programme, Rs 2.5 m. were put at the disposal of the local District Magistrate for reclamation. In other words, the judiciary ordered the executive to take certain actions to rectify injustice caused, at least in part, by the negligence of the executive. In their order the judges noted that:

> this is the first case of its kind in the country involving issues relating to environment and ecological balance and the questions arising for consideration are of grave moment and significance not only to the people residing in the Mussoorie Hill range forming part of the Himalayas but also in their implications to the welfare of the generality of people living in the country. It brings into sharp focus the conflict between development and conservation and serves to emphasize the need for reconciling the two in the larger interest of the country. (World Wildlife Fund-India 1987: 93)

In 1987 the Supreme Court ruled that the mines be permanently closed on environmental considerations, but the court did not agree to close down permanently those mines which were needed for defence purposes and for safeguarding India's balance of payments. This exemption was caused by the intervention of the Tata Group whose lawyer argued that limestone from the area was essential to produce high grade steel for defence purposes. The Supreme Court asked the Government of India to specify the minimum total requirement of high grade limestone for the manufacturing of high quality steel (Rosencranz, Divan and Noble 1991: 229). The RLEK responded by showing that the Tata company was already obtaining high grade limestone from the Jaisalmer area.

The Supreme Court passed at least five comprehensive *interim* orders before its final judgement in August 1988, which closed 101 mines. By 1989 only three mines were allowed to operate for the duration of their licence. The last mine, which is owned by the Uttar Pradesh state, closes in 1996.

The Doon case culminated at a very important point in time: that is, just before the 1986 Environmental Protection Act was passed. The case led to changes in the Mines and Minerals (Regulation and Development) Act of 1957 so that a lease may be prematurely terminated and reclamation would take place at the lessee's expense. Further, a change in the Mineral Concessions Rules of 1960 empowered the Department of Environment, Government of India, to screen all applications for mining licenses (World Wildlife Fund-India, 1987: 43).

A direct spin-off from the case was the declaration of the Doon valley as an ecologically fragile zone under the Environmental Protection Act of 1986 and the Uttar Pradesh Special Areas Development Act rather than an industrially backward area entitled to subsidies. For a period, the Doon Valley Board was chaired by the Prime Minister himself.

Had environmental laws been clear and had enforcement mechanisms been efficient, it would not have been necessary to go to the lengths required in the Doon case to stop mining operations. It was the insufficiencies of the existing system which compelled the Supreme Court and a small NGO to play an important and innovative role.

Other actors could have played that role, but failed to do so. The state Forest Department was only marginally involved in the case. Considering that the mines occupied 800 ha. of reserved forest and that the mines caused erosion in the mountains, this passivity is noteworthy. The Forest Department, for example, did not seek the approval of the Government of India for renewal of leases under the Forest Conservation Act of 1980 which requires the permission of the Central Government for releasing forest lands for non-forest activities. The Forest Department found that a clearance was not required as the leases had been granted *before* the Forest Conservation Act was passed. The Supreme Court, on the other hand, concluded that continued mining violated the Forest Conservation Act (Rosencranz, Divan and Noble 1991: 230).

Subsequent to the Doon case, environmental litigation has increased all over India. More than 4000 cases regarding environmental pollution were pending in various courts in 1991. However, the success rate has been very low. Activism has increased but judicial and executive passivity remains.

Factors Determining Outcomes

According to Kaushal, the outcome of the campaign hinged on several factors. Acquiring support from many quarters was essential. The political parties supported the RLEK, as did local civic associations such as Friends of the Doon and Save Mussoorie

Society. Their arguments also appealed to people in Delhi who were told that the climate in Delhi would be affected by environmental degradation in the Doon valley. Another factor, according to Kaushal, was that, 'the movement was not spoiled by fair-skinned admirers from the West'.

Apart from the factors identified by Kaushal, other factors may be mentioned. First, the factor of Kaushal himself and 'his' NGO. The RLEK began in the 1970s as an unregistered body working with the tribals in the Uttar Pradesh hills, and gained some experience in influencing policy by contributing to the enactment of the Bonded Labour Abolition Act in 1976 (RLEK, n.d.).

Second, the virtues of the Doon Valley and Mussoorie hill station helped focus attention on the case. The area is known for its natural beauty. Moreover, it is intimately connected with elite-formation in India by virtue of its private schools and by being the locale for the training of elite cadres within civil administration, forestry, the police and the army. It is also a popular place of retirement. This means that the area is home to a stratum of people above the average district administration in terms of seniority and social status. The cities of Mussoorie and Dehra Dun have a well-developed civic culture. The area is thus a virtual repository of childhood and adolescence memories for the Indian elite, including several Prime Ministers. According to Prashant Bhushan, who appeared for the petitioners: 'The administration acted promptly in the Doon Valley case . . . because pressure beyond the courts was exerted. Then prime minister Indira Gandhi took a keen interest in the case as her family had close connections with the valley for generations' (quoted from Khanna 1992). Third, the Doon valley is a centre of high level science, particularly natural science. Members of these institutions were called upon in their official capacities to pronounce on the technical merits of the case. Fourth, the area has other avenues of income. It is not chiefly dependent on the limestone mines. Other places cannot easily get the kind of a hearing which the Doon valley obtained. Tellingly, limestone quarrying continues in the hills *beyond* Mussoorie (Khanna 1992; Roychowdhury 1993).

The PIL case could have been linked to quarrying in other Uttar Pradesh hill areas to secure their closure, too. According to Kaushal, he contacted Sundarlal Bahuguna while preparing the initial affidavit in 1983, suggesting that Bahuguna provide a list of mines in Tehri and affidavits from affected people. Bahuguna replied that since he did not believe in the courts of law, he would not approach them (Kaushal, personal communication). Outside the Himalayas, limestone quarrying takes place in many other parts of India. The state of Rajasthan has around 30 000 mine leases including the limestone mines in Jaisalmer as well as a very large number of mines in the Aravalli Hills. Very little has been done to regulate mining in that state save, to a minor extent, in and around the Sariska National Park (Shankar 1993; Sjöblom and Singh 1993).

Fifth, as noted by Rosencranz, Divan and Noble, the central government and the Supreme Court were largely in agreement on the case. This undoubtedly strengthened the campaign. The quarrying was largely undertaken by small private entrepreneurs. Had the state been the sole entrepreneur, the court might have found it more difficult to close the operations. The state of Uttar Pradesh was, in fact, engaged in mining. Their mine was one of the biggest and it is the last to be closed. Similarly, the defence interests involved also made it more difficult for the court to impose a blanket ban.

Despite these ifs and buts, the Supreme Court did, in fact, order the mines to be closed and the Doon limestone case thereby provided a model and set a precedent for other pieces of NGO-intervention to follow in other parts of India. Kaushal came out of the battle against mining with his relations to the government intact, or even enhanced. The government awarded him the prestigious Padam Shri award, and he became a lecturer at the Lal Bahadur Shastri National Academy of Administration in Mussoorie which trains and grooms the uppermost layer of civil administrators in India.

Intervention on Behalf of Tribal Pastoralists

Subsequently, Kaushal resigned his position at the National Academy of Administration to take up the cause of the *Van Gujjars*, a Muslim tribe of pastoralists.[5] The Gujjars are presently threatened with eviction from the forests south of the Doon valley, which are to become a national park. According to Osmaston and Sale (1989: 93), the park was notified in 1983 and established in 1987 as an elephant reserve, with Rajiv Gandhi as one of the prime movers. However, the park is not really established yet as the Gujjars have refused offers of a resettlement of rights pending which the present sanctuary cannot be elevated to the status of a national park.[6]

There are both similarities and differences between the Doon mining case and the case of the Gujjars. The Doon case pitted the interests of the few, mainly the lease-holders, against the interests of the many. In case of the Gujjars in Rajaji, the interests of a smaller group of forest users are pitted against those of a more abstract generality of people, who aspire to protect wildlife and forests.[7]

In the PIL case against mining, scientific reasoning was extensively employed. A similar scrutiny of the Rajaji situation is not likely to lead to a high degree of scientific consensus. One of the institutions which the government may approach to obtain 'hard scientific facts' is the Wildlife Institute of India which is located in Dehra Dun. So far, this institute has not come out in support of the Gujjars. Since scientific support is an important factor for the success of environmental movements, an unclear scientific verdict will make it more difficult for the NGO and its constituency to succeed.

In 1992, the Government of India launched Project Elephant. Its proponents consider the present situation in the park area unsound because lopping of branches for cattle fodder and grazing have turned more than half the area into scrub unsuited for elephants (Ministry of Environment and forests 1993: 29–30; see also Khati 1993a: 403, and 1993b: 20).

According to Ravi Chellam from the Indian Wildlife Institute, the biotic pressure on the Rajaji forest is heavier than in, for example, the Gir National Park in Gujarat, which is inhabited by Maldhari pastoralists. He ascribes the intensive lopping of trees by Gujjars to the denser tree cover and the higher levels of erosion in Rajaji which limit grasslands. The elephants which numbered about 552 in 1993 are also responsible for part of the degradation (Ravi Chellam, personal communication).[8]

On a more conciliatory note, Project Elephant admits that: 'Large forest areas in Uttar Pradesh have been replaced by Eucalyptus Plantations . . . between 1966 to 1976, one-third of the 1660 Sq. Kms. of the most suitable elephant habitat was converted into monoculture of Eucalyptus and other such quick growing species' (Ministry of Environment and Forests 1993: 29). Further examples could be added (see Gooch, Chapter 12 above). This fuzziness regarding the causes of degradation provides the RLEK with an opportunity to blur the issue by an 'indirect issue oriented attack' to use Ellefson's terminology (Ellefson 1992): that is, by pointing to other causes of degradation.

In the mining case, the RLEK gained support from the Central Government, sidelining the Uttar Pradesh government and the Uttar Pradesh courts. The situation is different in the case of the Gujjars. Rajaji National Park is largely centrally funded and administered. The Ministry of Environment and Forest in New Delhi is directly involved, and it must contend with pressures both from conservationist NGOs and from NGOs supporting tribal rights.

As regards the Supreme Court, it has not, so far, supported the Gujjars. In a case filed in the Supreme Court (but not by RLEK), the court upheld the right of the Forest Department under the Indian Wildlife Act to evict the Gujjars from the proposed National Park. Given the relatively weak position of the Gujjars in the eyes of the law, it seems likely that RLEK will not rely on the courts to solve the present conflict. Instead, it has stressed entitlement rather than litigation. It has used three main arguments.

1.   An argument stressing *sui generis* tribal rights of entitlement to 'survival' and culture. This argument is based on international human rights conventions and buttressed with Indian policy statements (see, for example, *The Indian Express*, 31 January 1993). However, the RLEK must avoid the idea that these rights can be equated with ethnic and national rights to self-determination which would seriously weaken the reputation of the NGO and its clients in the eyes of the establishment (see Maheshwari 1993).

2.   An argument stressing the superior resource management practices of tribals. To survive in forests in the long run requires intimate knowledge of the terrain and sustainable resource utilization practices. As the tribals have – until others intervened – lived in the forests 'for centuries', they *ipso facto* possess such capabilities. This argument often proceeds by questioning the resource management capabilities of the present manager, the allegedly corrupt Forest Department.[9]

3.   An argument creating a positive image of the Gujjar Muslims as simple and poor but handsome vegetarians deceived and neglected by the government.[10]

As already indicated, the arguments on resource use are difficult to bolster scientifically in the present case. On the other hand, it is equally difficult for the government to proceed with the eviction of Gujjars in view of its stated policy of accommodation, the general 'heat' surrounding the topic of eviction elsewhere in India, and in view of India's National Forest Policy which stresses participatory management. By early 1994, the Ministry of Environment and Forests had 'in principle agreed to manage the country's 500-odd protected areas jointly with members of local communities to mitigate current conflict over wildlife parks and people' (Kapoor 1994).[11]

THE AGA KHAN RURAL SUPPORT PROGRAM

The NGO now to be discussed is a high-profile conglomerate compared to the RLEK but it, too, works in large measure by breaking new ground in the relation between the government and people. The AKF is one of several organizations built by the present Aga Khan. His Highness Prince Aga Khan Shah Karim al-Huseini is the 49th Imam of the Imami Ismailis who consider the Aga Khan to be the temporal and spiritual successor to the Prophet Muhammad. The origins of this Shiite sect can be traced to 760 AD. Ismailis pay a tax or tithe (*zakat*) amounting to 5 or 10 per cent of their income to the Aga Khan. A judgement in the Bombay High Court in 1866 established his title to all communal property of the Ismailis, thus enabling the then Aga Khan and his successors to create strong institutions through which to redistribute their accumulated wealth (Morris 1958). They have done this to an exceptional degree, combining their religious status with a detailed understanding of the modern world. At present, the Aga Khan Development Network encompasses both commercial and philan-thropic institutions, and operates in more than 25 countries.

AKF was established in 1967 as a private, non-denominational philanthropic organization. Programme expenditure in 1992 was US$ 27.3 m. with a donor commitment of a further US$ 124 m. The focus of the AKF is on East Africa and South Asia, and it has an office in New Delhi (Islam 1991).[12]

The AKRSP was created in 1984 as a non-denominational organ-ization. It is active in a number of villages in three districts of Gujarat. Within these villages 'Spearhead Teams' and 'Village Organizers' of the AKRSP have established 'Village Organizations', including 'Women's Development Organizations'. No attempt has been made to link Village Organizations in one village with those in other project villages in order to create a wider social movement.

AKRSP's focus is on the community management of natural resources, and its project portfolio includes watershed management, wasteland development, joint forest and joint irrigation management, bio-gas development, animal husbandry, credit and savings schemes, and training programmes (AKRSP 1992).

The chairman of the board of directors of the AKRSP is Dr I.G. Patel, ex-governor of the Reserve Bank of India and ex-chairman of the London School of Economics. The first chairman of the NGO was Dr V. Kurien, one of the most prominent leaders of the cooperative sector in India. Other members of the board include (or included) Ratan Tata, heir to the biggest industrial house in India, and Anil Agarwal, the well-known environmentalist. The board also has as members prominent Ismailis from Bombay.

The staff of the AKRSP is mostly young, and highly competent and motivated. It is recruited from all over India and from different religious backgrounds. The Chief Executive Officer, Anil Shah, retired as Secretary, Rural Development, Government of Gujarat and joined the AKRSP in 1984.

This NGO is obviously not a spontaneous product of ordinary villages of Gujarat, but as much an outside agency seeking to penetrate the villages as the state. What makes it special is its very solid foundation in terms of support and financing, the sophistication of its approach and methods, and its relation to government.

Latest Methodology

The methodology of the AKRSP is participatory. It is based on Rapid Rural Appraisal (RRA) methods developed in the late 1970s. RRA is a technique of information gathering which is neither as time-consuming as detailed anthropological fieldwork and large-scale sociological or economic surveys, nor as superficial as the kind of 'rural development tourism' often practised by international consultants. RRA uses available material such as published works, maps, censuses and local experts and employs group interviews and informal, but structured, conversations with local people (Chambers 1985).

The AKRSP began using RRA around 1987–8, learning the techniques from Chambers and others. AKRSP has added to RRA by developing new forms of Participatory Rural Appraisal (PRA), Participatory Rural Appraisal and Planning, and Participatory Monitoring. PRAs often involve 'transect walks' with different groups of villagers in the village and its surroundings, and drawing of 'ground maps' directly on the ground with available material as legends. Such maps are then transferred to paper. These are later compared with new ground maps to establish a system of monitoring and evaluation. In the experience of the AKRSP, most villagers are able to map the natural resources of a village and willing to share this information with outsiders who care to listen to them (see World Resources Institute 1991; Chambers 1992; Society for the Promition of Wasteland Development 1992b; Shah, Hardwaj and Ambastha 1993;). These methods have been widely adopted by donor agencies and others.[13]

Policy Influencing as a Way of Promoting Replication

The central figure in AKRSP's 'policy influencing' has been Anil Shah. Like many other Indian civil servants who retire in their mid-fifties Shah made a career move to the non-governmental sector which enabled him to continue dealing with his erstwhile juniors and colleagues still in government service. The importance of appointing a senior Indian Administrative Service officer as chief executive of an NGO should not be underestimated as such an ex-officer is treated according to his seniority and accorded appropriate respect, even after retirement.

As Chief Executive Officer in the AKRSP, Shah has slowly, persistently and politely been prevailing upon government to modify and reform its policies, laws, rules and regulations as well as, to some extent, its style and manner of interaction with the rural population. As in the Dehra Dun cases, the interaction between the NGO and the government has been extensive.

Between early 1987 and mid-1990, AKRSP helped to push and draft the Government of India resolution enjoining states to establish JFM. JFM empowers organized villagers, with the assistance of qualified NGOs, to enter into agreements with the Forest Department to manage degraded public forest lands jointly and enjoy usufruct rights. In Gujarat, the local Forest Department officers had been reluctant to implement such scheme, but higher officers were willing to take a risk in the hopes that JFM would end illegal felling. Such felling occurred during the 1990 general elections when politicians had encouraged tribals to fell trees on government land and sell the wood. The National Forest Policy passed in 1988 provided a suitable framework for the scheme, and in 1989 the

AKRSP held meetings with the Society for Promotion of Wasteland Development and others in Delhi at which Anil Shah helped to devise a legal framework for JFM. In early 1990 the new Minister of Environment and Forests started talks with Anil Shah. The process of consultation involved 49 separate contacts with government officials in Gujarat and Delhi, but persistence paid off in the form of the 1 June 1990 Government of India circular directing state governments to introduce JFM (1992; Sethna and Shah 1993; and, for the full text of the order, see Society for Promotion of Wasteland Development 1992a).

Long before this breakthrough, NGOs elsewhere had pressurized government to legalize already existing schemes. The precursors of JFM were participatory schemes in Arabari in Midnapore district in West Bengal which started in the early 1970s. They were followed by projects in Sukhomajri village in Haryana. In both cases NGOs played a prominent role (Palit 1992, Sarin 1993a; Saxena and Gulati 1993). There were other schemes in Orissa, Rajasthan and Southern Gujarat.

From the Indian Government's point of view the JFM-reform process was masterminded by the government itself through senior officers who supported trusted field personnel in their experiments in joint forms of management.[14] Forest officers in both West Bengal and Haryana, in fact, performed important roles. Foreign donors may, on their part, trace the genesis of JFM to *their* influence. In particular, M. Poffenberger and J.Y. Campbell from the Ford Foundation in New Delhi seem to have been influential.

In any case, what occurred was the creation of an informal consensus which was eventually given a formal shape enabling the process to be repeated. To say that NGOs typically step into situations where government has collapsed, as Kothari has reasoned (see Westergaard 1992: 20), would be misplaced in the present case. The AKRSP acted as an innovator in close cooperation with government, but was also influenced by the global currents noted above.

THE VICISSITUDES OF NGO-ING

If NGOs and grassroots movements want to act as innovators and brokers in the manner described above, they need to maintain relations of trust with their beneficiaries and with the state. Further, it benefits them to maintain good working relations with NGOs sharing the same ideals and goals.

The level of selflessness or public-spiritedness of the leaders of NGOs are widely monitored with various degrees of sophistication by clients, the state and opponents. It would seem that in situations where it is difficult for villagers and others to know the past achievements and future prospects of NGOs, monitoring-by-reputation tends to become an important basis for assessment. In areas such as Uttar Pradesh, where NGO culture is weak and where society is perceived to be saturated with dishonesty, people are likely to attribute all sorts of motives to NGOs and their leaders, making it very difficult for NGOs to sustain a value-driven or *wert-rational* movement. For this very reason, however, an NGO (or any other actor which gain people's confidence) enjoys the status of a redeemer.

Returning to the campaign against limestone mining, this campaign received the support of other groups including the Chipko movement (*Chipko Andolan*). Chipko activists entered the campaign by supporting the struggle against one particular mine in Nahi Kala or Nahi Barkot. In the early 1980s members of the Delhi-based NGO *Kalpavriksh* visited Nahi Kala (Ashish Kothari, personal communication). Subsequently, *Kalpavriksh* secured media attention to the struggle against this mine which involved dramatic forms of protest such as partial burying of volunteers on approach roads in order to prevent trucks from reaching the mine. *Kalpavriksh* also filed a writ petition against the Nahi Kala mine.

The case of the Nahi Kala mine shows that even NGOs operating in the same area with broadly the same goal may find it difficult to cooperate. The difficulty, in this case, seems to have sprung partly from disagreement on strategies, that is, whether to concentrate on local action in the form of *satyagraha* (the Gandhian style of non-violent action aimed at the moral conversion of the opponent) or whether to count on the efficacy of legal action in the Supreme Court). Here it seems that the RLEK chose the more effective strategy, and that the Chipko movement and *Kalpavriksh* did not influence the outcome of the anti-mining campaign in the valley as a whole to any considerable extent. According to Sanjeev Prakash (personal communication), their contribution may have been to reduce the risk of failure by diversifying strategies, but in this case writ petition no. 8209 was the crucial event which closed the mines. Accordingly, the Surpreme Court acknowledged the role of the

RLEK (rather than that of other actors) in its judgement of 16 December 1986, which states: 'We must place on record our appreciation of the steps taken by the Rural Litigation and Entitlement Khendra. But for this move, all that has happened perhaps may not have come' (RLEK n.d.).

In terms of publicity, the Chipko movement itself benefited from the confrontations around the Nahi Kala mine. Thus, Vandana Shiva, the prominent eco-feminist and spokesperson of the movement, portrayed the confrontations around the mine as the 'Chipko movement in the Doon valley', making it virtually synonymous with the struggle against mining in the entire valley (Shiva 1991, ch. 10).

The Chipko movement in the Uttar Pradesh hills provides further examples of the problems and predicament of NGOs and other movements. In the early 1970s, the Chipko grassroots movement brought felling in government forests to a standstill by opposing 'outside' contractors and their labourers.[15] Mobilizing public opinion in favour of safeguarding the environment to secure the basic needs of the local population, Chipko activists became directly instrumental in furthering a moratorium on tree felling in the high regions of the Uttarakhand Himalayas.[16] Not only that, according to Shekhar Pathak: 'The Forest Conservation Act of 1980 and the very creation of the environment ministry are due to the consciousness created by Chipko' (see Mitra 1993: 32–3).

However, according to Aryal (1994) and others, Chipko has run out of steam for a number of reasons. One reason is the prolonged rivalry between its two major leaders, Sundarlal Bahuguna and Chandi Prasad Bhatt (Aryal 1994: 19).[17] While Bhatt has continued to work in the field of rural reconstruction with modest success, Bahuguna has concentrated on the fight against the Tehri dam, the 2400 megawatts hydroelectric project, which will submerge Tehri town and displace thousands. Bahuguna argues that the dam is an expression of fallacious development policies and a potential threat to the entire region as it is located in a seismically active region. However, as noted by Bandyopadhyay (1992), the anti-Tehri dam movement to a large extent has failed to gain the support of people in the hills. It is mainly citizens of Tehri town and nearby villages that oppose the dam, and for them the questions of the safety and the wisdom of the dam are often overshadowed by the question of compensation and re-housing in 'New Tehri' (Swami 1994). The anti-dam movement is finding itself in a recurrent dilemma: if a movement admits that the economic interests of its followers are its prime concern, it risks losing the support an undiluted environmentalist agenda may secure in India and abroad. If it stresses an ecological agenda, it risks losing the support of its local clientele, who may see their economic interests or livelihood rights compromised.

This dilemma has been resolved by the third constituent of the Chipko movement, the Marxist-oriented *Uttarakhand Sangarsh Vahini*, by moving decisively away from environmentalism. Activists from this movement have formed the Uttarakhand Revolutionary Party (*Uttarakhand Kranti Dal*) which campaigns for the creation of a separate hill state called Uttarakhand. In 1988–9, this party led the 'Cut the Trees Movement' (*Ped Kato Andolan*) during which trees were reportedly felled in 111 places where the Forest Conservation Act – the Act which was enacted partly due to Chipko – had postponed development projects. According to Bipan Tripathi of the *Uttarakhand Kranti Dal* (who led Chipko activists in 1978), the Forest Conservation Act has delayed thousands of development schemes on forest lands in the hill region (Mitra 1993: 35; Aryal 1994: 20). The Act requires that prior permission be obtained from the Ministry of Environment and Forests in New Delhi before non-forest schemes may be undertaken on forest land.

CONCLUSION

In the right circumstances, NGOs are capable of empowering people, of strengthening civil society, and of helping people secure their rights. In this chapter, however, rather than stressing the organic relation between people and NGOs, I have argued that some NGOs are brokers and catalysts seeking a structured dialogue between government and citizens to create innovative solutions to intractable problems. The type of NGOs described in this article are elite organizations using their influence on behalf of, and for the good of, the non-elite. As Webster (1993), Dhanagare (1993) and others have pointed out, NGOs are not an alternative to the government. I would add that the NGOs studied here are, in fact, dependent on a functioning government.

Though NGOs are seen to promote democracy, NGOs often sideline existing democratic institutions and create groups of their own design. In India, the tendency to belittle the work of political parties by pointing out that politicians are corrupt, combined with the Gandhian ideal of 'going-to-the-villages' to build a true and direct democracy, makes it convenient for NGOs to circumvent the elected bodies.

NGOs often criticize the government for wasting money but, as noted by Brett, NGOs do not necessarily operate cost-effectively as project implementors (Brett 1993). Some Indian NGOs have squandered funds as profusely as the state. An NGO in Kerala, for example, spent Rs 1.3 m. on afforestation, but only six trees survived.[18]

Rather than in the promotion of economic efficiency or representative democracy, the contributions of the NGOs studied lie in their ability to devise and promote sensible solutions to pressing problems, involving both the government and the clients in new ways. The NGOs, through close and long-term interaction with their clients, imbue people with the courage to act (Bandyopadhyay 1993) and enhance their self-esteem by glorifying their indigenous (or bourgeois) selves. In this goading process of 'controlled empowerment', the clients become more monitored, more literate and better informed, often more involved in market operations, and more capable of making use of modern institutions, such as courts. While the leaders of NGOs are expected to be honest and upright, and even selfless, the clients, on their part, respond by learning how to act as citizens with responsibilities towards a broader set of others. Simultaneously, the government officials are encouraged to become more knowledgeable about the demands, rights and problems of the citizens, more responsive and attentive, and more courageous in solving problems.

References

AKRSP, *Annual Progress Report 1992* (Ahmedabad).

Aryal, M. (1994), 'Axing Chipko', *Himal*, Vol. 7, No. 1, pp. 8–23.

Baar, C. (1990), 'Social Action Litigation in India: The Operation and Limitations of the World's Most Active Judiciary', *Policy Studies Journal*, Vol. 19, No. 1, pp. 140–50.

Bandyopadhyay, J. (1992), 'Sustainability and Survival in the Mountain Context', *Ambio*, Vol. 21, No. 4, pp. 297–392.

Bandyopadhyay, J. (1993), 'Imbuing people with the courage to act', *Down to Earth*, 30 April.

Bhagwati, P.N. (1985), 'Social Action Litigation: The Indian Experience', lecture delivered 17 May 1985, at the Sri Lanka Foundation Institute International Centre for Ethnic Studies, Colombo, Sri Lanka.

Brett, E.A. (1993), 'Voluntary Agencies as Development Organizations: Theorizing the Problem of Efficiency and Accountability', *Development and Change*, No. 24, pp. 269–303.

Chambers, R. (1985), 'Shortcut Methods of Gathering Social Information for Rural Development Projects', in M.M. Cernea (ed.), *Putting People First: Sociological Variables in Rural Development* (Oxford: Oxford University Press), pp. 399–415.

Chambers, R. (1992), *Rural Appraisal: Rapid, Relaxed and Participatory* (Brighton; Institute of Development Studies), Discussion Paper 311.

Dhanagare, D.N. (1993), 'NGOs and Foreign Funding', *Man and Development*, June 1993, pp. 133–45.

Ellefson, P.V. (1992), *Forest Resources Policy: Process, Participants and Programs* (New York: McGraw-Hill).

Farrington, J. and D.J. Lewis (1993), '"Roles" in NGO-Government Relationships: A Synthesis from the Case Studies', in J. Farrington and D.J. Lewis (eds), *Non-Governmental Organisations and the State in Asia: Rethinking Roles in Sustainable Agricultural Development* (London: Routledge).

Gadgil, M. (1983), 'Forestry with a Social Purpose', in W. Fernandes and S. Kulkarni (eds), *Towards a New Forest Policy: People's Rights and Environmental Needs* (New Delhi: Indian Social Institute) pp. 11–33.

Guha, R. (1989), *The Unquiet Woods: Ecological Change and Peasant Resistance in the Himalayas* (Delhi: Oxford University Press).

Islam, S. (1991), 'Imam for all seasons', *Far Eastern Economic Review*, 14 November, pp. 64–6.

Johri, A. and N. Krishnakumar (1991), 'Poverty and Common Property Resources: Case Study of a Rope Making Industry', *Economic and Political Weekly*, 14 December, pp. 2897–902.

Kapoor, A. (1994), 'Govt to manage wildlife parks with local people', *Times of India* (Delhi edition), 15 January.

Khanna, A., (1992), 'Public interest litigation: The interminable wait for justice', *Down to Earth*, 15 August, pp. 33–6.

Khati, D.V.S. (1993a), 'Man and Forest: The Gujjars of Rajaji National Park', in A.S. Rawat (ed.), *India Forestry: A Perspective* (New Delhi: Indus), pp. 401–8.

Khati, D.V.S. (1993b), 'Problems in Paradise, Gujjars in conflict with Rajaji', *Sanctuary*, Vol. XIII, No. 4, pp. 14–21.

Kothari, A. P. Pande, S. Singh and D. Variava (1989), *Management of National Parks and Sanctuaries in India: A Status Report* (Delhi: Indian Institute of Public Administration).

Madsen, Stig Toft (1996), *State, Society and Human Rights in South Asia* (New Dehli: Manohar).

Maheshwari, A. (1993), 'Gujjars want to manage forest', *Hindustan Times*, 6 April.

Menski, Werner, (1990), 'On the Limits of Public Interest Litigation', *Kerala Law Times*, No. 26, pp. 45–7.

Ministry of Environment and Forests (1993), *Project Elephant (Gajatme)* (New Delhi).

Mitra, A. (1993), 'Chipko: An Unfinished Mission', *Down to Earth*, 30 April, pp. 25–35.

Morris, H.S. (1958), 'The Divine Kingship of the Aga Khan: Study of Theocracy in East Africa', *Southwestern Journal of Anthropology*, Vol. 14, No. 1, pp. 454–72.

Osmaston, B.B. and J.B. Sale (1989), *Wildlife of Dehra Dun and Adjacent Hills* (Dehra Dun: Natraj).

Palit, S. (1992), 'People's Participation in Forest Management', *The Indian Forester*, Vol. 118, No. 7, pp. 447–55

Rawat, Ajay S. (1993), 'Reclamation and Afforestation of Abandoned Mines in Doon Valley', in A.S. Rawat (ed.), *India Forestry: A Perspective* (New Delhi: Indus), pp. 383–99.

RLEK (n.d.), *Rural Litigation and Entitlement Kendra* (Dehra Dun).

Robinson, M., J. Farrington and S. Satish (1990), 'Overview', in J. Farrington and D.J. Lewis (eds), *Non-Governmental Organizations and the State in Asia: Rethinking Roles in Sustainable Agricultural Development* (London: Routledge), pp. 91–2.

Rosencranz, A., S. Divan and M.L. Noble (1991), *Environmental Law and Policy in India: Cases, Materials and Statutes* (Bombay: Tripathi).

Roychowdhury, A. (1993), 'Quarrying for trouble: Controversy over Himachal limestone mining', *Down to Earth*, 15 May, pp. 25–32.

Sarin, M. (1993), 'Change needed in forest protection customs', *Down to Earth*, 28 Feb.

Saxena, N.C. and M. Gulati (1993), 'Forest Management and Recent Policy Changes in India', *Wastelands News*, February–April, pp. 52–7.

Sethi, B.K. (1976), 'Environmental Effects on the Industrialisation of Dehra Dun', *Northern Flash*, 12 December.

Sethna, A. and A. Shah (1993), 'The Aga Khan Rural Support Project: Influencing Wasteland Development Policy', in J. Farrington and D.J. Lewis (eds), *Non-Governmental Organizations and the State in Asia. Rethinking Roles in Sustainable Agricultural Development* (London: Routledge).

Shah, A. (1992), 'Joint Forest Management: Afforestation, Participation, Participatory Rural Appraisal', *Wastelands News*, May–July, pp. 40–4.

Shah, P., G. Hardwaj and R. Ambastha (1993), 'Gujarat, India: Participatory Monitoring', *Rural Extension Bulletin*, Vol. I (April).

Shankar, U. (1993), 'Aravallis: Digging their own grave', *Down to Earth*, 31 August, pp. 25–32.

Shiva, V. (1991), *Ecology and the Politics of Survival: Conflicts over Natural Resources in India* (New Delhi, Newbury Park, London: United Nation University Press, Sage Publications).

Sjöblom, D. and A. Singh (1993), 'An indigenous land tenure system is revived to rehabilitate a protected area: the case of Sariska National Park in Rajasthan', *Forests, Trees and People*, Vol. 22 (November) pp. 28–30.

Society for the Promotion of Wasteland Development (1992a), *Joint Forest Management. Regulations Update 1992* (New Delhi: Society For the Promotion of Wasteland Development).

Society for the Promotion of Wasteland Development (1992b), *Participatory Rural Appraisal (PRA) Methods in South Gujarat, India* (New Delhi: Society For the Promotion of Wasteland Development).

Swami, P. (1994), 'Tehri, Again', *Frontline*, 11 March, pp. 65–76.

Webster, N. (1993), 'The Role of NGOs in Indian Rural Development: Some Lessons from West Bengal and Karnataka', paper presented at the EADI VIIth General Conference, Berlin, 15–18 September.

Westergaard, K. (1992), *NGOs, Empowerment and the State in Bangladesh* (Copenhagen: Centre for Development Research Working Paper).

World Resources Institute (1991), *Participatory Rural Appraisal Handbook: Conducting PRAs in Kenya*, Prepared Jointly by The National Environment Secretariat, Government of Kenya, Clark University, Egerton University and The Development Centre for International Development and Environment (London: World Resources Institute).

World Wildlife Fund-India (1987), *The Fragile Doon: A Case Study* (New Delhi: World Wildlife Fund-India).

World Bank (1987), *The Aga Khan Rural Support Program in Pakistan: A Second Interim Evaluation*, World Bank Operations Evaluation Study (Washington, DC: World Bank).

.**Notes**

1. A more detailed analysis of the cases discussed here can be found in my PhD thesis (Madsen 1996). I would like to thank Ravi Chellam, Pernille Gooch, Mr and Ms Jagawat, Avdesh and Praveen Kaushal, D.V.S. Khati, Ashish Kothari, Staffan Lindberg, Kate E. Madsen, Sanjeev Prakash, Sudhir Rao, Anil C. Shah and Vandana Shiva for critical comments, and SAREC for financing the research presented here.

2. In 1993, approximately 30 Indian Rupees equalled US$ 1.

3. According to World Wildlife Fund-India (1987: 90), a quarter or a fifth of that area could have supplied an equal amount of limestone had a more rational method of extraction been employed.

4. In 1961 the Minister of Mines in Uttar Pradesh had tried to limit mining in the area, but the then Chief Minister reversed the decision and granted 20-year leases. The leases were made renewable at the behest of the lease-holder for another 20 years.

5. I met Kaushal in April 1993 on 22 January 1994. For details about the Gujjars and other groups involved, see Chapter 12 by Gooch in this volume and Johri and Krishnakumar (1991).

6. See Kothari, Pande, Singh and Vaniva (1989, ch. 1) for the legal status of national parks and sanctuaries.

7. Some officials estimate that 5000 Gujjars live in the Rajaji forest in the winter season while Kaushal's estimate is closer to 10 000 or even more.

8. See also Rawat (1993) for a discussion of the resource use of Gujjars.

9. See the editorial 'Unique opportunity for Kamal Nath' in *Down to Earth*, 31 January 1993, for a summary of the argument stressing the rights and capacities of Gujjars and the interests and constraints of the government. The editorial encourages the Minister for Environment and Forest, Kamal Nath, who, incidentally, was educated in Dehra Dun, to create the country's first people's national park in Rajaji. Anil Agarwal, the driving force behind *Down to Earth*, has unequivocally supported the case of the Gujjars.

10. See, for example, *The Himachal Times* (Dehra Dun), 'Van Gujjars demand control of Rajaji National Park', 5 April 1993.

11. See Roychowdhury (1993) for a summary of the debate on Joint Protected Area Management.

12. cf. also *Business India*, 'Distinguished Strategy', 23 November–6 December 1992.

13. For a systematic critique of AKRSP's major sister project in Pakistan, see World Bank (1987).

14. Interview with D.N. Tewari, Director-General, Indian Council of Forest Research and Education.

15. According to Aryal (1994: 17) and Mitra (1993: 31), local contractors may have been behind the initial mobilization against 'outside' contractors as they themselves wanted the contracts.

16. The moratorium expired, partially, in 1993.

17. See Gadgil (1983: 131) and Guha (1989: 180–4) for summaries of the substance of their respective arguments.

18. The *Times of India*, 'New Forest Policy on the Anvil', 30 April 1990.

Index